# THE OTHER/ARGENTINA

SUNY series in Latin American and Iberian Thought and Culture

Rosemary G. Feal, editor
Jorge J. E. Gracia, founding editor

# THE OTHER/ARGENTINA

*Jews, Gender, and Sexuality
in the Making of a Modern Nation*

AMY K. KAMINSKY

Cover image: *Archeology of a Journey*, 2018. © Mirta Kuperminc. Used with permission.

Published by State University of New York Press, Albany

© 2021 State University of New York

All rights reserved

Printed in the United States of America

No part of this book may be used or reproduced in any manner whatsoever without written permission. No part of this book may be stored in a retrieval system or transmitted in any form or by any means including electronic, electrostatic, magnetic tape, mechanical, photocopying, recording, or otherwise without the prior permission in writing of the publisher.

For information, contact State University of New York Press, Albany, NY
www.sunypress.edu

**Library of Congress Cataloging-in-Publication Data**

Names: Kaminsky, Amy K., author.
Title: The other/Argentina : Jews, gender, and sexuality in the making of a modern nation / Amy K. Kaminsky.
Other titles: Jews, gender, and sexuality in the making of a modern nation
Description: Albany : State University of New York Press, [2021] | Series: SUNY series in Latin American and Iberian thought and culture | Includes bibliographical references and index.
Identifiers: LCCN 2020031728 | ISBN 9781438483290 (hardcover : alk. paper) | ISBN 9781438483283 (pbk. : alk. paper) | ISBN 9781438483306 (ebook)
Subjects: LCSH: Jews—Intellectual life—Argentina. | Jews—Civilization—Argentina. | Argentina—Ethnic relations. | Jews—Identity.
Classification: LCC F3021.J5 K354 2021 | DDC 982/.004924—dc23
LC record available at https://lccn.loc.gov/2020031728

10 9 8 7 6 5 4 3 2 1

*To the next generations:*
*David, Sarah, Adam, and Elliot;*
*to Jonathan, of blessed memory;*
*and*
*in memory of Sarah May*

# CONTENTS

List of Illustrations ... ix

Preface ... xi

Acknowledgments ... xvii

1  Planting Wheat and Reaping Doctors: Another Way of Being Argentine ... 1

2  Modernity, Cosmopolitanism, and Anxiety ... 21

3  Provisional Identity ... 47

4  Family Stories and the Invention of Memory ... 67

5  Jewish Legibility and Argentine Self-Fashioning ... 91

6  Incidental Jewishness ... 123

7  Embedded Jewishness: Memory and the State in Times of Terror ... 141

8  Troubling Difference: Jewishness, Gender, and Transgressive Sexuality ... 171

By Way of Conclusion ... 197

| | |
|---|---:|
| Notes | 201 |
| Bibliography | 217 |
| Index | 231 |

# ILLUSTRATIONS

Figure 1.1  Children's mural of the arrival of the SS *Weser*.  15

Figure 1.2  Children's mural in Moisés Ville.  16

Figure 4.1  Mirta Kupferminc, *On the Way (En camino)*.  88

Figure 4.2  Mirta Kupferminc, *Arqueology of the Journey (Arqueología de un trayecto)*.  89

Figure 5.1  Mirta Kupferminc, *To Be a Witness (Ser testigo)*.  113

Figure 5.2  Guillermo Kuitca, *El mar dulce (The sweetwater sea)*.  116

Figure 7.1  Mirta Kupferminc, *Ghosts at the Lodz Ghetto (In Daniel Kupferminc's memory) [Fantasmas en el ghetto de Lodz (En memoria de Daniel Kupferminc)]*.  151

Figure 7.2  Mirta Kupferminc, *That Place (Ese lugar)*.  152

Figure 7.3  Marcelo Brodsky, *NEXO 7: LOS CAMPOS (NEXUS 7: THE CAMPS)*.  166

# PREFACE

At the Ottawa Conference of Inter-American Women Writers in May of 1978 I found myself sitting around a table with a bunch of mostly Argentine writers and critics when someone observed that every single one of us in that room was Jewish. I no longer remember who exactly was there: Saúl Sosnowski and Pablo Urbanyi, for sure. Evelyn Picon Garfield and Marta Paley de Francescato, I'm pretty certain. What was notable about that moment was that being Jewish had nothing to do with why we were at that particular conference. For most of us, beyond our professional interests as writers and academics, another identity issue was part of what brought us there as literary scholars, women, and/or as Latin Americans. But the realization that all of us in that room were Jewish made a momentary difference, a sense of another, unexpected, kind of belonging. And of course, by no means all the Argentines at the conference were Jewish—Marta Lynch was there, as were Griselda Gambaro, Alicia Jurado, Elvira Orfée, Luisa Valenzuela, and her mother, María Luisa Levinson. To my recollection, no one presented a paper dealing with Jewishness in Ottawa. The Latin American Jewish Studies Association—LAJSA—would not be established for another four years, and feminist studies generally paid little attention to the fact of Jewishness within feminist activism or scholarship. What was perhaps the earliest lesbian-feminist Jewish anthology, *Nice Jewish Girls*, would be published in the US in 1982, coinciding with the founding of LAJSA. Jewishness was beside the point yet somehow meaningful for those in that room in Ottawa. My own interest in Jewishness as an area of scholarly investigation was decades in the future, a result of my bumping into Jewish-themed texts and Jewish-named writers, filmmakers, and visual artists in my research and teaching, until it seemed inevitable that I pay attention. The present book is the outcome of this slow gestation.

*The Other/Argentina* is deeply indebted to the growing body of research on gender, sexuality, and the modern nation, especially in relation to the field of Jewish studies in the United States and Europe. At the same time, it has been my intention to push the boundaries of that research, turning its gaze southward. Jewish studies in the US approaches the question of modernity largely by considering the triangle Europe–the United States–Israel, taking little note of Jewish communities and the way Jewishness means in other parts of the world. For its part, the impressive body of research in Latin American Jewish studies has barely been acknowledged by the US-based scholarly community. Conversely, the development of Jewish cultural studies, which has been revolutionizing Jewish studies in the United States over the past few decades, has thus far had little purchase in Latin America.

By limiting this study to Argentina, I open up some avenues and close off others. Jews are a minority in Argentina, but of all the countries of Latin America, Argentina has historically had the largest number, and proportion, of Jews in its population. Hence this book's focus on Jewishness in relation to Argentine self-fashioning, with regard to the position of Jews as simultaneously exemplary of, and the abjected other to, European modernity, and in the context of Argentina's own claim on a European identity in the face of Europe's refusal to accept any Latin American nation as its full equal. Argentina's Jewish history is certainly connected to that of other Latin American countries: many Jews leaving Europe or the Middle East who wound up in Latin America were hoping to get to the United States and landed instead in "the other America," sometimes Mexico or the Caribbean, Venezuela, Brazil, or Uruguay, and often Argentina. For the most part they reproduced a version of life in the old country in their new places of residence—they built synagogues and formed burial societies, created community centers, learned a new language but did not forget Yiddish and Hebrew, and held on to old rituals as well as to a sense of connectedness with Jews beyond their borders. Nevertheless, Jewish history in Argentina is distinguished by at least three factors: (1) the deliberate creation, by a German Jewish philanthropist, of Jewish settlements designed to create a Jewish homeland far away from the perils of Europe; (2) the immigration policies of postindependence Argentina that, in its desire to bring Europeans to settle, eventually expanded the list of the invited to include Jews; and (3) the Argentine elites' belief in their own difference from the rest of Latin America—that theirs is a modern European nation, with all the attending baggage surrounding Jews as both a part of and apart from whatever it is that constitutes Europe and modernity. These three intersecting phenomena suggest that Jewish ethnicity signifies somewhat differently in Argentina than it does in other parts of the continent.

Still, the very idea of Jewish modernity, even in its least nuanced form, challenges the Catholic Latin America to which Argentina belongs. In that worldview, Jews represent an intensely premodern cultural landscape thankfully superseded by Christian enlightenment.[1] Deeply held prejudices against Jews mark the Argentine cultural imaginary. Jewish and Gentile writers alike make use of the competing cultural, and deeply gendered, myths of Jews as an ancient people and as prototypical of modernity. The Jew is a complex marker: Luisa Valenzuela's liminal Israeli translator who scales walls and is unfazed by locked doors and windows in her 2010 novel *El Mañana* (The Mañana) vexes all borders and commonplaces. Erin Graff Zivin, recalling that the wandering Jew is a Christian trope, calls Jewishness "the wandering signifier."

My exploration of the traces of Jewishness in texts that may not be explicitly specific to Jews does not aim to excavate some essential Jewish nugget buried in Argentine soil, but rather to understand the different meanings that Jewishness carries in Argentina, and how sexuality and gender, as both lived experience and ideology, help code such meanings. Because gender, imbricated with sexuality, is an organizing principle of identity, it is inescapable as an effect of cultural texts, and it is a crucial category of analysis in teasing out the ways the Jewish presence in Argentina has affected that country's effort to establish itself as a modern nation. The project of thinking Argentine modernity through its relationship with Jewishness, gender, and sexuality would seem to rely on the presumption that its nodes of engagement—Argentina as a modern nation, Jewishness, what counts as manly or womanly, and normative as opposed to transgressive sexualities—are sturdy and constant. But Argentine identity has been contested since the foundation of the nation, and Jewishness bears different meanings for Gentiles, to say nothing of the schisms about its meanings among Jews themselves. The meaning of Jewishness shifts with the generations, among different Jewish communities, and within individuals. For its part, gender relies on constant reiteration; and, thanks to Foucault, we know that sexuality has a history. All these terms—Argentina, modernity, Jewishness, gender, sexuality—are provisional and in flux, but at the same time they have accrued a kind of solidity that allows us to use them with the expectation that they function to communicate in ways that are mutually, if provisionally, comprehensible.

Any understanding of culture, history, and society must take into account the politics of gender, and of the specificity of the local.[2] Riv Ellen

Prell, for example, argues convincingly that in the United States the process of Jewish assimilation is rife with anxiety, and that the strains caused by the simultaneous desire to maintain Jewishness and become American reveal themselves in expressions of loathing within the Jewish community that are expressed along internal fault lines of generation and, especially, gender. In the popular culture of the twentieth century she finds evidence of Jewish men who complain that Jewish women are too demanding and materialistic, Jewish women who object that Jewish men are egotistic and spoiled. If these internal anxieties exist within the Argentine Jewish community they are less visible as cultural—and especially literary—representations, possibly because the domestic fiction and the marriage plot that are central to Anglo-American narrative fiction are far less important in Argentina.[3] Shari Jacobson's argument that European Jewish orthodoxy is embraced by Argentine women of Syrian Jewish ancestry as a path into modernity confirms Prell's observation that ideas about Jewishness and modernity are locally produced, often in surprisingly distinctive ways.

Feminist and queer perspectives in Jewish cultural studies have opened the door to considering gender and sexuality in theorizing Jewish modernity. Daniel Boyarin, like Prell, is utterly convincing in his argument that Jewishness is a marker of difference connected to gender and sexuality, and I believe this claim holds true in Argentina. Still, the distinct material reality of Jews in Argentina may call into question some of the basic assumptions of Jewish cultural theorists in the US and Europe. Jews in Argentina are part of a larger Jewish history, but there are aspects of their experience that are specifically, and tellingly, Argentine. Argentina's status as a refuge for Jews escaping the pogroms of the late nineteenth century and the Holocaust of the twentieth, as well as for Nazi war criminals after the Second World War, fictionalized by (among others) José Pablo Feinmann in *Heidegger's Shadow* (*La sombra de Heidegger*), Edgardo Cozarinsky in *Lejos de dónde* (Far from where), and Paola Kaufmann in *The Lake* (*El lago*), and its particular history of immigration—inviting Jews to settle there, but only after the rest of Europe had been exhausted as a source of immigrants—highlight Argentine ambivalence toward Jews. For some Jews in Argentina, assimilation may represent full participation in and acceptance by the nation, but it may also afford a kind of protective coloration that allows one to pass. The specificities of Argentine Jewish history also affect the representation and cultural meanings of the gendered Jewish body. The feminized body of the Jewish male and the nurturing body of the Jewish mother are deeply rooted in Western tradition generally, whereas the abject body of the Jewish prostitute and the lacerated body of the Jewish torture victim acquire particular meanings in Argentina. César Tiempo's *Versos de una . . .* (Poems of a . . .), Nora Glickman's *Una tal Raquel* (Some woman named Raquel), and Patricia Suárez's *Las polacas* (The Polish girls) exemplify the former, while Alicia Partnoy's *The Little School* (*La escuelita*), Sara Rosenberg's *Un hilo rojo* (A red thread), and Nora Strejilevich's *A Single, Numberless Death* (*Una sola muerte numerosa*) are instances of the latter. Furthermore, icons of Argentine Jewish masculinity include not only the peddler and the scholar, but also the Jewish gaucho and the urban tough, troubling conventional readings of Jewish masculinity. The title character of Edgardo Cozarinsky's *The Moldavian Pimp* (*El rufián moldavo*) is a swaggering Jewish pimp, and the heroes of Marcelo Birmajer's *Tres mosqueteros* (Three musketeers) recall their past as urban guerrillas.

Mutually comprehensible meaning relies on narrative, and in this book I look at particular forms of storytelling (fiction, feature films, and theater rather than history and journalism, for example) to examine the ways that Jewishness and gender, inflected by sexuality, have played a part in the production of Argentina as a modern nation. The biting satire of Diana Raznovich's plays and Ricardo Feierstein's novelistic interrogation of memory itself severely undercut the nostalgic idealization that characterizes Gerchunoff (1910). Read together with Alicia Steimberg's wit (1971) and Ana María Shua's gentle irony (2000), these texts are part of an edifice of elegy, satire, humor, and memory. The journal *Hispamérica*, founded and edited by the tireless, brilliant Saúl Sosnowski, has unobtrusively showcased the work of Jews without announcing it as such, subtly marking Argentina as Jewish territory.

Here as in what follows I name only a few of the many extraordinary writers, filmmakers, and visual artists whose work bears on the interplay of gender, Jewishness, and modernity in Argentina. There is no way I could have included discussions of all of them in this one book. I hope that my efforts here serve to encourage others to take up this work and move it in directions that I have not envisioned.

n.b.: a note on titles. Where published translations exist I use the English title first, followed by the Spanish. Where there is no official translation, I give the Spanish title and offer a provisional rendering into English.

# ACKNOWLEDGMENTS

It took me many years to research and write this book, and many people and institutions helped me along the way. Leslie Morris, Michael Bernard-Donals, and Keith Cohen, warm and welcoming colleagues in Jewish studies at the University of Minnesota and the University of Wisconsin, thought it would be a good idea to include my perspective as a Latin Americanist in a DAAD-sponsored seminar on post-Holocaust literature. That was the beginning of my foray into Jewish studies. It continued with an extraordinary NEH Summer Institute, "Venice, the Jews, and Italian Culture," whose leaders, Murray Baumgarten and Shaul Bassi, thought I might have something to offer. I am forever grateful to them, and to my colleagues at the institute, who taught me so much. NEH later doubled down on me, with a magnanimous fellowship that gave me a year's leisure (in the classical sense of time to read, reflect, learn, and write) to concentrate on this project. The University of Minnesota was also truly generous, supporting my research with a multiyear grant-in-aid, travel grants, and a semester at its sterling Institute for Advanced Study.

Friends and colleagues have urged me along with encouragement and resources. I am especially grateful to Noni Benegas, Carla Manzoni, and Daniela Goldfine for introducing me to crucial materials I would not otherwise have found. I also want to offer my deepest thanks to Marcelo Brodsky, Guillermo Kuitca, and Mirta Kupferminc for their generosity in permitting me to reproduce their artwork. I am forever indebted to Judith Katz for telling me I really should write this book; it was her idea that we visit Moisés Ville, a trip we would have found far more difficult to manage had it not been for Ken Kaminsky's world-class driving skills. David Kaminsky made the transition from kid to colleague during the course of this project. His insight has proved invaluable.

## ACKNOWLEDGMENTS

From the moment that Rosemary Geisdorfer Feal generously invited me to submit my manuscript to the SUNY series in Latin American and Iberian Thought and Culture, I have been enveloped in scholarly and professional welcome at the Press. I am deeply indebted to the anonymous readers of the manuscript for their attentive reading; the book is stronger for their suggestions. Editors Rebecca Colesworthy and James Peltz have been there for me with support and encouragement, and Jennifer Bennett-Genthner has been unreservedly patient with me in all questions of formatting and production. Kathy Dvorsky's careful copyediting has been a gift.

I am deeply indebted to the work and the friendship of Riv Ellen Prell, Leslie Morris, Saúl Sosnowski, Mirta Kupferminc, Alicia Partnoy, and Florinda Goldberg, who continue to inspire me. Long walks with Elaine Tyler May and long talks with Naomi Scheman have sustained me intellectually and emotionally. As always, Ken Kaminsky has been a source of strength and encouragement. This book is dedicated to the people he loves most in the world.

CHAPTER ONE

# PLANTING WHEAT AND REAPING DOCTORS
## Another Way of Being Argentine

The fabric that is Argentina is woven of many threads, not least of which are the warp and woof of cultures, languages, and beliefs of the people who made their way into that nation. In this book I search for one of the strands in the complex fabric of Argentine history and self-representation, the strand of Jewishness. I tug on the fibers of Jewishness in Argentina to test the strength of the weave that holds them, and I consider the patterns of nation and meaning they form in combination with the threads alongside which they lie and those with which they interlace. The fabled Argentine Jewish migratory route from the shtetls of Eastern Europe to the agricultural settlements of the pampas and to the urban centers of the nation gave rise to the sardonic observation that Jews came to the countryside of Argentina where they sowed wheat but reaped doctors, as their children went off to live in the nation's urban centers. This pattern is just one of the ways that Argentina's Jewish history resonates both with Jewish diasporas more generally and with Argentina's past as a nation of immigrants, even as the story of Jews in Argentina rings changes on other Jewish and Argentine migration and assimilation narratives.[1] Jewishness and Argentineity have been modified and inflected by each other so that Argentineity slips into Jewishness, just as Jewishness is another modality of Argentineity.

The very project of modernity in Argentina, the weaving of that cloth of many textures, relies, in part, on a submerged and troubled relationship to the paradox of Jewish otherness in, and identification with, the nation. It thereby claims a central place for Jewish-authored texts and the deployment of Jewishness, as an idea as well as an identity, in shaping Argentina's cultural landscape as a modern nation. As a multicultural immigrant nation with a large, and still largely ignored, indigenous population as well as a little-acknowledged history of African slavery and its aftermath, Argentina struggles with, and is enriched by, conflicting and interlacing meanings of religion, ethnicity, race, sexuality, and gender.[2] Visual artists, filmmakers, and writers, who often speak both of documenting their world and discovering it as they create, have often interrogated the meaning of Argentine modernity in relation to Europe and to the rest of Latin America. Literary and visual texts marked by complex representations of Argentina's sites of difference, tied to such critical moments in the nation's history as the rise of labor and anarchist movements in the early part of the twentieth century, Peronism in midcentury, the dictatorship and repression of the 1970s and 1980s, and times of economic crisis like those of the turn of the millennium are, therefore, critical sites for both exploring and temporarily stabilizing such meaning.

Argentina claims to be a modern nation, a claim that would be utterly precarious were it predicated only on the nation's political and economic status in the world. Instead, Argentine modernity rests on a balance between unitary national identity and a mix of often-subdued internal differences that may trouble such unity but that also link the nation to a globalized cosmopolitanism. Both close and symptomatic readings of Argentine literary, visual, and cinematic texts to examine cultural representations of difference, give ample evidence that Argentine modernity is predicated on such a balance. The texts I call upon, mostly by Jewish-identified authors, a category that is hardly uniform or unambiguous, give ample evidence that Argentine modernity is poised between a unitary sense of nationality and a range of marginalized ethnic, racial, sexual, and gender identities.

For its part, Jewishness holds multiple meanings related to Argentina's claim to modernity.[3] In the context of Argentina's struggle to claim a place in the modern world, Jewishness is, among other things, a matter of cultural representations and elisions. At times Jewishness is salient, for good or ill. For Jewishness is a productive irritant that, in Argentina as elsewhere, refuses to dissolve completely. Making their way into the very stuff of the immigrant nation, Jews and Jewish culture inflect national identity in ways that are embedded in Argentina's vibrant literary and visual cultures. Argentina's Jews are associated with urban life and rural development, capitalism as well as socialism, medicine, psychoanalysis, and intellectual and artistic pursuits—in other words, with modernity. Nevertheless, theorists of modernity often consider it as a purely European phenomenon, and in fact

European modernity produces itself against the colonial, raced, and feminized other that includes both Jews and Latin America. This is the modernity of the atomized subject that has come under so much feminist scrutiny, but it is also one that is almost immediately recovered for community by the (distinctly masculinist) social contract. Modernity is necessarily globalized insofar as it produces itself against the other from without, as well as in contrast to the other within.

The familiar if somewhat tired argument that Latin America has never been part of modernity, but rather has always been postmodern, derives from the notion that the singular, European (unmarked but for that reason no less masculine) subject can never have been fully transplanted onto American soil: that the *criollo* was by ancestry Spanish, but by history and geography American.[4] The embrace of hybridity came much later, but it sealed the (post)modern pact as forever and necessarily marked by the incorporation of at least one of its others. One observer, Adolfo Colombres, distinguishes between "dominant modernity," the modernity of the Enlightenment, which "aspired to put reason at the service of liberty and justice" (95) but lost its way and became an obsessive religion of progress (95) and "our [Latin American] modernity," produced through the diversity of Latin American cultures, traditions, belief systems, and histories (106ff.). Nevertheless, despite his attention to class differences, Colombres's Europe is ethnically monolithic, excluding Jews and other minorities, and both his Europe and his America are hetero-masculine, with room neither for women or sexual minorities.

On the other hand, the dominant strains in Jewish cultural studies approach the question of modernity with little reference to Jews outside Europe, the United States, and Israel. Until the quite recent entry of feminist and queer perspectives in Jewish cultural studies, gender and sexuality were not taken into account in either the affirmation or the theorization of Jewish modernity. Still, even this narrow understanding of Jewishness makes space for the suggestion that Jewishness and modernity are linked. Despite having absorbed European understandings of Jewishness, Argentina, as a hybrid nation, necessarily modifies the conventional European view of Jewish difference. Jews remain outsiders among more easily assimilated immigrants to the nation, but because most Argentine Jews *are* European, they are not so "other" to the dominant culture as are indigenous people and Afro-Argentines. The recent exodus of Jews from Argentina is another mark of Jewish difference, but these new Israelis, Europeans, and North Americans identify also as Argentines.[5]

As languages and narrative systems, English and Spanish both inscribe actor and action in relation to some other. Written narrative implies a multiplicity of subjects circulating among the subject of the sentence, the narrative voice, and the author her or himself, and always presupposes at least one subject-receptor, the reader or listener. Nevertheless, the indirect complement of the verb, the one who is not its subject and whom I am loath to call its object, may stand in a relation of alliance, friendship, and trust. It is a relationship that Martin Buber calls I/Thou, in which the encounter between the two is not the monological relationship between subject and object, but rather an encounter between subject and subject, in which both may undergo a certain transformation as a result of their coming together. In the encounter between Jews and Argentina, both are changed, and both grow.

This discursive ground is not without moments of conflict. Two foundational texts of Argentine Jewishness, Julián Martel's antisemitic, urban *The Stock Market* (*La bolsa*, 1891), and Alberto Gerchunoff's *The Jewish Gauchos of the Pampas* (*Los gauchos judíos*, 1910), which stakes a Jewish claim to Argentina's iconic pampas, frame the contested meanings of Argentineity and Jewishness.[6] Subsequent writers have embraced and rewritten the emblematic figure of Gerchunoff's Jewish gaucho, while *The Stock Market*'s blatant antisemitism persists as a symptom of anti-Jewish sentiment.

The pseudonymous Martel published the foundational (if noncanonical) antisemitic text of Argentina, *The Stock Market*, within two years of the arrival in the port of Buenos Aires of the steamship *Weser*, which carried the first group of Russian Jewish immigrants headed for a rural life in Argentina. Less than twenty years later, Alberto Gerchunoff, a descendant of one of the *Weser* passengers, wrote his own story of Jewishness in Argentina. Gerchunoff's *The Jewish Gauchos*, like Martel's *The Stock Market*, stakes a claim to authentic Argentineity; each organizes that claim around radically different representations of the Jewish immigrant and diametrically opposed views of the value of Jewishness to Argentina as a modernizing nation. What is more, both Martel and Gerchunoff implicitly represent both Jewishness and Argentineity in distinctly gendered and sexualized ways as they develop an understanding of Jewishness in relation to its bearing on Argentina as a modern nation.

The urban setting of *The Stock Market* troubles traditional masculinity, which, in the city, is challenged not only by the domestic demands of the bourgeois Catholic woman, but, more overtly, by what the narrator describes as a veritable invasion of immigrants. The modernity of industrial-era civilization is a cause of anxiety. Among the trappings of that civilization, the brightly lit home that Luis Glow, the novel's embattled hero, provides for his loving but implicitly demanding wife, Margarita, and their children both symbolizes the enlightenment of modernity and testifies to the rash, ostentatious spending that threatens the traditional, conservative family. The newly developing capitalism that promises Argentina entry into the modern economic world is shot through with the danger of degeneracy, corruption, and deceit. In *The Stock Market*, these dangers are embodied in the figure of the Jewish speculator. He is not the only corrupt figure in the novel, but he is unmistakably the source of corruption. Textual anxiety about the inappropriate entry of Jews into the fabric of polite society finds an echo in distress over class mobility. A conversation between Glow and his friends expresses astonishment and not a little dismay that a former waiter is now hobnobbing with the gentry and can no longer be berated by his (erstwhile) social betters. It is the Jew, however, whose presence most threatens the social order. Martel's Jewish man is deficient in his unhealthy body; described in feminine terms, he is both degenerate and dishonorable:

> The one who mangled these French words with German teeth, and not the purest German at that, was a pale, blond, lymphatic man, of short stature, and in whose disagreeable and effeminate face could be observed an expression of hypocritical humility, which earmarks the Jewish race through a long period of servility. He had small bloodshot eyes, like the descendants of the tribe of Zabulon and the hooked nose typical of the tribe of Ephraim. He dressed with the flashy showiness of the Jew, who can never quite acquire the noble distinction which characterizes the man of the Aryan race, his antagonist. His name was Filiberto Mackster [*sic*] and he had the title of Baron which he had bought in Germany believing that this would lend importance to his obscure name. (1948, 33–34)

> [El que lo hablaba, masticando las palabras francesas con dientes alemanes, y no de los más puros, por cierto, era un hombre pálido, rubio, linfático, de mediana estatura, y en cuya cara antipática y afeminada se observaba esa expresión de hipócrita humildad que la costumbre de un largo servilismo ha hecho como el sello típico de la raza judía. Tenía los ojos pequeños, estriados de filamentos rojos, que denuncian los descendientes de la tribu de Zabulón,

y la nariz encorvada propia de la tribu de Ephraim. Vestía con el lujo charro del judío, el cual nunca puede llegar a adquirir la noble distinción que caracteriza al hombre de la raza Arya, su antagonista. Llamábase Filiberto Mackser y tenía el título de barón que había comprado en Alemania creyendo que así daba importancia a su oscuro apellido. (1891, 35–36)]

Mackser's physical degeneracy is echoed by the social and moral corruption embodied by his young associate, a man engaged in sex trafficking, slavery, and pro-Jewish propaganda:

> He was accompanied by a young man, countryman and fellow believer, who practiced the white slave trade, supplying the brothels of Buenos Aires with all the beauties which supply the German and Oriental markets. He also wrote for a daily evening paper, in whose columns he lent important services to the interests of the Jews, quite often winning public approval for them. He was, besides, president of a club of slave traders. (1948, 34)

> [Iba acompañado de un joven, compatriota y correligionario suyo, que ejercía el comercio de mujeres, abasteciendo los serrallos porteños de todas las bellezas que proporcionan los mercados alemanes y orientales. También escribía en un diario de la tarde, en cuyas columnas prestaba importantes servicios a los intereses judíos, consiguiendo muchas veces dirigir la opinión en favor de éstos. Era, además, presidente de un club de traficantes de carne humana. (1891, 36)]

Martel's schematic description of Mackser and his sidekick crams a cartload of stereotypes into these short passages. Between them, the Jewish men are sickly, pale, short of stature, unpleasant to look at, effeminate, affected, hypocritical, servile, flashy, corrupt, and quite possibly homosexual:

> Pale blond, sickly, and of short stature, God only knows what strange bonds united him to the Baron de Mackster [sic], whom he seemed to treat with extreme consideration. (1948, 35)

> [Pálido, rubio, enclenque y de reducida estatura, sabe Dios qué extraños lazos lo unían con el barón de Mackser, al que parecía tratar con exagerados miramientos. (1891, 37)]

The religiously suspect, sexually degenerate Jew is part of an international conspiracy to take control of the new nation's sources of wealth:

> The Doctor [Glow] knew that the Semite was an envoy of Rothschild, the English banker, who had sent him to Buenos Aires to operate in gold and to exercise pressure on the market. What the Doctor didn't know was that Mackster [*sic*] had the assignment of monopolizing, with the help of a strong Jewish syndicate, the principal productive sources of the country. (1948, 35)

> [No ignoraba el doctor que aquel semita era un enviado de Rothschild, el banquero inglés, que lo había mandado a Buenos Aires para que operase en el oro y ejerciese presión sobre la plaza. Lo que el doctor no sabía era que Mackser tenía la consigna de acaparar, de monopolizar, con ayuda de un fuerte sindicato judío, a cuyo frente estaba él, las principales fuentes productoras del país. (1891, 37)]

Mackser and his partner mimic Gentile ways in a manner that is always insufficient: they mangle both French and German, and their attempt at elegance inevitably misses the mark. The older man affects a language and a title to which he has no right and, in an echo of the scurrilous *Protocols of the Elders of Zion*, is the envoy of an international Jewish conspiracy bent on taking over the nation's economy.[7] Mackser's companion traffics both in women and in propaganda, and he writes pro-Jewish columns for the press. A third Jewish character, a moneylender who refuses to lend the protagonist funds when he learns that he is the financially ruined Glow, is a similar caricature.[8]

*The Stock Market* is blatantly antisemitic in its condemnation of Jewish lust for money, accusations of treachery, and the suggestion of an international, antipatriotic conspiracy that would undermine not only the naive blond protagonist but the ever-whiter nation he embodies as well. Martel marshals the culturally available hate-mongering stereotypes quite overtly, but he is only a bit more circumspect about the way the feminization of the villain depends on a pejorative valuation of femininity itself. His depiction of modern bourgeois femininity debases the image of the idealized wife and mother, whose upkeep and desire for social advancement underlie the protagonist's eagerness to enter into a shady deal in which he becomes the victim.

The innocent protagonist loses all his money by trusting the persuasive Jewish-led cabal, but in the end he was never all that innocent. His plan to make a killing in the stock market (a practice in which someone is necessarily left as loser) is already corrupt, already contaminated by the pull of modernity, even without the Jewish agent of overt dishonesty. The civilized modernity that Glow craves is built upon a foundation of barbarism. The blazing lights of the house that advertise his hoped-for success as a speculator edge toward making literal the metaphor. The house built on (failed) speculation cannot stand. Glow cannot afford to keep it up; all that light emanating from it might as well mean that it is burning to the ground.

The central cause for anxiety in *The Stock Market* is modernity itself, which cannot keep its masculine, European, Christian purity intact. Just as Jewishness—here in the debased form of modern capitalist practices—underpins modernity, the masculinist modernity of the West needs the feminine: the house in the city with all its lovely furniture and its decorative woman and children who are (remembering Veblen) the very proof of modern masculine success. Although Luis Glow originally fell in love with Margarita in the purest way, all love and beauty and romanticism, she is much more practical—even mercenary—than he:

> His wife, who was quite ambitious and who seemingly had married him because he was a rising young man, had dreamed of driving him to reach a very high position (the Doctor didn't even suspect this); she also induced him to go into politics. And the sly girl hadn't made a bad choice because, among his contemporaries, he was the one who showed the most promise, the one who would go farthest, but—The Stock Market swallowed him. (1948, 89)

> [Su mujer, además, que era ambiciosa, y que quizás, al casarse con él sabiendo que era un joven de esperanzas, había soñado en impulsarlo a subir alto, muy alto (esto el doctor ni lo sospechaba), también lo inducía a meterse en política. Y no había elegido mal la pícara muchacha, porque de la generación de Glow, él era quien más valía, quien iría más lejos; pero . . . ¡Se lo tragó la Bolsa! (1891, 93)]

Both the wife and the stock market have their claws into Glow; he is the blue-eyed innocent.

Margarita is beautiful, richly attired, and sexually appealing. The danger suggested in her voluptuous body is expressed in the metonym of her hair, described as both "rebellious" and "provocative." Martel's increasingly overwrought description of her ends with a comparison to a deadly snake:

> tall and with a slightly rosy whiteness which meant ardent and young blood; black, shining, enormous, fascinating Andalusian eyes; wavy, rebellious hair which was darker than her eyes, if possible, and on whose waves lay a small golden hat which seemed to be shipwrecked like a gold-masted ship, a toy on that sea which at every instant overflowed in the form of a provocative lock of hair on the narrow Greek forehead, giving an excuse to the small agile hand to throw it back with a movement of affectionate familiarity; wrapped in a luxurious bronze-colored velvet coat whose folds let one guess the exciting form of a body which had reached the height of splendid development; high breast, full throat which rose in a soft curve to lose itself in a swan skin wrapped around the neck like a snow-white viper. (1948, 92)

> [alta, blanca, con esa blancura ligeramente sonrosada bajo la cual se adivina la sangre ardiente y joven; de ojos negros, relampagueantes, ojos andaluces, enormes, luminosos, fascinadores, el pelo ondeado, rebelde, sin reflejos, más negro, si cabe, que los ojos, sosteniendo en sus olas de tinta una gorrita dorada que parecía naufragar, como bajel de mástiles de oro, juguete de aquel mar que a cada instante se desbordaba en forma de provocativo mechón sobre la angosta frente griega, dando pretexto a una manecita ágil y regordetona para echarlo atrás con un movimiento lleno de familiaridad cariñosa; envuelta en lujoso abrigo de terciopelo bronceado, cuyos pliegues dejaban adivinar las formas incitantes de un cuerpo llegado al apogeo de su espléndido desarrollo; alto el seno, la garganta llena y turgente, escapándose en suave curva para ir a confundirse con la piel de cisne arrollada al cuello como una víbora de nieve. (1891, 96–97)]

Health, high color, sensuality, and rich clothing all come together in this description of beauty, excess, and danger. Margarita is far more astute than her husband, perceiving that he is likely to be swindled, and she is suspicious of the dishonorable people he is dealing with. While Glow is giddy over the prospect of investing in an underhanded scheme to make cheap liqueur, Margarita has been following the stock market with a dispassionate eye. She is a better judge of investments and has a cooler head than her husband. It is he who makes the showy display of burning lights in every room in the house, and when she chastises him for his ostentatious waste, he blames her for not being at home to greet him. Refusing to stay quite in her place as the angel in the house, Margarita begins to embody the transgressive woman whose monstrosity lurks beneath the surface. Her sexuality is firmly accounted for within the novel, but her superior economic acumen is another link, however domesticated, to the Jewish threat against which the naive Glow has no defense other than his antisemitism, which is not sufficient to check his greed.

Luis Glow, whose first and last names both suggest the light of modernity, and whose title, Doctor, bestows society's recognition of a secular formal education and perhaps even wisdom, ends in a descent into madness, destroyed by the stock market, which drives him "insane, insane forever" (1948, 195) [¡loco, loco para siempre! (1891, 311)]. In his delirium, he succumbs to a beautiful temptress who turns into a monster, entrapping him in her claws, stabbing him with her quills, and breaking his body. In its seductive beginnings, what will become that nightmare vision is reminiscent of Margarita herself, with her serpentine neck, bare arms, and warm breast, "the most beautiful creature that his eyes had ever beheld" (1948, 194) [la criatura más hermosa que habían contemplado sus ojos (1891, 310)]. Just before she reveals her true nature as a horrible beast, Glow, trapped in his own desire, "tasted all the joys of love and of satisfied vanity" (1948, 194) [probó todos los goces del amor y de la vanidad satisfecha (1891, 310)]. Once he is ensnared in her embrace, she turns into a hairy, reptilian, sharp-edged monster that identifies itself as the stock exchange, associating Margarita with the temptress stock market in its deadliest incarnation.

The lure of the material—of the feminine, of sensual delight and vast wealth—makes Glow seek out the monster, the deformed, literally grasping and clutching beast that, however seductive, is also metaphorically the Jew with whom it has been identified through the course of the novel. The all-engulfing feminine materializes in this nightmare in which the stock exchange is personified and made monstrous at the same time. Here Martel conjures the fear of castration, images of the vagina dentata, and the terror of being engulfed by the feminine, which he has already associated with the degenerate Jewish cabal at the center of the corrupt and corrosive stock exchange. Not for nothing did Martel choose his pseudonym; the medieval warrior's hammer deals a fierce and wicked blow to Jewishness, femininity, and modernity.

In order to function, modern urban financial success requires the very system of corruption that the Jew is conscripted to embody in this novel. The young capitalist earns his money by investing (i.e., by speculating), not by exchanging his labor for wages, or by exploiting Argentina's natural resources, or even by dint of inheritance. These more straightforward means of earning a living are intimately connected to the rural life that Alberto Gerchunoff claims as deeply Jewish, once the Jews have left their shtetls and come to Argentina.

In contrast to *The Stock Market*, Alberto Gerchunoff's *The Jewish Gauchos of the Pampas*, set in autochthonous rural Argentina, makes the case that Jews are ideal Argentines. Gerchunoff embraces the gaucho myth as well as the project of development, the scene of robust, implicitly reproductive sexuality and the modernization-cum-Argentinization of Jews who, nevertheless, keep their Jewishness intact. Gerchunoff stakes a claim for Jewish Argentineity that is also vigorously and normatively masculine without relinquishing the settlers' deeply held Jewishness.[9] By naming their town Moisés Ville, in honor of the Jewish baron who bequeathed them the land and reminiscent of the biblical figure who led their ancestors out of slavery in Egypt, the Jewish settlers tie the place to a particularly Jewish strain of patriarchy, one that makes a place for women as sexual beings. Unlike Martel, Gerchunoff has no need for a demonized feminine sexuality. His Jewish women settlers are healthily fertile, as if in sympathy with the land. The majority of them are willing adjuncts to their husbands and dutiful daughters to their fathers. The desire they arouse is destined to be contained within a marriage in which they are expected to be productive, not ornamental.

Gerchunoff's Jewish men are the ideal rural males in their physical prowess, but they also epitomize Jewish masculinity in their dedication to study. Women are necessary for reproduction and for male sexual delight. Gerchunoff's earthy Jewish women settlers are the antidote to the consumerist beauty of Glow's wife in *The Stock Market*, but in other ways they are not that unlike Margarita, prized for their beauty and their capacity to reproduce. In both texts the women are secondary, present in relationship to the men who value them. But whereas Margarita is the decorative wife who permits Glow to display his affluence, Gerchunoff's hardy Jewish women are productive, hardworking participants in the colonial project. Still, in their voluptuousness, both Gerchunoff's Jewish milkmaid and Martel's bourgeois wife are described with a lasciviousness that is only recuperated by their containment in sanctioned masculine desire.

This is not to suggest that Gerchunoff displays no anxiety about the perils of assimilation. These are gender-coded as well: he tells the story of the insufficiently demure young woman who runs away with a real—not a Jewish—gaucho. For although the Jewish men who are his heroes live in the countryside and learn to drink maté, ride horses, and handle a knife, they are new settlers, not the often-itinerant cattle-herders of indigenous and European ancestry named by the term *gaucho*. Only their connection to rural Argentina makes it possible for Gerchunoff to so strategically call these Jewish settlers gauchos. Ironically, the Jewish gauchos (the name stuck) are part of the modernizing project of rural development, a project that in essence does away with the real-life gaucho. They are willing, if not necessarily self-aware, pawns in the national goal of ethnic cleansing, displacing the indigenous inhabitants of the land.[10] Their part in the modernizing project culminates with migration to the cities as subsequent generations chose to leave the agricultural colonies in favor of higher education, the professions, and the world of commerce. In all of this, Gerchunoff and subsequent cheerleaders for Jewish participation in the project of making Argentina, make the case for a specifically Jewish Argentineity.

As the cultural valence of transgressive sexuality changes, as gender queer and sexual transgression (particularly women's embrace of their sexuality and of desire itself) tip toward the positive, the meaning they lend to any text also must shift. A feminist perspective radical thirty years ago but now perfectly mainstream, for example, reveals the crude underlying sexism of Martel's *The Stock Market* of a piece with its antisemitism and homophobia. It also reveals similar attitudes concerning women's proper place in Gerchunoff's *The Jewish Gauchos*, highlighting the shared heteronormativity of both texts.

Although both *The Stock Market* and *The Jewish Gauchos* are part of the project of modernity—colonization, development, urbanization, assimilation, and the policing of gender—the contrast between the two texts' understanding of Jewishness in that project could not be more stark. Gerchunoff's Jew is integrationist, assimilationist, and nationalist, while holding on to religious tradition. The healthy Jewish body of the Jewish gaucho and his family, and the appropriate sexuality of desirable women and men who build those families, stand in stark contrast with Martel's sickly, sexually suspect, cosmopolitan Jew. For both, the ideal male is the handsome protagonist with his charming wife and beloved children, the ideal, heterosexual, reproductive head of household who provides the model for the benignly patriarchal state.

Given the obsessive connection between sexual degeneracy and Jewishness, it is no surprise that *The Jewish Gauchos* and subsequent texts petitioning for Jewish admittance as trustworthy, respectable Argentine citizens cleave so strongly to heteronormativity and sexuality in the service of reproduction. The Gerchunoff character who all but drools in the presence of a lusty young Jewish farmer's daughter is displaying a state-sanctioned masculinity that is in concert with patriarchal norms. Women's own desire is subdued in the text, except as a counterexample, and even there the breach is well within the bounds of heterosexual propriety. The young woman who runs off with her Gentile suitor establishes a marriage with him. Her behavior may be devastating to her Jewish family and community, but it also serves to reinforce the bonds of heteronormativity between Jewishness and Argentineity and even presages the assimilation-cementing intermarriage that becomes so common in later generations.

Nothing less than the right to full nationality is at stake in Jewish masculinity, an observation rendered obvious in any consideration of Argentine Jewish texts that deal with Israel. The tension of the other-as-same within the nation that wreaks havoc on Jewish masculinity in Argentina (and elsewhere in the diaspora) is resolved in straightforward Zionist masculinity, the fully realized Jew as rightful inhabitant of the land. The Jewish man in these texts does not have to deal with his Jewishness as *another* way of being fully part of the nation; in Israel he can claim untroubled belonging. In Daniel Burman's *The Empty Nest* (*El nido vacío*, 2008), for example, the Israeli son-in-law is the ideal man who bests the Argentine father in the competition for the daughter's love. More importantly, he is the Jewish writer as supermacho, winner of prizes and famous throughout the world.[11]

In Jewish Argentine texts that figure Israel, Jewish claims to heteronormative masculinity are often bound up with the warrior figure of Israeli nationalism. Elías, the protagonist of Marcelo Birmajer's *Tres mosqueteros* (Three musketeers, 2001), moves to Israel to become a spy to help protect Jews as a direct result of his inability to protect his two friends in Argentina when they became urban guerrillas and were captured by the paramilitary. Zionism is a masculine project in these, and other, Argentine Jewish texts. In Burman's *Lost Embrace* (*El abrazo partido*, 2004) the father has long ago left his family and gone off to Israel. He is eventually absolved of the abandonment of his wife and son when it is revealed that he left because his wife was unfaithful to him, effectively trampling on his masculinity. When he returns, it is as an Israeli war hero, but he is also physically scarred—his missing arm is a kind of castration that is also a sign of heroic masculinity, a visible sign of a damaged virility recuperated by sacrificing himself for the land of absolute Jewishness and absolute Jewish masculinity. The film ends with the father and son marching together arm in arm, a reconciliation that leaves the mother behind. The war-hero father embodies ideal masculinity for the son. Israel in these texts is clearly a space of Argentine masculine Jewish desire, where Jewish manhood can be rewritten, as it was on the pampas.

Gregorio Tavosnanska's 1999 novel *Ydel, el judío pampa* (Ydel, the pampas Jew) can be read as an homage to *The Jewish Gauchos*, abiding as it does by the values, and even more deeply by the themes, of Gerchunoff's foundational text. Published close to a century after *The Jewish Gauchos* but set in around the same period, Tavosnanska's novel is structurally more complex than Gerchunoff's series of vignettes, and, with the inclusion of a Black character who describes his life before and after slavery, he is more sensitive to the racism of the era than Gerchunoff. Nevertheless, his Ydel (the Yiddish form of Judah, a name that translates literally as "Jew") is a hypermasculine figure who loses his virginity on the boat to Argentina and whose sexuality is subsequently properly channeled in marriage. The older woman who initiates him, and who makes the experience of the voyage a time of pleasure and delight only the two of them share, is called Raquel, a name long associated with Jewish prostitution in Argentina.[12] Once Raquel teaches Ydel to please women sexually she conveniently disappears from the text, allowing him to be both an expert lover and a good husband. Raquel essentially dissolves into the city; the woman who is marked as sexually free has no place in the productive—and reproductive—countryside.

Ydel makes a Jewish home on the pampas anchored by his wife and father, but he also enjoys the freedom of the journey by horseback that makes him a true Argentine man. Tavosnanska contrasts him not only to his wife Fany, who has somewhat less than happily given up the communal life of the small agricultural settlement, where women enjoy each other's company in carrying out their domestic duties, and who fears the weapons her husband has learned to use, but also to his elderly father, who represents the old country and the old ways. The old patriarchy gives way to the new. Unlike his father, Ydel learns Spanish, drinks maté, rides his horse, and dresses in the gaucho garb that allows freedom of movement on horseback and protects him against the cold. Ydel is proud of his skill with the *facón*, the short-handled knife that any self-respecting gaucho must learn to wield. He is also proud that he makes up for taking his wife away from women's companionship by providing her with sexual satisfaction. Her desire satisfied, she is not only unquestionably, but also unquestioningly, subordinate. Like Gerchunoff, Tavosnanska inserts his exemplary Jewish male into the most Argentine of settings, making and remaking the case for Jewish Argentineity rooted in proper masculinity. The story is his; dominant narratives of generation and gender assure that. Nevertheless, Tavosnanska's retelling of the foundational story is less sanguine about the adaptation of Jews to Argentina and vice versa. Even the bitterest episode of *The Jewish Gauchos*, in which Gerchunoff memorializes the death of his father at the hands of an angry gaucho, is burnished by the author. In *Ydel*, on the other hand, Tavosnanska does not minimize the hardships of settling the land. Nor does the narrative nurtured and proffered to tourists by the handful of Jewish women of contemporary Moisés Ville who are dedicated to maintaining and transmitting the Jewish history of their town.

About a hundred years after the first boatload of Russian Jews landed in Buenos Aires, the schoolchildren of Moisés Ville, as if in homage to Gerchunoff, were invited to create a rosy picture of the settlement of that Jewish village on the pampas and a happy coexistence between immigrant Jews and their already-Argentine neighbors. The charming murals they painted decorate the walls surrounding the Moisés Ville museum on the Argentine

Figure 1.1. Anonymous. Children's mural of the arrival of the *SS Weser*. Source: Amy Kaminsky.

pampas, depicting the arrival of the steamship *Weser*, bringing smiling Jewish immigrants to the shores of Argentina. Nearby, the artists have joined traditional Jewish symbols—the Star of David and the menorah—with icons of Argentine nationalism—the flag, the map, the nation's colors—to celebrate both the nation's welcome of these immigrants and the Jews' embrace of Argentine national identity. Between these two images is a darker one, linking the Holocaust to Argentina's 1976–1983 dictatorship (see chapter 7).

Indeed, the Jews of the *Weser* came at the invitation of the Argentine government, intent on filling the land with Europeans and scuffing the traces of the indigenous people they had pushed off this fertile land. What happened to the *Weser* travelers does not make for joyous murals; you learn about that only by entering the museum itself. In other words, that story is legible to those who go beyond the triumphalist story of immigration and assimilation.

In 1881 the Argentine government, which had begun its invitation to immigrants years before as a way to populate their new nation with industrious European stock, extended its reach to those it had formerly

Figure 1.2. Anonymous. Children's mural in Moisés Ville, including map of Argentina with Jewish, indigenous, and national symbols. *Source*: Amy Kaminsky.

eschewed: Eastern European Jews. The eugenicist impulse to create a racially superior nation was not entirely abandoned, and the Jews, like the Italians who constituted such a large percentage of Argentina's immigrants, were not thought to be of the caliber of the British, French, and Germans who preceded them and were welcomed somewhat more ambivalently.

The original group of approximately one hundred and thirty families (just over eight hundred people) that sailed on the *Weser*, led by their rabbi, arrived in Argentina from Ukraine in 1889. They had agreed to purchase land from Rafael Hernández, who reneged on the deal, leaving the immigrants stranded. A second landowner agreed to sell them property on which to settle, and after several weeks in the Immigrants' Hotel, an overcrowded holding area meant to house two thousand but sheltering three times as many, the Weser Jews made their way to the pampas town of Palacios in hopes of meeting up with the agent who had promised them their land. He did not appear.

Why did these landowners feel they could do this? Were they simply scoundrels? Did these immigrants simply seem less than human to them? Was their being Jews a factor?[13] Without the land they had been promised, this small band of Jewish immigrants could not build themselves proper shelter, so they remained over the winter in the railway station where they had been abandoned. Those who survived did so thanks to the charity of the railway workers who gave them food. One hundred and eighty died, including more than seventy children. The following spring, Wilhelm Lowenthal, a Jewish agronomist visiting from Europe at the request of the Argentine government, passed through the station where the travelers were encamped. He heard their story and brought it to the attention of the authorities, and upon his return he prevailed upon Baron Maurice von Hirsch to buy land in Argentina to set aside for Jewish settlers escaping antisemitic violence in Russia and Poland.

Rafael Hernández's brother, José, authored what is arguably the national epic of Argentina, *The Gaucho Martin Fierro* (*El gaucho Martín Fierro*), which mythologizes and laments the gaucho, whose way of life is eroded by the arrival of the new immigrants. His poem documents the violence of gaucho life; it is a testament to a brutal brand of masculinity. *Martín Fierro* can be read as a paean to violence, violently extirpated. Chillingly, the great poet's brother performed a real act of violence of his own that ended in the death of scores of children and adults. After the winter was over, their families carried their bodies to what would become Moisés Ville, led to their new home by their Italian settler neighbors. The children were among the first to be buried in the town cemetery; their graves are marked by the long grass of the pampas, at the edge of the crowded rows of headstones of their parents and subsequent generations. The stories of some of those people can be read through their gravestones: the dead are identified as mothers and fathers, daughters and sons, wives and husbands. Sometimes their professions are engraved in those stones, and sometimes the nature of their deaths. Family plots indicate generational continuity, and the grandest headstones signify wealth or stature in the community. At the edge of the cemetery, but within its walls, lie a handful of suicides—testament, I imagined as I stood in front of them, to the struggle to adjust to life in such a harsh and strange place.

The origin story of the journey of the *Weser*—the struggle to survive, the leadership of their rabbi, and the rescue by Lowenthal and later Hirsch—has become part of the mythology of Argentine Jewish history. The retelling of this tale in Jewish immigrant narratives is one of the means of creating a legible Jewish past for Argentina.[14] Jewish Argentine history is not separable from Argentine history tout court, but when told by Jews it is often inflected for Jewishness. The old joke about Peruvians descending from the Incas, Mexicans descending from the Aztecs, and Argentineans descending from boats becomes a Jewish tale of Exodus in the *Weser* story, and that story in turn encapsulates the story of the Jews who followed them. The voyage narrative is malleable: stories of Jews crossing the sea also include the voyages of women lured to Buenos Aires by men promising marriage but turning them out as prostitutes and ships filled with Jews trying to find refuge from the Holocaust. It has also been about sexual initiation (*Ydel*) and the birth of the new Argentine child (in Angélica Gorodischer's short story "Camera Obscura" (La cámara oscura, 1991). The Jewish tales of the sea journey and subsequent fraught entry into Argentina intersect with stories of other immigrants, some coming down from those same boats.

These Jewish immigrants were becoming part of a community of Argentines even as they made the crossing, as depicted in the popular television miniseries *Vientos del agua* (Winds of water, 2006). The very Jewishness that separates these immigrants from others binds them to those others as part of an immigrant nation. Tzvi Tal, writing about the image of Jews in David Blaustein's 2007 documentary, *Hacer patria* (Forging a nation), observes:

> [T]he story of the Jewish family is the story of the Argentineans, whose collective projects and national narratives have fragmented without the emergence of a political force that awakens popular

confidence and might channel it into necessary social reform. The courage of the Jewish immigrants who set sail for an unknown world in Argentina, and the effort they made to rebuild their lives and assure a better future for their children, are characteristics worthy of emulation by any Argentine confronting the consequences of neoliberalism and globalization. Despite the minoritarian residue of antisemitic xenophobia, the majority of the Argentine people recognize themselves in the cinematic images of the erstwhile "Russians" [i.e., Eastern European Jews] and identify with the small triumphs of the Jews of the film. (my translation)

[(L)a historia de la familia judía es la historia de los argentinos, cuyos proyectos colectivos y narrativas nacionales se han fragmentado sin que surja una fuerza política que despierte la confianza popular y pueda encauzarla en una imprescindible reforma social. El coraje de los inmigrantes judíos que se embarcaban hacia un mundo desconocido en Argentina, y los esfuerzos que dedicaron a reconstruir sus vidas y asegurar un mejor futuro a sus hijos, son características dignas de emulación por todo argentino que se enfrenta a las consecuencias del neoliberalismo y la globalización. Pese a la remanencia minoritaria de posturas xenófobas antisemitas, la mayoría de la población argentina se reconoce en las imágenes cinematográficas de los otrora "rusos" y se identifica con los pequeños éxitos y miserias de los judíos de película. (2010)]

Novelist Ernesto Sábato also links Jews and other immigrants as constitutive of an Argentine national character, in an overt and purposeful way, placing Jews more centrally in that formula. As María Rosa Lojo notes, in *Abaddón the Exterminator* (*Abaddón el exerminador*), the author's alter ego, Sabato (sans accent), remarks:

My theory about the new Argentina . . . The result of three forces, three great nations: Spaniards, Italians, and Jews. If you think about it a little you'll see that our virtues and our defects come from there. Yes, of course there are also Basques, Frenchmen, Yugoslavs, Poles, Syrians, Germans. But what's fundamental comes from there. (my translation)

[Mi teoría sobre la nueva Argentina . . . Resultante de tres fuerzas, tres grandes pueblos: españoles, italianos y judíos. Si lo pensás un poco verás que nuestras virtudes y nuestros defectos vienen de ahí. Sí, claro, también hay vascos, franceses, yugoslavos, polacos, sirios, alemanes. Pero lo fundamental viene de ahí. (Sábato 193, ctd. in Lojo 53)]

Ricardo Piglia is another writer who associates Jewish with Italian Argentina, but in a far more muted way. In *The Absent City* (*La ciudad ausente*), Piglia names his protagonist Russo, a common Italian name that is, as well, a pun on "ruso," or Jew. Not quite collapsing the two, Piglia rather sets them in an oscillation in which each is held in tension with the other. Russo, despite the complexity of his name, is not particularly marked by immigrant ethnicity. Instead, discursively linked to the Argentine avant-garde writer Macedonio Fernández (by preserving the soul of Macedonio's dead wife), he is quintessentially Argentine.

For Sábato's Sabato and, more discreetly, for Piglia, Jewishness is constitutive of Argentineity. These two Gentile authors subsume Jewishness into Argentineity: their implicit metaphor is the melting pot. Most of the Jewish-identified writers and artists discussed in this book, on the other hand, maintain the integrity and distinctiveness of Jewishness in the face of a sometimes-hostile dominant culture that is being claimed, also, as one's own. For Piglia and Sábato being Argentine means being just a little bit Jewish; for the Jewish artists, filmmakers, and writers we will meet in this book, being Jewish is another way of being Argentine.

CHAPTER TWO

# MODERNITY, COSMOPOLITANISM, AND ANXIETY

Argentina constitutes itself as a nation by imagining not just a territory and a shared cultural archive-in-progress but also a population, yet it can hardly found itself on a claim to an always-already present "folk" rooted in the land from time immemorial. The founding myth of modern Argentina is, rather, of a virgin land that merely needed to be cleared of the annoyance of nomadic, uncivilized beings who had no culture or history of their own to speak of. As the nation was established through the nineteenth and early twentieth centuries, the contestation over exactly who would constitute the Argentine citizenry worked within certain loose parameters. "To govern is to populate" ran the motto of Juan Bautista Alberdi, the intellectual author of Argentina's constitution of 1853. The tried-and-true method of impregnation of the local women, followed by years of raising the babies they bore, was too slow a method, and Alberdi's project was in fact to dilute indigeneity to the point of extinction in order to build a modern nation. So Alberdi proposed filling the nation with ready-made adults, immigrants willing to work to "make America."

This phrase, whose common meaning refers to making a comfortable life for oneself in a land offering opportunity, quite literally signifies the creation of the continent (and in this case the nation) itself.[1] The sovereign subject whose agency underwrites the project of nation-making is the fundamental actor of European modernity. Moreover, Argentina's claim to modernity, closely tied to the nation's self-representation as essentially European, relies on those sovereign subjects. The modern subject is characterized by agency, the ability to make choices and fashion one's life. Immigration, understood as the decision to leave a perilous (or even simply unsatisfactory) home behind and grab the opportunity to make one's own life, to "make" or "do" America—*hacer la América*, is in this sense a modern undertaking.

At the same time, European modernity rests, in part, on the suppression of its own internal others. Because Jews are both avatars of cosmopolitan European modernity and modern Europe's abjected other, they occupy a complicated place in this construct. Within a fervently Eurocentric Argentina, Jews are among the marginalized others of the nation, remaining outsiders among more easily assimilated immigrants. On the other hand, because most Jewish immigrants to Argentina are from Eastern Europe, they are less "other" to the dominant culture than indigenous people, Asian immigrants, and Afro-Argentines.

As Anna Tsing demonstrates, there are multiple modes of modernity that, in the case of former colonies, rely on contact and resignification as functions of the historical specificity of any single nation. Although a version of resignification takes place in Argentina, the desire for Europeanness on the part of the cultural (and often political) elite effectively mimics European modernity.[2] Moreover, as Beatriz Sarlo has argued, because of its location at the periphery, geographically and historically, Argentina's modernity trembles with anxiety. If modernity is, as Mary Louise Pratt contends, "Europe's (or the white world's) identity discourse, as it assumed global dominance," then Argentina's aspirational whiteness and Europeanness is at the heart of its also aspirational claim to modernity.[3]

In the mid-nineteenth century, shortly after Argentina gained its independence from Spain, the government commissioned scouts, sent out to recruit likely immigrants to the new nation. Men and women both were enticed by promises of wealth, of rich land to farm and a growing industrial center that needed workers. Full citizenship, however, with its full rights of suffrage and responsibility was reserved for men.[4] The desire of the national leaders to sculpt a particular kind of citizenry is evident in the trajectory of the recruitment effort. The first, most desirable immigrant recruits were the British and northern Europeans, valued for their racial purity, surely, but also for a work ethic that was presumed to be an effect of Protestantism. England, Germany, and Switzerland were the nations Alberdi himself favored. Only in the last years of the immigrant recruitment process were Eastern European Jews invited to participate in the project of Europeanizing the nation.

The liberal elites who spearheaded the immigration campaign hewed to the dichotomy between civilization and barbarism that was so eloquently—and problematically—articulated by Domingo Faustino Sarmiento in his classic *Facundo*, where civilization was founded in European liberalism. The stark Manichean nature of the mantra "civilization versus barbarism," the absolute distinction drawn between the two, has plagued Argentina's political history: liberals and conservatives, Federalists and Unitarians, the right and the left, have staked their claim to civilization, disparaging their rivals with the charge of barbarism. Each side represents the other as irredeemably mired in the subhuman condition that is barbarism, unfit for human company: ignorant, coarse, backward, unenlightened, with implications of brutality on the one hand and chaos on the other. Civilization is always defending itself against barbarism, but just who is civilized and who is a barbarian has always been up for grabs. For the *Unitarios*, those urban, largely anticlerical supporters of a strong central government of the early nineteenth century, warm to the precepts of the French and American revolutions, the Federalists (the rough and ready frontiersmen who valued a decentralized government) were barbarous, virtually lawless clans, led by strongmen on horseback. For those Federalists, the tenets of civilization as they understood it—strong masculine leadership in both the public and the domestic spheres, and a strong church—were threatened by liberal ideas. Their motto, in fact, was "Mueran los salvajes unitarios"—Death to the Unitarian savages.[5] In the mid-nineteenth century, European immigrants would serve to give the new nation a boost into civilization; by the end of that century the landless peasants coming off the boat into Buenos Aires who could not even speak the language of their new homeland were construed to be in need of civilizing by the established citizenry. In other words, as the first group of immigrants became Argentines, barbarism began to be attributed to those who followed them.

One subtext of the civilization versus barbarism trope is its claim to modernity: to being part of the civilized world, acceptable at the table where modern nations meet. The barbarians are alien, and they are inevitably associated with what is unassimilable to modernity in the emerging Argentine nation of the nineteenth century, namely Blackness and indigeneity. These signs of the non-European are repressed or cast out discursively and, in far too many cases, literally.[6] For the nation aspiring to modernity, Jewishness oscillates between civilized modernity and primitive barbarism. Catholic Argentina did not identify itself as purposefully not-Jewish, except by default, but neither did it embrace Jews as among those who would be not just the skin and flesh, but also the bone and marrow of the nation.

As a hybrid nation, Argentina necessarily modifies the conventional European view of Jewish difference. Buenos Aires in particular may be thought of as a modern global city in part because of the cosmopolitanizing presence of Jews, insofar as Jewishness in the modern era signifies both Europeanness and a loose relationship to nation. The city's cosmopolitanism is then, in part, a function of its Jewish citizens and global Jewish culture. Moreover, modernity itself is both embraced and reviled in Argentine culture writ large, in part as it is connected to Jewishness.

It is not surprising, then, that the ultimate cosmopolite, Victoria Ocampo, the founder of the self-consciously modern, Europhile cultural journal *Sur* was, as Borges tells us, called an upstart Jew by Argentine society. Her family was part of the nation's oligarchy, but their name suggested to some an ancient Jewish ancestry, a great-great grandparent who converted to Catholicism sometime during the pogroms of the fourteenth century in Spain, or—at the latest—faced with expulsion in 1492. Borges himself was proud of one of his possibly Jewish ancestral surnames.[7] Still, Ocampo's real connection to Jewishness has more to do with her participation in the making of a modern culture in which Jews were ambiguously emblematic of the modernity they sought and admired.

Waldo Frank was one of the cosmopolitan Jews involved in the establishment of Ocampo's *Sur*. Frank grew up in a genteel assimilated Jewish home in New York; he was later beaten up on the streets of Buenos Aires by attackers who considered him a Bolshevik Jew. Frank envisioned *Sur* as the fusion of Victoria Ocampo's knowledge of European modern culture and the passionate commitment to the promise of Latin American literature espoused by the Jewish Argentinean publisher Samuel Glusberg. It didn't happen that way; Frank eventually saw that Ocampo was far more interested in European modernism than in the emerging Latin American culture that Glusberg promoted (Frank 170–71).

Victoria Ocampo was just one of Argentina's elites who embraced a European version of modernity for her nation. Decades later, José Pablo Feinmann's *La crítica de las armas* (The critique of weapons) explores Argentina's late twentieth-century national malaise in the figure of a neurotic protagonist and his relationship with his Jewish and Catholic family. The novel opens with the narrator's decision to kill his aged, paranoid, but frustratingly resilient mother. Convinced of her own grandeur and fearful of being poisoned by jealous rivals, she is, as are so many Catholic mothers in novels of the dictatorship and especially of exile, symbolic of the nation.[8] But the narrator is not allied with his father either. He rejects his father's Judaism, and he has colluded with his brother to take the operation of the family business from the older man. He is both/and and neither/nor in relation to his mother and father. Cathected to and in rebellion against both parents, the novel maps the character's Jewish/Catholic neurosis onto the nation.

Argentine Jews, living their lives, do not of course experience themselves as mere markers of otherness or cosmopolitanism. Santiago Kovadloff, for one, argues that Jews themselves entered modernity when they left Europe and came to Argentina between 1890 and 1930. His elegant distinction between Eastern European Jews as a spatial people, ghettoized in part by their own need for self-preservation, and Argentinean Jews who, entering into a new nation as citizens, became part of an historical process that, in fact, did alter the meaning of their Jewishness, may be productively read through Julia Kristeva's taxonomy of time. What Kristeva characterizes as the monumental time of never-changing eternal verities, lived as the cyclical time of ritual, is, in effect, caught in spatiality.[9] That Kristeva associates this temporality with women is another way of naming it nonmodern and nonhistorical, and is consistent with the association between women and Jews in Western culture. Historical time, the temporality that Kristeva associates with masculinity, reinserted into constricting space with the military coup of 1930 in Argentina, is a sign of modernity, associated with progress, agency, citizenship, and secularism. For Kovadloff, Jews enter into modernity when they leave the shtetl and cross the ocean, becoming citizens. For Kovadloff this transition from space to time implies moving from an atomized, isolated community experience that at the same time is obstructed by the majority society, toward an experience of global and reasonably equitable interchange with a larger society that, although majoritarian, does not not define itself in opposition to its minorities, but even creates itself on the basis of them. Emigrating, then, would mean moving from a denigrated identity to "the validation of the self" [la convalidación del ser propio (80)]. What I have been thinking of as "another way of being Argentine," Kovadloff calls "a new modality of Argentineity" [una nueva modalidad de lo argentino (80)] that makes possible the identity "Argentine Jew."

Kovadloff's assessment is, ironically, largely consonant with the anti-immigrant argument that developed in the early 1900s, when the civilization-barbarism divide was inverted such that Argentina was no longer the barbaric new country in need of the civilizing effects of European immigration but rather the civilizing influence on the European underclass swarming into its capital. Yet from the distance of almost a century, he is also eager to recognize that Argentina, as much as the Jews who came there, has been altered by this encounter in what he calls the "consubstantiation" of Jews and Argentina. The mutual construction of Argentina and its Jewish community in largely positive ways (despite inevitable tensions and conflicts) was made possible, he argues, by the democratization of the nation between 1926 and 1929 (80). However, Kovadloff goes on to show that Jews are once again excluded from full Argentineity during the right-wing military regimes that took power periodically, starting in 1930, preparing the way for the veritable demonization of Jews during the 1976–1983 junta.

Kovadloff nuances his analysis by inserting it into a gendered framework (i.e., the doctrine of masculine dominance underlying *patria potestad*). This paternal power, which Kovadloff understands to be a function of Catholic theology, is at odds with Jewish laws of lineage, in which one is Jewish by virtue of being born of a Jewish woman. Kovadloff argues that the authorizing function of the maternal disqualifies Jews (i.e., Jewish men; women are by virtue of their femininity not full citizens to begin with) from full participation in the nation. We might understand Kovadloff's analysis to be predicated on the anxiety of the paternalist Argentine state, itself founded on the paternal imperative of Catholicism, when challenged with the foundational claims of maternity. Still, Kovadloff elides the patriarchal nature of traditional Judaism. The near pun modernity/maternity encapsulates a contradiction within dominant discourse, in which claims to belonging hearken to a paternal line that supersedes the maternal. Patriarchal structures underlie the modern state, modeling the rational, benevolent father in charge of the family that is the nation. At the same time, Jews of all sorts, be they devout or be they atheists, deeply engaged with the Jewish community or loosely attached to it if at all, may be modern Argentine subjects.

For her part, Beatriz Sarlo incorporates Jewishness into Argentine modernity with her placing of artist Xul Solar's peripherally modern image at the very beginning of *Una modernidad periférica* (A peripheral modernity), her study of Argentine modernity. Among the scattered signs, symbols, and figures in the painting she discusses are those she recognizes as stars of David. The Jewish reference is quietly present for all to see, part of the hybrid nature of the modern(izing) nation.[10] Similarly, Juan Gelman hides Jewishness in plain sight in his construction of Argentina.

Gelman's long, angry, and mournful poem "Pensamientos" (Thoughts), written in October of 1967 at the behest of Casa de América in Cuba to commemorate the death of Che Guevara, is, as well, a meditation on his own nation. It includes the changes he rings on the refrain, "I am from a country" [soy de un país], whose variations include lines that enmesh cosmopolitanism and Jewishness in the nation:

> I am from a very complicated country
> Latineurocosmopolurban
> criolejewpolespanportuitalire
> according to the texts (my translation)
>
> [soy de un país complicadísimo
> latinoeurocosmopoliurbano
> criollojudipolacogalleguisitanoira
> según dicen los textos (181)]

and later

> I am from a country where they let Comandante Guevara fall:
> the military men the priests the homeopaths
> the public auctioneers
> the Spanish refugees the Jewish masochists
> the owners
> the workers also for now (my translation)
>
> [soy de un país donde al comandante Guevara
> lo dejaron caer:
> los militares los curas los homeópatas
> los martilleros públicos
> los refugiados españoles masoquistas judíos
> los patrones y
> los obreros también por ahora (182–83)]

Gelman's inclusion of Jewishness in an Argentina that bears the burden of responsibility for Guevara's capture and death takes two forms. In the first of these stanzas, the poet makes an Argentine melting pot out of the very words of immigration, identity, and modernity pressed together into a single enjambed adjective, "latinoeurocosmopoliurbanocriollojudipolacogalleguisitanoira," which breaks down more or less as Latino-Euro-cosmopolitan-urban-Creole-Jew-Pole-Spaniard-Portuguese-Italianire. The virtually unpronounceable portmanteau is a linguistic enactment of the complexity of Argentineity: urban and rural, cosmopolitan and nationalist, European and Latin American, Jewish and Polish, Iberian and Italian, all elided into a single breath-defying utterance.[11] The ethnic components of this unwieldy Argentineity are just this side of being pejorative insofar as terms Jew, Pole, *Gallego*, and *Tano* have been tarnished with a derogatory corrosive. "Jew" and "Pole" bear the residue of antisemitism; "Gallego" is a mildly offensive metonym for Spaniard, as is "Tano" for Italian. It is just a little ironic that the poet shies away from taking responsibility for the Argentineity he names so extravagantly: he blames "the texts" for this concatenation. Yet the texts—the stories—circulating around Argentina are precisely that complex, that enmeshed, that self-contradictory. In Gelman's poem, being Jewish is another way of being Argentine, at least to the extent that the elements of the adjective can be isolated, but at the same time he includes it within the dense weave that is Argentineity. Gelman's inclusion of Jewishness here is far from the celebration of what we now call cultural pluralism as Gerchunoff dreamt it, however. For Gelman it is about sharing the responsibility for Che Guevara's death, for abandoning his ideals and either working actively toward his murder or being complicit in it. Gelman does not distinguish between the two; if Jewishness is to be part of Argentineity it is not exempt from accountability.

In another apparent paradox, the Argentina Gelman describes is cosmopolitan and urban, but at the same time it is "criollo," a term denoting that which is authentically Argentine and attached to the rural landscape, in contrast to the urban, multicultural capital. The criollo, however, is most decidedly not a member of the indigenous population; he is, rather, analogous to the "real American" (white, Christian, small-town, heterosexual) of the United States. Yet the paradox is only apparent. Natan Sznaider, in his discussion of Jewish political thought in Europe, does not see the nationalism embedded in a term like "criollo" as antithetical to cosmopolitanism. Rather, he links cosmopolitanism to "particular national attachments as potential mediators between the individual and the global horizons against which identifications unfold" (7). Indeed, much of the cultural capital that has accrued to rural "criollo" Argentina has been consolidated in the urban center and what Angel Rama fortuitously dubbed "the lettered city," most famously the celebration of the gaucho in José Hernández's *The Gaucho Martin Fierro* and the mourning of the passing of that figure in Güiraldes's *Don Segundo Sombra*, but also in Gerchunoff's *The Jewish Gauchos of the Pampas*, which was written and published in Buenos Aires years after Gerchunoff himself had left the Jewish colonies for the capital.

The link between nationalism and cosmopolitanism seems particularly apt in the case of Argentina, a nation created out of a colonial struggle to claim an identity in opposition to an imperial power and out of competing internal factions. Argentina is a settler nation, with all the cruel history of attempted genocide against indigenous peoples the term implies, and with the former colonists' zealous claim to the nation once they gained independence from Spain. Modernization and nation-building in Argentina are functions of Europeanizing the nation, and they go hand in hand with genocidal wars whose goal was ethnic cleansing. Wiping the earth clean of indigenous people would free up their lands for the taking. Rhetorical genocide is part of the equation, and even Gelman omits indigeneity, as well as Blackness, from the Argentine mix of his overstuffed adjective.[12]

As we have seen, newly independent Argentina deliberately sought European immigrants to promote its policy of national whitening and recruited those Europeans with varied levels of enthusiasm. Nineteenth-century racial categories were largely national, regional, and ethnic; thus Northern Europeans (German, British) were most prized; Italians and Jews less. The Argentine elite declares its nation white, its culture universal, its literary traditions European, and its Indians gone. It ignores its own African heritage and the presence of Asians. There is resistance to this erasure, of course, but the overwhelming image that Argentina now presents to itself and the world is still that of the most European of Latin American nations. So it is not entirely surprising that Gelman should bond cosmopolitanism to nationalism in the absence of aboriginal Americans, Blacks, and Asians.

The Jewish presence, on the other hand, is part of what makes Argentina cosmopolitan and thereby modern; Jews themselves are swept into modernity by their embrace of an Argentineity they help create. Sznaider notes that in relation to cosmopolitanism, Jews are not exceptional but rather exemplary, in the sense that they stand as an example of the struggle for difference-in-equality of the cosmopolitan order. In (albeit unacknowledged) accord with the feminist critique that universalism submerges marginal identities into a norm derived from the hegemonic site of its articulation, Sznaider contrasts universalism's homogenizing impulse with the cosmopolitan embrace of difference.[13] The universalizing desire underlying the emancipation of France's Jews, for example, emerged as the expectation that they would abandon their religious and other group ties. Sznaider argues implicitly that modernity in Europe requires a cosmopolitan (in contrast to a universalist) stance, and explicitly that Jews were cosmopolitan before Europe was. The link between cosmopolitanism and the modern ties Jewishness to modernity, and this tie is absorbed into Argentina's sense of, desire for, and claim to modern nationhood. Leonardo Senkman makes a similar argument when he avers, more generally, that

> Latin America's Jews were . . . part and parcel of the region's shifting involvement in the global arena. At the same time, they adjusted themselves to the road of diverse forms of modernity in the Atlantic setting. (2008, 125)

Senkman soon settles in and focuses his discussion on Argentina, whose road to modernity with reference to transnational Jewishness is his primary object of scrutiny (125). Pointing out that modernity at the periphery bears the weight of paradox, Senkman argues that Latin America forges its modernity in opposition to North American (and to a lesser extent) European neocolonialism as well as in imitation of the global North (126). For their part, Jews in the agricultural colonies established institutions such as synagogues and schools for reproducing the past and maintaining a cohesive identity and religious practice. They also established publication venues for Yiddish-language books and built theaters to attract an international circuit of Jewish theater, making small towns like Santa Clara and Moisés Ville part of a cosmopolitan Jewish world.

"Making—or doing—America" for the later flows of Argentine immigrants meant being able to claim an Argentinean identity rooted in cosmopolitanism, but for Jews and others, that did not mean giving up a sense of belonging to another history or culture as well. In Argentina the immigrant melting pot is rather like a minestrone soup whose ingredients are altered but not dissolved in the cooking, and whose dominant flavor is Italian. The new immigrant longs to be accepted by and into the receiving nation, but not to be erased by it. The cosmopolitanism of the minestrone nation emerges from the desire for a new national identity at the same time old identities remain deeply felt.

Argentinean Jewish cuisine has been similarly traditional and assimilationist, from the time the first settlers came to the agricultural colonies. Ritual kosher slaughter was established early on, and local bakeries, as well as Jewish grandmothers, prepare Eastern European delicacies like knishes and honey cake to this day. Nevertheless, following a recipe for gefilte fish in a compilation of traditional recipes sold at the Moisés Ville museum, there is one for "fake fish," acquiescing to the reality of available ingredients in that landlocked, riverless town. In place of the traditional carp, it calls for ground beef. Jewish Argentineity is a modern invention as much as it is a continuation. Meat-based gefilte fish may be the perfect metonym for the singularly Jewish Argentine identity of the agricultural colonies. Like the Jewish gaucho it exceeds its internal contradiction to get to a deeper truth.

Traditional foods remain important markers of identity and, significantly, of the coming together of cultures. In one brief scene from Alicia Dujovne Ortiz's autobiographical novel *El árbol de la gitana* (The Gypsy woman's tree), shared food in a Jewish home on the pampas suggests cultural interchange:

> It's like the coral snake, poetically remarked the peon, who, when he smelled the coming storm, had stayed in the house of the *Moishes*, drinking maté with matzoh. (All translations from this text are my own.)
>
> [—Parece la víbora de coral—dijo poético el peón que, al oler la tormenta, se había quedado en casa de los moishes tomando mate con matse. (200–01)]

The alliterative pairing of matzoh and maté, the emblematic food and drink of Jews and gauchos respectively, testifies to cultural convergence. The ritual of sharing maté, the gourd and metal straw passed from person to person, implies trust and camaraderie, while matzoh is central to the ritual Passover meal in which Jews are enjoined to bring the stranger to the table. The simple refreshment of matzoh and maté does not erase difference; rather it connects people across that difference, and the reality of taking into one's own body the food or drink of the other calls into question radical separateness. The slightly derogatory undertone of both "peon" and "Moishe," terms each might use for the other, creates a trace of tension that unsettles the ritual hospitality of both Jews and the pampas with its suggestion of the somewhat-wary relations between Gentile cattlehands and Jewish settlers.

Immigration and affiliation with the nation are functions and signs of modernity, but as we have noted Jewish immigrants also bring with them cultural baggage that associates them with antiquity. European modernity, linked to both the emancipation of women in the form of education and, eventually, suffrage and full citizenship, and to the integration of Jews into the body politic, including unlocking the gates of the ghetto and the end of sumptuary and other laws setting Jews apart, did not mean the end of sexism or antisemitism in Argentina or elsewhere.[14] However much modern democratic states tolerate religious diversity and espouse gender equality, the otherness of Jews, like the otherness of women, remains a strong cultural norm. Senkman (1992) reads Marechal's foundational novel, *Adán Buenosayres* (Adam Buenosayres), for example, as a critique of modernity in which

Jewishness is attached to immigration, squalor, and by extension criminality, and in which the idea of women's equality is ridiculed.

The otherness of Argentine Jews is in part a function of their being seen as both more ancient and more postmodernly cosmopolitan than the Gentile Argentines among whom they live. Jews are a spectral presence even as they assimilate, and occasional unease and fear find expression in antisemitism. Jews themselves are not ghosts, but a very old world shadows each Jewish subject. Jews themselves, as a minority, and as a historically suspect minority at that, cannot hope to determine the meaning of Jewishness for the culture as a whole. Nor, given the nonhierarchical structure of Judaism with its lack of an ultimate authority, should it be remarkable that the meaning of Jewishness is contested from within as well. It is not surprising that Jews express anxiety about how actions taken by other Jews will be interpreted by the Gentile power structure. Good public relations matter. Although the current term "spin" connotes a facile, superficial, and often cynical effort to influence interpretation, the way Jewishness is understood by the Gentile world can be a matter of survival.

The question is, then, do Jews themselves see themselves as oscillating between modernity and premodernity? As a question about assimilation and the preservation of tradition, the answer would be yes—that is Gerchunoff's project, as well as that of Raquel Mactas, who, like Tavosnanska, writes directly in Gerchunoff's shadow. It is also the project of those—Jews and non-Jews alike—who claim that the still-unsolved 1994 bombing of the Asociación Mutual Israelita Argentina, the Buenos Aires Jewish cultural center known by its acronym, AMIA, was an attack on Argentina, not just on the nation's Jews.[15] Many also believe that the AMIA bombing was indeed about international antisemitism working hand in hand with the local variety, linked to anti-Zionism, as it followed on an attack on the Israeli embassy in Buenos Aires. That incident has had less traction in local historical memory precisely because the embassy was foreign territory, while the AMIA building is an Argentine space as much as it is a Jewish one.

The very desire for assimilation, by Jews and Gentiles both, underlies the claim that the AMIA bombing was an attack on Argentina. As a claim made by many non-Jews as well, it is a demonstration of the notion that Jewishness is not only compatible with Argentineity, but also that Argentine Jewish institutions are just that—both Jewish and Argentine. Jewishness, Argentineity, and cosmopolitan modernity are mutually constitutive even when they are not fully compatible.

As Kovadloff's notion of consubstantiation suggests, Jewish assimilation into Argentine society is also assimilation into modernity, and that is not an unclouded good. Full entry into modernity, figured as the city, holds a threat to Jewishness in Raquel Mactas's *Los judíos de Las Acacias* (*The Jews of Las Acacias*), where the author suggests an urban-rural distinction that links the city to a worthy but perilous future and the countryside to a desirable past. Despite Mactas's bleak representation of rural Jewish life, the older generation of Jews of the agricultural colonies about whom she writes are ambivalent about sending their children away to the modern city, since to do so means a loss of Jewish practice and, ultimately, identity. The radical mobility of immigration of one generation eases the way for internal migration in subsequent ones, so it is no wonder that many of the children and grandchildren of the original colonists continued their modern, peripatetic ways and moved to the city, overtly cosmopolitan and overtly threatening. Just as the criollo version of the Argentine countryside is fully complicit with the modern world it purports to resist and from which it ostensibly offers a respite, the Jewish countryside in Argentina is an insufficient bulwark against assimilation.

Jewish anxiety about modernization and deracination is a version of the Argentine anxiety about being modern that is similarly centered on the urban-rural divide. Here it is instructive to heed Mary Louise Pratt's observation that, in the periphery, modernization, understood as instrumental rationality or capitalist development, may in fact hinder modernity, defined as normative rationality leading to self-actualization and self-determination.[16]

Jewish Argentine internal migration is not just a matter of moving from the agricultural colonies to the cities; it happens within the city as well. One of the two stories Daniel Burman tells in his 2000 film *Waiting for the Messiah* (*Esperando al Mesías*) is a Jewish coming-of-age tale in which the protagonist, Ariel, struggles to escape what he calls the bubble of his Jewish neighborhood in Buenos Aires. As he sees it, unless he leaves he will merely be repeating the lives of his parents, circumscribed in a very small world. Nevertheless, his way out of the Jewish world depends to a great extent on his having been part of it. He learns his trade as a videographer recording weddings and bar mitzvahs, and by making a travelogue of his own neighborhood, the archetypically Jewish district of Buenos Aires. Ariel tries to leave behind the life that is laid out for him by abandoning his childhood sweetheart Estela, who is fully enmeshed in the community (she teaches music to children in the Jewish community center and performs religious rituals) in favor of a Gentile colleague in a lesbian relationship who, ironically, is fascinated by and identifies with what she sees as his otherness as a Jew. For her part, and despite her misery at losing the boy she loves, Estela has no problem being both Jewish and Argentine, traditional and modern. She installs a karaoke machine in Ariel's father's small café to bring in a younger, more modern, clientele; and, in a poignant scene, dances a tango with the older man.

Modernity is associated with the sort of anomie that Burman's Ariel experiences. Nevertheless, the subject who takes center stage in his existential aloneness is still legible when he is a member of the dominant group. The outsider, in contrast, is not visible, and his or her meaning is unclear. Sergio Chejfec's protagonist in *My Two Worlds* (*Mis dos mundos*) experiences himself as being invisible, and his desire to be seen, not even as a native of the place but acknowledged at all, resonates not only with modern Jewishness in multicultural spaces, but with the dilemma of the migrant and the exile more generally.[17] Chejfec's narrator, an Argentine Jewish writer visiting Brazil, is not simply unseen: his right to be present in the space he is passing through goes painfully denied or unacknowledged. He is shooed off benches by people who he imagines claim sitting rights by virtue of their coming to those same spots every day. In one painful scene he thinks he is being hailed by someone who in fact is calling to someone else, and he embarrassedly recedes to his proper unnoticeability. He is invisible, nonexistent in the fabric of a modern city that is not his own.

In contrast to Chejfec's outsider (not just as a Jew, but more importantly as an Argentine in Brazil), apparently resigned to his marginality, are those men who find a joyful connection to the national body by way of affiliating with a local or national sports team. Raanan Rein's study of Jewish soccer in Argentina makes the point amply, without losing the nuance of Jewish difference. Soccer was a path to Argentineity, but there was specifically Jewish soccer in Argentina as well, with Jewish soccer teams connected to cultural clubs. There were clubs made up of exclusively German or Eastern European Jews, as well as clubs in which Jews of all backgrounds played. Moreover, Jewish boys (some of whom also played in the Jewish clubs) played on neighborhood teams with non-Jews. Integrated teams marked the player's Jewishness at the same time that they welcomed the player himself.

Toward the end of *Mestizo: A Novel* (*Mestizo*), Ricardo Feierstein's novel of identity and otherness, the author momentarily interrupts the disjointed, nonlinear narrative with a father-and-son outing to a soccer game. The amnesiac protagonist momentarily sets aside his struggle to bring to consciousness a crime he has witnessed, the memory of which he hopes will heal him and make him whole (and if this sounds like a postdictatorship national allegory, it is). This episode, unlike the rest of the novel, is presented in the graphic novel form of the *fotonovela*, reinforcing soccer's place in popular culture.[18] This highly accessible form, visual as well as verbal, is linear and, apparently, seamless. Whereas in the rest of the novel, the stuttering narrative overtly suggests the protagonist's struggle with what he can know, the pictures and words of the totalizing graphic form imply that everything of importance is told. The graphic novel is familiar, accessible, and a source of pleasure. The content of the episode is similarly reassuring; the shared exhilaration of the soccer match gives both the protagonist and his son the sense of belonging to the majority for the first time. As fans of the winning team, they are part of the nation, not its other. *Mestizo*'s utopian celebration of a national identity in fact exceeds the nation: "The differences fade into a common carpet of humanity" (335). The details are both global and Argentine, with references to the dictatorship and the kerchiefs of the Mothers of the Plaza de Mayo, but the terms are postnational, generational rather than strictly geopolitical, and the tone is ecstatic:

> The ill-considered (and brave) youthful fascination for the rapid and violent changes, the passion for life, the care of nature, and the pacifism necessary in a world that charges toward holocaust, all, all, and all of us are here, majorities and diverse minorities in this group of faces that are filled with hope and white kerchiefs that, like a new and definitive hymn to joy, unites memories and portraits in the trees built by our heart. Because all History (construction of the tree) will only be a metaphor for the central meaning: mestizos and survivors. We start to advance down the wide avenue singing, singing, always singing, the rest of life ahead of us, and the memory of the identity (Jewish and Latin American blossom, plural and yearning) found in us, recovered for all times. (2000, 335)

> [La alocada (y corajuda) fascinación juvenil por las modificaciones rápidas y violentas, la pasión por la vida, el cuidado de la naturaleza y el pacifismo necesario en un mundo que corre hacia el holocausto, todo, todo y todos estamos aquí, mayorías y minorías diversas en este grupo de rostros preñados de esperanza y pañuelos blancos que, como un nuevo y definitivo himno a

> la alegría, une recuerdos y retratos en los árboles construidos por nuestro corazón. Porque toda la historia (construcción del árbol) no será sino una metáfora del sentido central: mestizos y sobrevivientes. Comenzamos a avanzar por la ancha avenida cantando, cantando, siempre cantando, un resto de vida por delante y de la memoria de la identidad, por fin y de una sola vez (brote judío y latinoamericano, plural y anhelante) encontrada en el nosotros, para siempre recobrada. (1994, 360)]

The complex narrative lines of *Mestizo* come together here with the promise of the healing of the nation (the novel's action ends in 1983) and the possibility of, in Raanan Rein's terms, becoming a Jewish Argentine. After the familiar clarity of the graphic novel section, the narrative revisits the story that David, the protagonist, has been trying to piece together; now the chaff has been sifted out and the narrative thread that had been buried in it emerges. David and Eduardo's success in becoming one with the rest of the nation via soccer is an Argentine phenomenon. It contrasts with his father's boyhood memory of playing soccer with the Gentile boys in his Polish village. Tolerated when he scored goals, he was berated as a Jew when he missed a penalty kick, a moment that made him understand that he could never claim full membership in the nation:

> I kicked and missed and my teammates yelled at me: "What are you doing, Stinking Jew?" That made a great impression on me. My family lived there for as many generations, perhaps before many of the ancestors of these Ukrainians and Poles, and nevertheless they saw themselves as rulers of the country, and they yelled "Stinking Jew" because I missed a penalty kick. There and then, I understood that we could never be equals. The Jews would never assimilate in those lands. (2000, 51)

> [Yo tiré y salió afuera. Y los compañeros me gritaron: "¡Qué hacés, judío de mierda!." Eso me impresionó muchísimo. Mi familia vivía alí desde hacía un montón de generaciones, posiblemmente antes de muchos de los antecesores de esos ucranos y polacos. Y, sin embargo, ellos se sentían los dueños del país y me gritaban "judío de mierda" a mí porque erré un penal. Ahí entendí que nunca podríamos ser iguales. Los judíos no se asimilarán jamás en esas tierras. (1994, 63)]

The achievement of cultural mestizaje crystallized in the soccer match requires a receptive nation; Argentina does this, however imperfectly. Nevertheless, the incorporation of David and his son into the "majority," which implicitly clears a path to David's recovered memory and his sense of identity, is deeply gendered, unrelentingly masculine. Of all the figures portrayed in this episode, whether players or fans, not one is a woman. Unlike the rest of the novel, in which dissonance, absence, and lacunae are encoded as sources of anxiety, the missing element here is glossed over; Jews may become part of the soccer nation, but only if they are men. Moreover, the masculinity bestowed on soccer players, and by extension their fans, is precisely what the Jewish man presumably lacks. Andrés Neuman's *Una vez Argentina* (Once Argentina), for example, recounts the childhood memory of playing soccer, which gave the narrator a sense of teamwork, of knowing his body, and protection from being considered a nerd. The heteropatriarchal culture of soccer both presupposes normative masculinity and confers it on its participants. Through soccer, national belonging, if not citizenship itself, is coded masculine. "Manuel's Dream," a section of Feierstein's *La logia del umbral* (The lodge of the threshold) that recalls the immigrant neighborhood of the family's past, includes the memory of the local soccer team in which young, virile men, newcomers from a variety of backgrounds, perform an idealized version of Argentineity (127, 129).

In Argentina, soccer has been enlisted as a balm of inclusion and a sign of national unity to draw attention away from deep social and political injury. Radios in clandestine prisons were set to soccer matches in which torturers and victims cheered the same team. In Martin Kohan's novel *Dos veces junio* (Two times June), the match is quite simply conscripted for national unity by the dictatorship. The very sense of cohesion that the protagonist and his son find in *Mestizo* holds the possibility of a very false sense of unity and the sharp edge of otherness.

Soccer can soothe or channel the anxiety of the violence of modernity. As early as 1948, the film *Ragged Football* (*Pelota de trapo*) takes soccer as a national identifier that excludes Jews but also holds out the promise of assimilation. In it, Don Jacobo is a shopkeeper who has both a soccer ball in his window that the local boys want to buy and a son who wants to play soccer. He is stereotyped as a comically unscrupulous Jewish businessman who raises his prices daily, keeping the coveted soccer ball out of the reach of the children. His son, however, contains the promise of assimilation. Within the worldview of the film, that desire precludes Jewishness as a kind of Argentineity, since it is premised on the child's dissatisfaction with his own Jewish difference. When a little girl, the child of Italian immigrants, asks him his name, he tells her that it's Abraham, but that he doesn't like it. He does not need to specify that his disaffection lies in the fact that his name is Jewish, and therefore different. (—¿Cómo te llamás?—Abraham, pero no me gusta. ["What's your name?" "Abraham, but I don't like it."]) She goes on to ask him if he is a *ruso*—literally, "Russian"—like his father, and he replies that he's not, that he's Argentine. Offering the solidarity of one second-generation immigrant to another, she tells him that her mother is Italian. But unlike "Italian," *ruso* is an ambiguous signifier. In the Argentine context it means not only Russian, but Eastern European Jew more generally. So when Abraham says he is not a *ruso*, he is denying more than a national identity in order to claim full participation in the country of his birth.

The comically and relatively mild antisemitism discernible in the characterization of Don Jacobo illustrates Josefina Ludmer's argument that Argentine modernity's unpleasant face is often drawn as Jewish. In her magisterial study of the trope of crime in Argentine literature, Ludmer scrutinizes the links between Jewishness and criminality in the Argentine imaginary. It may seem ironic that a people historically constricted by three sets of laws: those imposed by Jewish religious strictures; those imposed by the state on all its citizens; and those imposed by the state on Jews specifically—typically regarding where they could live, the kinds of clothes they could wear, the professions available to them, and special taxation—should also be linked to society's fear of outlaw behavior. Yet the triple set of laws implies an underlying fear, both within and without, of Jewish transgression. Insofar as the outlaw is literally outside of the law, criminality is only one version of outlaw-hood. By Christian lights, the Jew is always already an outlaw.

Ludmer both comments on and enacts the anxiety around the relationship of Jewishness, Jews, and the modern Argentine nation in *The Corpus Delicti: A Manual of Argentine Fictions* (*El cuerpo del delito*). Citing Sebreli's *La cuestión judía* (The Jewish question) on the liberal roots of antisemitism in Argentina, Ludmer offers a catalog of antisemitic stereotypes in foundational Argentine texts, enumerating the assumptions about Jews that feed anti-Jewish sentiment, including "Jews as usurers, as simulators or criminals of truth, and as antipatriots who act politically on both sides and provoke chaos" (154). Ludmer argues that, effectively, Jews are a cultural artifact of money:

> "The Jews" are always the *representatives of money*, and the narrative that includes them is an economic narrative: banks, stock

exchanges, and gold. "The Jews" are the sign of the money sign: a sort of representation squared. Or better yet, "the Jews" are the representatives of money, which is in itself *an apparatus of representation*. (155)

She goes on to add the link of sex to the chain that connects Jews, money, and criminality. "Jews as usurers, simulators, and men, effeminate men, who sexualize money and power (and who are linked to prostitution)" (155). Arguing that Jews are represented as deviously involved in politics, playing both sides, Ludmer notes that they "are the antithesis of the 'high culture' of 'the aristocracy' (and of 'the nation'), and they are invariably contrasted with a figure of 'truth'" (156). Ludmer signals a certain disquiet of her own, echoing the dominant society's anxiety vis-à-vis Jews and Jewishness, in writing disrupted by asides, emphases, and, especially, scare quotes:

> The "stories of Jews" are *fictions of exclusion*; they put into evidence a group of symbolic differences relating to truth, and also a group of empirical differences (a voice-language or a different gaze); these differences are placed "in crime" and in relation to the state. The political and economic "story" of "the Jews" (seen clearly when read from the perspective of crime: "in" the world of crime) appears in Argentina in antisemitic pamphlets from the end of the nineteenth century through the present. (154, original emphasis)

Ludmer's reading of the conflict between "truth" and "Jew" in the context of crime derives from her analysis of dominant-culture texts. When Jews themselves take up the question of truth, Jewishness, modernity, and crime, the story is likely to be somewhat different. Jewish writers do explore these relationships, but they read and represent them from within, often with greater nuance. The Jewish confidence man, for example, may be more complicated than he first appears. In Edgardo Cozarinsky's story "Budapest," the artist-turned-forger David Lerner goes to Hungary, where his mother was born, to swindle an old woman out of a painting that had been stolen, and that she had kept, during the upheaval after the Second World War. A peripatetic Jewish Argentine, he had long ago left Buenos Aires for Paris and stopped painting his own work. As Lerner moves more deeply into his ancestral past, he begins to shed both forgery and falsehood. Finding his way more or less into his mother's Budapest, Lerner advises the woman he had meant to victimize to keep the painting, thus allowing her to avoid winding up with the forgery he would have painted.

Stories of Jewish criminality that are linked to sexuality, especially those about the so-called white slave trade, which scandalized and horrified proper Jews during the early part of the century, have become somewhat burnished over the course of nearly a century.[19] The women who were trafficked have been undergoing a slow transformation from victim to agent. One of the earliest literary Jewish prostitutes, César Tiempo's pseudonymous Clara Beter, is cast as a sympathetic victim. Tiempo invents this figure as the author of a book of poetry whose title, *Versos de una . . .* (Poems of a . . .), drops into coy silence rather than pronounce the word "prostitute." Clara Beter's name combines clarity with bitterness in a bilingual pun, just as the writer's lifelong pseudonym translates the German and Yiddish of Zeitlin into César Tiempo. He ventriloquizes the prostitute, writing in her voice in a manner that evokes a kind of prurient sympathy. *Versos de una . . .* is Tiempo's first serious publication, and the character's story of her homeland and her family, recalled in the first poem through a nostalgic haze, resonates with his own autobiography. According to Eliahu Toker, the book quickly sold thousands of copies in its three editions (31). As Esther Díaz suggests, the fictional Beter struck a chord in the numerous men who wrote to this male-authored creature because she combined the sexual availability of the prostitute with the repentance and the sense of social solidarity so appealing to the working men of her era (183). Consider the following lines from the poem "A un obrero" (To a worker), in which the fictional Beter speaks not of her own exploitation, but rather that of the laborer whose pain she can help assuage:

> All naked I offer myself to your natural desire,
> bite my breasts, crush my body,
> I want to offer you this celebration of flesh
> so that you might forget the harshness of your days.
> . . .
> I know that you suffer; your life is the bitter
> life of all the sad workers
> . . .
> How comforting it is to feel merciful!
> . . .
> you who suffer so deserve the ephemeral
> celebration that my body wants to offer you. (my translation)

[Toda desnuda me ofrezco a tu instinto,
muerde mis pechos, estruja mi cuerpo,
   quiero brindarte esta fiesta de carne
para que olvides tus días acerbos.
   . . .
   Sé que padeces, tu vida es la amarga
vida de todos los tristes obreros,
   . . .
   ¡Cómo conforta sentirse piadosa,
   . . .
tú que así sufres, mereces la efímera
fiesta que quiere brindarte mi cuerpo. (in Toker 1997, 69–70)]

The overt sexual imagery of the first stanza borders on a sadomasochism that the speaker herself invites. The worker's desire is simply his human nature ("*instinto*"—"instinct"—is the word in the original), and any pain she might experience in the encounter is recuperated for the reader as a "celebration of flesh" offered to assuage his suffering. We may find a covert reference to the prostitute's own exploitation in her articulation of that of the worker, but the speaker never suggests that she herself is harmed or diminished by their encounter. Quite the contrary. Moreover, this particular poem submerges the commercial aspect of prostitution: the speaker offers her body as both a gift and the workingman's due. The putatively male, heterosexual reader gets to enjoy the eroticism of the poem in its direct address; he is invited to bite and crush the whore's body and to identify with the oppressed laborer for whom she abjects herself. But Tiempo goes even further, attributing satisfaction to the poet/prostitute, who is comforted by her own abjection, which she frames as an act of mercy and simple goodness that her body itself desires to offer her interlocutor.

Considerably more complex is the figure of Raquel Liberman. This real-life woman, born in Warsaw in 1900, was already married and a mother when she immigrated to Argentina in 1922 to join her husband. He died shortly thereafter, and she spent several years as a prostitute before taking on the Zwi Migdal, the criminal gang that had trafficked her. Liberman has become something of a heroine; certainly she was a survivor. Her story has been taken up in fiction, biography, film, and drama. Playwright and scholar Nora Glickman's biography of her suggests that Liberman may have made the choice to enter prostitution as a means of survival, saving money to buy her way out and denouncing the Zwi Migdal to the police, and only much later making her way to freedom. Glickman went on to bring the story of Liberman to a popular audience with her play *Una tal Raquel* (Some woman named Raquel). Humberto Costantini, who barely traced the edges of Jewishness in most of his work, left two volumes of an incomplete, and at this writing still unpublished, novel, *Rapsodia de Raquel Liberman* (Rhapsody of Raquel Liberman) when he died.

In her introduction to *Una tal Raquel*, Glickman recalls that the family of Raquel Liberman hid the story of their grandmother from the children in the family, but that her granddaughter, after the first shock of recognition upon seeing her grandmother's photograph attached to the story of the Jewish prostitute, was eager to learn about that grandmother. The story that appealed to the granddaughter was one of victimization as well as courage, choice as well as coercion. According to Glickman, the real Raquel lied about her marital and maternal status to get into Argentina, negotiated with her pimp for a cut of the money she earned, tried to buy her way out of prostitution, denounced the Zwi Migdal to the police (who were corrupt and of little assistance), and went to the Jewish ladies' rescue society for help. In other words, Liberman used all the resources available to her, first to survive and support her children and then to extricate herself from prostitution.

We might remember Kovadloff's thesis that Jews are modernized when they come to Argentina, in considering Elsa Drucaroff's *El infierno prometido: Una prostituta del Zwi Migdal* (The promised Hell: A prostitute of the Zwi Migdal). Dina, the young protagonist of the novel, first opts for modernity at home in Poland, when she chooses, against her mother's will, to continue studying after primary school. Her mother predicts that she will "wind up in Buenos Aires," already a code word for prostitution in the Eastern European Jewish imaginary in the early 1900s; but Dina also experiences Buenos Aires as the very site of modernity she was reaching for when she insisted on continuing her studies. In Drucaroff's novel, modernity is of a piece with both education and women's sexual victimization:

> Ah, Buenos Aires: a place without earth or snow or mud or shame or pogroms, or stores of potatoes rationed out to get through the summer. Paved streets, tiled sidewalks, carts filled with food, pockets filled with coins. Everywhere stone and cement and walls so solid and warm for those who live inside, foreign to her. Everything modern, so modern. Everything strange, cold, threatening. A place to get lost in.

But although she was incapable of freeing her damp hand from his, the city was beautiful, as lovely as it was terrifying; although she hated Hersch Grosfield, although she was there to do something horrible, she could not escape the joy of the speed of the car, of her new clothes, of the parade of people, of this world that bustled outside the car window. And of being far away, very far away. (my translation)

[Ah, Buenos Aires: sin tierra ni nieve ni barro ni vergüenza ni pogroms, ni depósitos de papas que se racionaban para pasar el verano. Piedras en las calles, baldosas en la vereda, carros repletos de alimentos, bolsillos repletos de monedas. Todo piedra y cemento y paredes tan sólidas y abrigadas para los que viven adentro, ajenas para ella. Todo moderno, tan moderno. Todo extraño, frío, amenazante. Un lugar para perderse.

Pero aunque era incapaz de soltar su mano húmeda de la otra, la ciudad era hermosa, tan hermosa como aterradora, aunque odiaba y temía a Hersch Grosfield, aunque estaba ahí para hacer algo horrible, no pudo evitar la alegría de la velocidad del auto, de su ropa nueva, del desfile, de ese mundo que bullía por la ventanilla. Y de estar lejos, muy lejos. (56)]

As one of only two girls in her village (and the only Jewish one) to go on to high school, Dina opts for modernity against her mother's furious objections. The educated woman is the fallen woman, and both are associated via the mother's pronouncement with Buenos Aires. In fact, the mother's prediction comes true. A classmate rapes Dina, who comes home disgraced, and the only solution the family sees is to send her off with a Jewish Argentinean scouting for new prostitutes. He offers marriage, but given the mother's earlier statement, they know—even if they want to deny it—that the offer of marriage is a cover.

María Inés Krimer's 2010 novel *Sangre kosher* (Kosher blood) recalls and updates the story of the Zwi Migdal and the Jewish sex trade. When a young Jewish woman named Debora disappears, her father hires Ruth Epelbaum, a detective who has been a librarian and archivist for the Jewish community to which she belongs. The character of the detective shares a surname with one of the real-life leaders of the Mothers of the Plaza de Mayo, so the search for Debora inevitably resonates with the search for the children who disappeared during the period of the dictatorship. In the introduction to her short story, "Shabat," Krimer tells about her own family's connection to the Jewish crime organization: a sister of her grandfather's was a Zwi Migdal prostitute who eventually married one of the crime bosses, was widowed, and then ran her own brothel. Krimer says that this story was never told by the men in the family, rather it was passed down through the women. This is another sort of Jewish assimilation story; the secret that threatens the family's legitimacy (as Jews at all in one case, as respectable Argentines in the other) is entrusted to the women, who keep it alive through the generations. It appears that the men would just as soon forget, or perhaps they cannot be trusted with such explosive information.

Krimer again updates the Zwi Migdal story in 2011, setting her novel *La inauguración* (The inauguration) in the present and chillingly telling the story of contemporary sex trafficking that again resonates with the state terror of the 1976–1983 dictatorship. A young woman commits a pointless theft of a cheap hair-straightening iron, and as she runs away from the police she comes upon a woman beaten nearly to death, who, it emerges, was trying to escape from a prostitution ring. The protagonist, trying to help the dying woman, is kidnapped by the men who left the woman to die and is terrorized into submission. The violence done to the women resonates with political violence: as they dump the dying body of the woman, one of the men assures the other that her body will sink down into the mud because this is a spot where the military dumped subversives. Political violence and gender violence merge in this place. There is nothing overtly Jewish, nothing folkloric about this prostitution ring. It is banally, transnationally Argentine (a pamphlet the protagonist finds advertises Caribbean, Paraguayan, and Polish women), but the head of the ring is known only by a Yiddish-derived nickname: Buby. Nothing but that name suggests that he might be Jewish, and when he quotes the Christian Bible the implication that he is Jewish is further compromised. Like Ruth Epelbaum in *Sangre kosher*, the resonance of the name stands on its own.

The protagonist of *La inauguración* herself is hardly an innocent, but her moral standing is ambiguous. She enters into a sexual relationship with her mother's boyfriend and eventually kills him and runs away; her falling into the hands of a prostitution ring is the direct result of her having committed a theft, but also of trying to help a woman she found beaten severely. Once she is in the house where she is being kept in anticipation of being sold as a prostitute, she believes she can seduce the man in charge who claims her sexually and with whom she derives her own sexual pleasure.

The lines of desire and of morality are complex; pleasure and desire are not always channeled in politically agreeable ways.

Other retellings of the story of the Jewish sex trade also reconfigure the women involved as more complex characters. Some, like Krimer's aunt, struggle against their own victimhood by entering into partnerships with their exploiters and trafficking other women. Borges's fictional Emma Zunz prostitutes herself deliberately in order to take revenge on her father's betrayer so that the mesh of victim/victimizer is utterly unravelable. Others scramble their way to respectability, sometimes by buying their way out of prostitution, more often by marrying a client and establishing a family. Mario Szichman's Dora, in the morbidly comic *At 8:25 Evita Became Immortal* (*A las 20:30 la señora entró en la inmortalidad*), eventually escapes prostitution, but not the fear that she will join those women who never make their way out, buried in the thieves' cemetery established by the Zwi Migdal, beyond the border of the welcome and the legitimate, in death as in life.

Gendered stories of anxiety, of women who refuse simple victim status as prostitutes but rather take practical control of their situation—marrying their traffickers, exploiting other women, seducing their captors—are quintessentially modern. They disrupt patterns previously held to be natural, they upset the entrenched order of society, the family, the nation. If, as feminist political theorists have argued, the modern nation-state models itself on the patriarchal family, women who do not conform to the model of controlled sexuality (virgin bride, chaste wife, mother of legitimate children), or whose presence reveals the underside of a masculine sexuality and camaraderie expressed in the space of the brothels, threaten the stability of the nation as it wishes to imagine itself. This anxiety, however, is part and parcel of modernity itself. Modernity's refusal to settle into permanent patterns, its openness to innovation, its invention of the sovereign social subject, all potentially produce unease as a companion to the promise and possibilities it holds out.

CHAPTER THREE

# PROVISIONAL IDENTITY

Like the Jewish prostitute, whom we have come to understand differently as the last century progressed and turned, the meaning of Jewishness itself shifts with the teller and the times. For this reason, Jewishness as a rhetorical device can function as a gauge of its own place in Argentine self-fashioning. Patricio Pron's epigram, recalled by Elsa Drucaroff in her very angry private letter to him, which he then published, answered, and subsequently deleted from his blog, encapsulates the flickering presence of Jewishness in the Argentine national consciousness: "An Argentine is a Spaniard who thinks he's North American and in reality is nothing but a poor Italian; which is why he suffers like a Jew."[1] This is one of many jokes that poke fun at Argentine self-aggrandizement, but its terms are telling. Here the core identity of Argentina is Spanish; the fundamental Argentine immigrants, still reproducing the initial gesture of conquest and colonization, are Spaniards. This construct is reinforced in popular culture. Juan José Campanella's 2006 television miniseries *Vientos de agua* (Winds of water) which follows the lives of immigrants to Argentina, begins in a village in the Spanish province of Asturias. The first of the characters to emerge as an immigrant is, thus, a Spaniard who befriends a Jewish man and an Italian woman on the boat. Though they all make the same journey and arrive at the same time, the series establishes the Spaniard as the primary frame of reference by placing him first in the scene of immigration. The miniseries goes on to focus on the Spanish émigré and his family.[2]

The two immigrant groups that undermine the self-importance of the dominant group (Spaniards who imagine themselves to be even more important in the world; i.e., North Americans—the sine qua non of capitalist modernity) are known via stereotype in Pron's little witticism: the poverty of the Italians and the suffering of the Jews. Both are evacuated of their meaning: the grinding poverty of southern Italian immigrants and the victimization of East European Jews are put into the service of a minor variation on those themes. Note that neither poverty nor suffering here is connected to particular practices that one group of Argentines might perpetrate on another, but rather they are ascribed to the nation as a whole. Nevertheless, the three groups invoked here as the reality of Argentina are, in fact, constitutive of Argentina's population, and their presence in this epigram both represents and reinforces their actuality in Argentine culture. Still, the Argentine "is" Spanish and Italian; the Jew who is present in the utterance is invoked not for himself, but as a metaphor for Argentine suffering. Jewishness emerges as a wavering presence in Argentina's consciousness of itself.

Argentine self-consciousness is a familiar trope; the nation's intellectual elite have long been fascinated with Argentina's identity.[3] Similarly, for Jewish writers and artists, until the establishment of Israel always in the minority in any nation of the world, Jewish identity has been a constant source of reflection. The long-held debates concerning the nature of Jewishness (Is it a religion? a race? Are Jews a nation? a people?) leave one with the sense that Jewishness as an identity may be real, but it is a reality that is always shifting. Its content is endlessly debated, and the best I can do here is invoke what seems to me to be the least constricting understanding of the term and reiterate that I have no desire to fix its meaning.

It is no surprise that the problem of identity has long been at the center of the study of Argentine Jewry, as scholars in a variety of disciplines consider the following questions: How can Jewish identity be maintained in the face of a culture of assimilation? How has Jewish identity been constituted textually? How is family memory conscripted in the telling to weave a dense fabric for a community whose identity as Jews might seem to undermine the project of being fully Argentinean? What, in fact, is the relationship between Argentine identity and Jewish identity? The Jewish community, *la colectividad*, provides Jewish clubs, friends, schools, and institutions designed to create and nurture strong ties and loyalties. The institutions of the *colectividad* have one sort of stake in identity; individuals have another. Both may be flexible, refracted through other modes of identity (national, political, gender, class, sexual). Identity is not unitary; it comprises an array of what we might call "identitemes": not only the aforementioned gender, nationality, class, and sexuality, but also occupation, ethnicity, and political affiliation—some more profoundly meaningful than others, but each in productive relation with its counterparts.

Furthermore, even national identity is internally fractured. Jews involved in the labor movement, Peronism, and the leftist opposition to dictatorship, for example, have often identified less with their Jewishness than with their political commitments. National identity itself was contested and strengthened as Jews and others were forced to leave Argentina during the dictatorship of the 1970s and 1980s. For psychological survival in exile, the individual must cope with an identity in flux. Moreover, an identity that is both nationally grounded in Argentina and predicated on uprootedness linked to Jewish diaspora provides a kind of stability that is nevertheless loosely anchored to place. Identity in exile must be stable, but it cannot be fixed. It is, rather, something like a narrative, in which the end is unlikely to be identical to the beginning, but in which the end is connected to the beginning as it gathers new matter to it. In exile, identity is disrupted and performance of identity can be recuperative. Identity, particularly national identity, is rife with implications not only of belonging, but also of power.

In 1983 historian Leonard Senkman virtually established the field of Jewish Argentine literary studies with his masterful book whose very title, *La identidad judía en la literatura argentina* (Jewish identity in Argentine literature), announces this central preoccupation with Jewish identity in Argentina. More recently, Raanan Rein asks, when bringing the terms "Jew" and "Argentine" together, which one is the noun and which is the adjective? Is it a matter of Jewish Argentines or Argentine Jews? Which is the stable term that is set off balance by the surprising modifier? Considered differently, the fact of the modifier ("Jewish" for the noun "Argentine," as much as "Argentine" for the noun "Jew") signals the instability of identity itself, so easily thrown off kilter by the intrusion of the disruptive adjective. This is especially true in the case of Jews in this relatively new nation for which the claim to modernity is crucial. The precariousness of the noun-adjective relationship is heightened in Spanish, where there is no difference at all between the form of the adjective and that of the noun ("*judío argentino*" and "*argentino judío*"), and only their placement in relationship to each other signals which term is the noun and which the adjective. Argentina's assimilationist culture encourages Jews to aspire to an Argentine identity, yet Jews at various stages of assimilation (or ambivalent about it) render problematic the very idea of a singular identity. Senkman traces the story of Argentine Jews as it shifts from integration and assimilation, in the line opened by Gerchunoff, to exile and loss of nation subsequent to the dictatorship. This unmooring from nation is a major shift. I would add, though, that in this post-nation moment, Gentile post-exiles are also what Senkman calls post-Argentines, as much as their Jewish counterparts are. Thus, just as Argentine nationality can be read through Jewish Argentineity, so can the disintegration of Argentineity. After exile, no one can count on the nation as a stable place to be, or as a stable source of identity. It is perhaps ironic that in receiving countries in Europe and North America, Argentine exiles are most likely to be perceived not in terms of their nation, but as part of a larger migration of Latin Americans, even as individuals' sense of their own national identity is intensified.

The claim to Jewish identity is similarly precarious, even treacherous. In his novel *Mestizo*, Ricardo Feierstein suggests as much as he thinks identity via a bunch of official documents that are strewn and muddied at the moment of his protagonist's trauma, the moment in which he has apparently seen his old friend shoot a woman. Although Schneiderman actually retains most of his memory, his sense of his own identity seems to be about being able to create a coherent narrative out of the scattered pieces of paper, which have been smeared with (and thereby obfuscated by) mud, and confused, blown around, thrown out of order.

To maintain that a form or an attitude is Jewish is a shaky proposition; finding traces of Jewishness in texts in which only the author's signature suggests that there might be something Jewish here, comes close to claiming an essence of Jewishness that will make its way to intelligibility if we only try hard enough. This is dangerous territory, and I want to name it as such. Is it better when Jews themselves engage in this practice? Is it so different from antisemitic pronouncements that there are essential Jewish traits? If we believe we can hew to principles of scholarly objectivity, there can be no clear answer. However, as scholars, our goodwill—or malice—matters. Utter objectivity is impossible, and it is only when we leave behind the pretense of disinterest that we can try to be clear-eyed about both ourselves and the object of our scholarly enterprise.[4] Yet in the interstices of texts, and in the spaces where identity recedes without disappearing altogether, places where Jewishness is a given, perhaps, and therefore goes unstated, Jewishness as a near absence resonates. In Argentina, narratives in which characters are marked Jewish by their names or associations, even as that identity seems otherwise peripheral, map a quiet Jewish terrain for the nation.

The landscape of Jewish culture in Argentina, as elsewhere, is made up of three broadly definable parts. One group consists of texts and objects that are part of transnational (even prenational) Jewish culture, primarily those linked to Jewish law, theology, spirituality, and mysticism. A second comprises objects made by Jews that have no apparent Jewish content. These include scholarly work across disciplines, including history, philosophy, literary and cultural criticism, the social and hard sciences, as well as novels, music, dance, and visual art. The third group includes work that explores Jewishness in its larger historical and cultural context and that context in relation to Jewishness. That third group has been the site of most of the intellectual labor around Argentine Jewish art and literature, and with good reason. It is the place where Argentine syncretism and the survival of Jewishness come together. It is where Jewishness is visible, where it is both sturdy and malleable, and the question of identity is at its core.

Nevertheless, identity, particularly Jewish identity in the contemporary world and national identity at a moment that some are calling "postnational" is no longer self-evident or stable. The wealth of scholarly work in Argentine Jewish literature and history derives from the impulse to erect and maintain the edifice of Jewish identity in Argentina. It makes sense. It is easy to be scornful of identity when that which you hold yourself to be is not in any existential danger. For Jews, who faced annihilation in the living memory of some and in the historical memory of many more, asserting a presence in the world and meaning in a national culture is an act of survival. Moreover, it is Jewish-identified scholarship that has brought attention to these Jewish-authored texts. Much like other identity-based scholarship (for example, feminist work on women, or queer work on gays, lesbians, transgender, and nonbinary people), the texts they attend to—however worthy and brilliant—often languish outside the cultural mainstream until identity-driven scholarship brings attention to them. Of course, mainstream cultural analysis is also largely identity-based. The difference is that the un(re)marked identity of the cultural and national elite dovetails genteelly with its own agenda. Identity-driven scholarship does a service, not least by troubling hegemonic complacency and showing the way to a more expansive cultural landscape. On a more profound level, it calls into question the unstated assumptions that underpin culture and nation, ultimately undoing any reliance on a stable set of meanings, including its own.

Yet even though bringing attention to the importance of the Jewish presence in Argentine culture is a necessary, healthy, and culturally broadening corrective, too much insistence on Argentine Jewish identity constrains our thinking. Not every effort made by a Jew will have Jewishness as its driving force. What a Jew does is not always about Jewish identity. Ana Katz's film *A Stray Girlfriend* (*Una novia errante*), for example, is a psychological portrait of a young woman abandoned by her boyfriend. It is scrupulously free of ethnic markers of any sort. As Saúl Sosnowski (1987) has so eloquently argued, the focus on Jewish identity as the primary theme of Jewish authors limits the possibilities of the scholarly enterprise on this very corpus. Other scholars have wrestled with the problematic as well. Darrell Lockhart, for example, distinguishes between "Jewish writers" and "Jewish writing" before deciding to include both in a study whose title, *Latin American Jewish Writers*, favors the former. Florinda Goldberg, in her impeccably researched and tightly presented study of the range of approaches to textual Jewishness, opts for the second formulation: Latin American Jewish writing.[5]

My own intention when I began this study was to set aside questions of identity in favor of questions of meaning. Specifically, I wanted to ask, and answer, the question, what does Jewishness mean in the context of Argentine modernity? But of course naming Jewishness implies identity, just as naming Argentineity does—there is no way around it. My own private shorthand title for this book, the first name of numerous computer files scattered on my desktop, eventually to be deposited in an array of similarly named folders, was "JA," short for "Jewish Argentina." I mention this because the formulation is so deeply rooted and so deeply problematic. Clearly, the question of identity cannot be avoided; indeed one of the fundamental issues addressed by this study is, in fact, the very notion of Jewish identity, especially as it relates to the nation. For identity shimmers. It is like an energy, produced in the spaces between the self and its circumstances—history, body, what others have to say, rolling toward each other and away, spinning on axes, bright and dark in turn. Orbs rub against each other, pulse and bump, their edges worn away by friction, but also accreting matter as they take density from each other; rough gives way to smooth and becomes rough again.

In his study of Jewish political thought in modern Europe, Natan Sznaider refers, perhaps more helpfully, not to Jewish identity, but to "the Jewish condition." I hedge with that "perhaps" because although a condition is flexible, likely to change through time and across place, the definite pronoun (*the* Jewish condition) roots it back down and implies that it is unitary and unchanging. *The Other/Argentina* is propelled in part by the energizing and exhausting tension between unitary solidity on the one hand and instability and internal fracture on the other, not just of Jewishness but of Argentina as a nation. Sznaider in fact asks the same question that vexes me, although he does so in the context not of Argentine history and culture, but rather with reference to European political thought:

Is there such a thing as a Jewish Europe or a Europe of the Jews? Can one even speak of Jewish voices or a Jewish epistemology without reducing thought to a matter of origin and birth? (1)

Stealing a page from feminist thought can help answer Sznaider's question. Gayatri Spivak richly articulated what many feminist scholars and activists had already been practicing: a strategic essentialism that maintains a culturally constructed identity around which to mount political action. Strategic essentialism carries with it a whiff of the battlefield, a foundation in an oppositional social movement that questions the ways in which notions of the feminine have been deployed against women and certain men, and which therefore needs to be held on to in order to combat inequality even as the whole notion of an essential femininity must eventually be undermined in order to finish the job. I would suggest modifying Spivak's locution and call my practice here "provisional essentialism." Provisional essentialism, like the strategic version, is makeshift and temporary, but it does not purport to undo identity in quite the same way. It can be dismantled, but it provides a useful structure for addressing a culturally constructed, but no less real, entity.

The meaning of Jewishness discernible within intellectual and artistic engagement resides in perpetual motion between modernity and the premodern. It occupies the spaces circulating between modern migration, European sophistication, and secular representation on the one hand and a connection to the tribal, a religious creed that predates Christianity, and the sacred written word on the other. This meaning, held by the dominant culture—not entirely of its own imagining, but of its shaping—sets the stage for differential power relations between Jews and non-Jews. Its different valuation of Jewishness and dominant Christian-ness must, of course, be negotiated by Jewish-identified subjects.

The answer to the question of what "is" Jewish comes down to the control of signification. The dominant, non-Jewish culture retains its discursive power, but Jews themselves can claim the authenticity of insider knowledge and experience. In this study, I have made a decision to privilege the work of Jewish-identified makers of art, film, literature, and music, whose struggle with the meaning of Jewishness necessarily engages with dominant modes of thought.

Gentiles are sometimes sympathetic, sometimes hostile, and sometimes indifferent to Jews and Jewishness. Jews may be, too. Not all Jews stick to topics like the Holocaust, for example, or with the production and maintenance of a visible Jewish community, even if they are Jewish-identified. That term itself has come to mean those who take themselves to be Jewish and who are actively Jewish in one way or another—religiously, culturally, culinarily, linguistically. Family ties, the memory of the ritual attached to the preparation and consumption of food, or of words in a Jewish language are among the affective and embodied ties to Jewishness. Foods eaten at family meals and words shaped in the mouth or caught in the ear are captured, represented, and produced in art and literature. Jewishness is about a shared history as well as a connection to a sacred narrative and body of teaching. It is also about practice—cultural as much as religious. It sometimes manifests in self-presentation (which may include anything from ritual garments to fashion choices), in what one cooks and eats, in where and how one earns a living. It is about a presence in space that looks both forward and backward in time. In Argentina, it includes deliberately acquiring land to carve out a space for survival in the face of European hostility. The establishment by Baron von Hirsch of the Jewish Colonization Association is a non-nationalistic, in fact assimilationist, gesture (despite the search for a place to establish a Jewish homeland, these colonies were not meant to stand as a separate Jewish nation), that at the same time maintained Jewish difference. The JCA colonies, like the subsequent Jewish Argentine writing and filmmaking they set in motion, were an experiment in self-assertion as both same and different—Argentines like any other, Jews to boot. The first Argentine Jewish narrative, one that every subsequent one has to reckon with, is the story of assimilation and identity in the colonies. The Jewishness of the settlers whom Alberto Gerchunoff would call Jewish gauchos not only would not interfere with Argentineity; it was (im)perfectly congruent with it. Indeed, the trope of the Jewish gaucho has remained powerful enough so that an urban and urbane writer like Edgardo Cozarinsky can productively invoke it as his own lineage in an interview on French television.

Grammatically, however, the subject of identification—the one who is doing the identifying—is ambiguous, and "Jewish-identified" can also be understood to mean "identified as Jewish by others." This is familiar—and disturbing—enough from the point of view of modern Jewish history, but I'd like to hold on to it long enough to allow for a positive or at least neutral understanding of such "Jewish identification," even if it often comes with a dusting of residual antisemitism, as the leftist militants in Cozarinsky's *Lejos de dónde* (Far from where?) demonstrate as they welcome the presumptively Jewish Federico into the student movement with the assurance that Jews are always welcome:

"Do you know how many Moishes are with us? As far as the organization is concerned you're just another Argentine." Then, letting a smile take over his face, "The finances of the organization, your people are the ones who manage them." (my translation)

[—¿Sabés cuántos moishes están con nosotros? Para la orga sos un argentino más.—Luego, dejando que la sonrisa le invadiese el rostro—las finanzas de la orga, son las tuyas, quienes las manejan. (123)]

At the very mention of inclusion, difference is inscribed, and the antisemitic association of Jews with money permeates the utterance.[6] Being Jewish may be another way of being Argentine, but here "other" is the operative term.

Argentine Jewishness is, then, also forged in relation to a dominant, sometimes overtly hostile, culture that sees Jews as "other." Ricardo Feierstein makes it clear that such otherness is powerful, but that it is anything but straightforward. In *La logia del umbral* (The lodge of the threshold), the secret society of the title is a self-fulfilling prophecy, a phantom organization created by Jews in response to Gentiles' belief that such a society exists. Jewish identity thus internalizes its otherness even as it protects itself from its own others. A central theme of Feierstein's *Mestizo: A Novel* (*Mestizo*) is identity as otherness, both of which terms I use uneasily, as shorthand for the meanings that congeal around them. To be the *mestizo* trumpeted in the title of the novel is to reject the drive for purity and homogeneity in favor of the layered richness of multiplicity. In *Mestizo*, Feierstein represents the complexity of otherness in a variety of forms: as an assimilated Jew, his protagonist negotiates life among both antisemitic Gentiles and his more deeply observant coreligionists. Jewish difference from the larger society thus shares space with the differences within Jewishness itself. The desire to differentiate, however, is challenged by the impossibility of purity. Ultimately, this covertly polemical novel argues, the greater good is served by acknowledging that in modern Argentina there can be no unblended race or religion.

Uneasy Jewishness takes another turn in José Pablo Feinmann's novel *La crítica de las armas* (The critique of weapons), which begins with an apparent claim to unproblematic Jewish identity, as the protagonist's father speaks in Yiddish. This initial situating of the narrative in an Argentine Jewish milieu is quickly undermined by the narrator's deeply ambivalent relationship to his own sense of Jewishness. The son of a Catholic mother and a Jewish father, Pablo Epstein (whose first name, not incidentally, echoes the author's) is the embodiment of bourgeois Argentine contradictions: his history as a leftist militant, for example, has not kept him from benefiting from the family business.[7] Perhaps most deliciously ironic is Pablo's citing Jewish law to prove that he is not Jewish, thus reinforcing the idea that he is. To whom does Jewish law matter? Certainly not to the Catholics he is trying to convince.

*La crítica de las armas* is replete with references to Argentine ambiguity about Jewishness, both the protagonist's own and that of the nation in general. The doctor who will overload Pablo's cancer-ridden body with radiation treatments admits to his own antisemitism, but he claims that his commitment to healing overrides his dislike of Jews. Pablo's self-proclaimed cowardice maps onto Jewish stereotype, and his cynical observation that being a child of survivors is the fanciest of Jewish credentials are moments of the former. In a further twist, he implicitly credits the character who claims this particular form of victim status with foreseeing the impending bloodbath of the dictatorship and urging the narrator to leave the country while he can.

Jews at various stages of assimilation, or variously ambivalent about it, render problematic the very idea of identity, even as Argentina's assimilationist culture and its undercurrents of antisemitism encourage Jews to aspire to an Argentine identity. Germán Rozenmacher writes of the first generation of Jewish immigrants and the precarious, not always successful integration into the new nation. The protagonist of his short story "Tristezas de la pieza de hotel" (Hotel room sorrows) embodies the anxiety of Jewishness within the character's own family. Still a peddler, he is the only one among them still mired in the poverty of the first generation. He is the only one who has not married, made an Argentine family, or succeeded economically. The story is triggered by the death of the protagonist's mother, the attachment to whom signals his inability to enter full adulthood, but also full Argentineity. Tellingly, the story's only overt reference to Jewishness concerns only the two of them, in the context of the successful assimilation of the rest of his own generation:

> What was he to his relatives but the nice bachelor uncle who came to visit? Maybe he was something else, not so pleasant. An enormous family filled with respectable people, all doctors, engineers, lawyers, all of them with plaques on their door, winners. Or if not, first class merchants, businessmen with millions

of pesos, wives, children, grandchildren. And he hadn't stopped being a peddler, stuck in his nickel-and-dime business. He saw himself five, ten, fifteen years back when his mother was still young and tried to advise him on the best way to do business, because she had always wanted to be a businesswoman, for the two of them to build an indestructible commercial enterprise from the moment both had gotten off the ship that had brought them from a tiny European town that might not even exist anymore. Just two Jews in a strange new city. (my translation)

[¿Qué era él para sus parientes sino el tío solterón y apacible que iba de visita? Quizá era algo más, no del todo agradable. Una vasta familia toda llena de personas respetables, todos médicos, ingenieros, abogados, todos con chapas en la puerta, triunfadores. O si no vendedores que [*sic*] primera clase, comerciantes con millones de pesos, mujeres, hijos, nietos. Y él no había dejado de ser un pequeño vendedor callejero, metido en sus negocios de tres por cinco. Se veía cinco, diez, quince años atrás cuando su madre era todavía joven y trataba de aconsejarlo sobre la mejor manera de hacer negocios, porque siempre había esperado ser una mujer de negocios, que los dos formaran una sociedad comercial indestructible desde el momento en que ambos habían bajado del barco que los había traído de un pequeñísimo pueblo europeo ahora quizás inexistente. Apenas dos judíos solos en la ciudad nueva y extraña. (10)]

The narrator's failure as an aspiring Argentine is ultimately linked to his inability to separate from his mother and the Jewishness she represents, and the concomitant failure to make his own family in and of Argentina. The protagonist, who is the visible sign of the immigrant roots of the family, narrates his estrangement from his relatives, an estrangement that the reader might well understand as the family's own anxiety about its recent escape from the precariousness of Jewishness.

Rozenmacher goes on to explore the radical loneliness of the unsuccessfully assimilated Jew in "*Blues* en la noche" (Blues in the night), in which a singer acclaimed in Russia as a young man is reduced to aged penury in Argentina. In the final scene, the elderly displaced artist performs not in a concert hall for a worshipful audience, but in his tenement apartment for a young boy who wants to learn to play the trombone. The old man puts on his stage makeup, but as it runs down his face it is as if his entire visage is disintegrating, as if his identity as an artist will no longer hold together. Being an artist had required him to mask his Jewishness in Russia, and it is only in Argentina that a Jewish identity has crept back up on him over the years of eking out his living among other immigrant Jews:

> And then he came to Argentina and began to tour, traveling second class, all over, giving concerts and recitals, always with other people, of course, because he knew that no one would come to listen just to him, and he sang as a synagogue cantor during the holidays in some colony in Entre Ríos, because even though he left the name Goloboff, he had once more recognized that he was Jewish, perhaps because he had to earn a living or because it was futile to pretend to be different, or because he felt terribly alone. (my translation)

> [Y entonces vino a la Argentina y empezó a rodar, en vagones de segunda, por todas partes, dando conciertos y recitales, siempre con otros, claro, porque sabía que a él solo no lo vendría a escuchar nadie, y cantaba como cantor sinagogal durante las fiestas, en alguna de colonia Entre Ríos, porque aunque se había dejado el nombre de Goloboff, había vuelto a reconocer que era judío, quizá porque necesitaba ganarse la vida o porque se dio cuenta que era inútil fingirse distinto, o porque se sentía terriblemente solo. (86)]

Here as in "Tristezas de la pieza de hotel" Jewishness is deposited primarily in the figure of the otherwise minimally developed character of an elderly woman. It is only when Goloboff's wife, an immigrant like himself, dies that the singer becomes observant, as though her role in their marriage had been to sustain the Jewishness of both.

In the case of Daniel Burman's *Waiting for the Messiah* (*Esperando al Mesías*), it is not the protagonist's mother who embodies Jewishness for the male protagonist; she dies early in the film. This role is performed instead by a young woman, the protagonist's longtime girlfriend. The principle is the same, however: in these male-authored texts, Jewish identity is fraught for the men, but it is simply a function of the women, whose reproductive work includes not just the labor of making a Jewish home and raising Jewish-identified male children, but seamlessly embodying Jewishness itself.

Migration, intermarriage, transnational lives, the demands of tradition, and the pull of modernity are all in play in the production of Jewish Argentineity in four films by Daniel Burman, all of which center on protagonists named Ariel. The quartet, consisting of *Waiting for the Messiah*, *Lost Embrace* (*El abrazo partido*), *Family Law* (*Derecho de familia*), and *The Tenth Man* (*El rey del Once*), can be read as progress toward a troubled assimilation that always has as its center the demands and the lure of the paternal. Burman plays with identity itself in the films. Each protagonist has his own story, but they are inevitably linked thanks to casting, naming, and personality traits that they share.[8] The first and youngest Ariel tests the waters outside the Jewish bubble in which he was raised, resisting the circumscribed world of his father. He strains against the expectations that he will take over his father's small business and marry the nice Jewish girl who already behaves like a daughter to the older man. The middle Ariel shifts allegiance from the mother to the mutilated but heroically Jewish father who is a hero of the Six-Day War; and the adult Ariel, married to a Gentile woman, submits to his own father as he enters paternity himself. The fourth Ariel leaves his New York fiancée behind as he returns to Buenos Aires to see the father who, from Ariel's point of view, always put his commitment to the Jewish community ahead of his responsibility to his son. Reading across the first three films, the broad narrative follows the Jewish son as he grapples with hetero-patriarchal norms, reconciles with the father, eventually steps into the role of father—and the law of heteronormativity. In each of the films family is idealized: the great tragedy of *Waiting for the Messiah* is the death of Ariel's mother, while Ani's accepting and loving mother and Ariel's warm—if suffocating—father stand in contrast to Laura's father, who has abandoned her emotionally and, for all practical purposes, materially. Similarly, in the film's second plot, a new holy family is formed, consisting of a working-class woman who has stayed faithful to her imprisoned husband, a formerly middle-class bank worker whose wife throws him out when he loses his job, and the baby he finds in the trash. *Lost Embrace* is all about the return of the father, as the son slowly learns that the family story he has lived with—that his father callously abandoned him and his mother when he went to Israel as a warrior—is less than entirely true. The beloved mother in this narrative was, in fact, unfaithful to her husband, who quietly left her to her lover. The happy ending in which father and son are reconciled, and the father (implicitly) forgives the mother, binds the family again. The very title of *Family Law* forewarns the viewer of the inevitability of heteronormative adulthood within the framework of the nuclear—but also extended—family. The mother in *The Tenth Man* is simply absent from the beginning. A brief reference to her reveals virtually nothing about her; the father has taken on the role of nurturer. In sharp contrast to the recovered hero-father of *Lost Embrace*, the father has never left the neighborhood. He, too, however, is a hero, as the key figure in a private charitable foundation that provides food, medicine, and other life necessities to the poor Jews of the historically Jewish Buenos Aires neighborhood, El Once.[9] It is the son who has left and who, at the beginning of the film, is preparing his return from New York to the old neighborhood and his father. The film charts the son's progress as he effectively becomes his father, assimilating not into the larger society but rather back into its Jewish community.

In contrast, Mario Szichman reveals the fissures set to undermine the apparently unified family in his three novels about the Pechof family, in which he takes aim at the quest for assimilation. The oldest Pechof brother pimps out his son to lure investors, promising them that the handsome young man will marry their less-than-beautiful daughters. He exploits the labor of his brothers, who in turn depend upon and despise him. The production of the outward sign of family unity, a family photograph, is delayed over and over as one brother refuses to show his face. Szichman particularly pillories the desire to assimilate in *At 8:25 Evita Became Immortal*. Among the family members trying to juggle Jewishness and Argentineity, one, Jaime, has a single goal: to reinvent himself as a Gentile with an aristocratic past. He hires a "manager" to teach him taste and manners and to fashion an illustrious Argentine history for him. In Jaime's rapacious rejection of his own history and the hilarious project of learning a whole new past, the joke is that Jaime never stops thinking in terms that center his Jewishness. He wants to enter a world of Gentiles but can't stop thinking of them as "other" to him—he wants to be a *goy*, but only a Jew would use that term. The only term he has for what he aspires to become is pejorative.

Argentine Jewishness is produced textually over and over again, a discursive formation that is also a material reality. As a minority discourse one of its projects is to assert itself in the face of the dominant culture that would either name it as other or swallow it up more or less whole. Its actual content is not, however, fixed. Edgardo Cozarinsky's *The Bride from Odessa* (*La novia de Odessa*) posits the fundamental question of what, in fact, constitutes Jewish identity in Argentina. The title story is about an overt decision to perform Jewishness to get to Argentina, a decision that raises the question of where identity resides and taking on the question of Jewish identity as it shifts from Europe to the Americas. Jewishness for the narrator (the last in the line of the family whose story this is) is not about belief; it is about food and about his family, and also about antisemitic treatment in such state institutions as school and the army. In Odessa, the eponymous bride is a Russian Orthodox servant working in a hat shop owned by a Jewish woman. She is the only non-Jew employed in the shop, and she is at the bottom of the pecking order, working for room, board, and the occasional tip from the store's wealthy customers. She makes the decision to assume a Jewish identity—literally to take on the identity of the young wife of a Jewish man who is about to immigrate to Argentina. Rivka Bronfman, the young woman engaged to the Jewish man who is about to embark for Argentina, does not want to go, so the Odessa bride, whose real name we never learn, uses her passport and lives out her life in Argentina as Rivka. Although Rivka's name is boldly stated, on the passport and by the woman who assumes it, the identity of the young man who will become the family patriarch is uncertain. Cozarinsky, channeling Cervantes, writes the paterfamilias into ambiguity: "The young man, whom we shall call Daniel Aisenson" (2001b, 4). The passport is an outward sign of identity, and escaping Czarist Russia on false papers is a familiar trope in the story of Jewish immigration. The bride reinvents herself as Jewish, and her children and grandchildren live their lives as Argentine Jews.

Family stories of this matriarch take shape around moments of her physical courage as a pioneer on the pampas (in one incident that reverberates with European anxiety, she shoots at some Gypsies who are rumored to be stealing children), and in her ultimate act of undeniable maternal sacrifice she dies giving birth to her tenth child. One story about this mythic great-grandmother is handed down secretively, however—the story of her replacing Daniel's legitimate wife. It is secret because her not being Jewish compromises her children's claim to Judaism: only a Jewish woman can produce a Jewish child. According to traditional Jewish law, then, the Odessa bride's children and the grandchildren of her daughters' line are not Jewish. It is the eldest daughter in each generation who is told the story, since it is her children and those of her younger sisters who are affected. Nevertheless, this Russian Orthodox woman becomes Jewish in the eyes of Argentine officialdom. She carries Rivka's immigration documents, and she inhabits and performs Rivka's life. As she proclaims joyfully on the Odessa steps: "I am Rivka Bronfman."

The bride from Odessa lives as, and thereby becomes, a Jewish mother and, posthumously, a Jewish grandmother, a canonically Argentinean one, settling the JCA colonies, with her stories of childbirth and bravery on the pampas. Her children and grandchildren are Jews in the eyes of the others who surround them, both Jew and Gentile, although knowledge of the Odessa bride's true ancestry would call that identity into question in the Jewish community.

Cozarinsky's "Émigré Hotel" (Hotel de emigrantes) echoes "The Bride from Odessa" in its destabilization of Jewish identity. This story takes place a generation later, during and after the Second World War, but is likewise narrated by a descendant of the protagonists. A fuller and more suggestive story, it tacks itself to reality at all its corners: the Spanish Civil War, the ship *Nea Hellas* and its famously rejected passengers, the desperation of reaching the very end of Europe, Lisbon, with nowhere else to go but toward the sea and America, with the Nazis threatening to swallow Europe whole.

Narrated by a young scholar, the grandson of an American heiress named Anne Hayden Rice and a German whom she met during the Spanish Civil War, it is the story of a threesome and of transnational, problematic Jewishness in the mid-twentieth century. Two inseparable German friends, the Jewish Theo Felder and the Gentile Franz Mühle, meet Anne, who becomes their lover. Trapped in World War II Europe, only she and one other can get out of Europe. The passport is in Felder's name, but it emerges that Mühle probably assumes his identity and goes to the US. The daughter of this couple, inhabiting postwar Jewish transnationalism, marries an Argentine she meets at Woodstock and goes with him to live on an Israeli kibbutz. Eventually they open a pizzeria in Tel Aviv. The young couple ultimately returns to Argentina, where they divorce. The narrator, Anne Felder's grandson, tries to piece together this family story from documents, letters, hotel registries, and other fragments, and finally he finds an old bookseller who may have known the original threesome. The story is necessarily fragmented, telling the Holocaust from the point of view of those in the relative safety of neutral Portugal, and including the casual antisemitism of commentators like Jean Giraudoux. Jewish identity in "Émigré Hotel" is fungible. Here, unlike in "The Bride from Odessa," there is no anxiety about the reality of Jewishness: Anne Rice becomes Anne Felder, marrying the man whose name marks him as Jewish. Her daughter, in turn, marries an Argentine Jew, and their son is the scholar who manifests no religious commitment, but whose commitment to digging out this story proclaims a sense of connection to Jewishness.

> The real Theo Felder—I write the word "real" but have no idea what that adjective means applied to someone who had given up

## PROVISIONAL IDENTITY    63

his identity (and what was perhaps still more important in the Europe of that time: his passport) in a loving gesture towards someone who was to use it for the rest of his life, and bequeath this foreign name to my mother. (2001b, 154)

[El verdadero Theo Felder—escribo "verdadero" pero no sé muy bien qué significa el epíteto aplicado a alguien que había cedido su identidad (y lo que en la Europa de 1940 era tal vez más valioso aún: su pasaporte) en un gesto de amor por el amigo que iba a usarla durante el resto de su vida, que iba a legar ese apellido ajeno a mi madre. (2001a, 136)]

The passport legitimizes identity, and even—once—survival (and here once again is the irony of the Jewish identity making migration possible). To assume the identity of another first seems a charade, but as the identity is performed it becomes real. Anne Rice takes on a certain Jewishness by taking on Felder's name, perhaps to the dismay of her relatives. Her daughter finds a Jewish husband, and the young couple goes to live in Israel. They return to Argentina and eventually divorce; the husband, when he remarries, chooses a psychoanalyst as his second wife—a caricature that reinforces both his Jewishness and his Argentineity. The postwar generation is part of the transnational youth culture of Woodstock. Their emblem is the globalized, but also quintessentially Argentine, pizza that makes its way to Israel. National and ethnic identity, so critical during the Holocaust, and conferred bureaucratically, by the passport, becomes nearly vestigial:

If it is true that Theo Felder transferred his identity to Franz Mühle so that he could emigrate to the United States, my grandmother found herself blessed with a married name that many would have considered unfortunate. . . . I wonder if she enjoyed upsetting her relatives, deeply rooted in New Hampshire, by becoming Mrs. Felder? Be that as it may, it seems her daughter, Madeleine Felder (who became my mother), inherited a destiny along with a surname: aged eighteen, at Woodstock, she met the man who was to become my father, one Aníbal Cahn, born in Argentina. (2001b, 133–34)

[Si es cierto que Theo Felder cedió su identidad a Franz Mühle para facilitarle la inmigración a los Estados Unidos, mi abuela se vio agraciada, sin buscarlo, por un apellido que muchos habrían considerado ingrato . . . ¿La habrá divertido irritar a sus parientes, tal vez aferrados a raíces en New England, convirtiéndose en Mrs Felder? En todo caso, su hija, Madeleine Felder, que iba a ser mi madre, pareció haber heredado junto con el apellido un destino: a los dieciocho años, en Woodstock, conoció al que iba a ser mi padre, un tal Aníbal Cahn, nacido en la Argentina. (2001a, 133–34)]

The slipperiness of identity is reinforced by the suggestion that the bookshop owner, a man named Campos who purported to know the trio, may be the real Felder. More to the point, the acknowledgment of the evidence of the identity switch is convincing but not entirely conclusive. Felder can be translated into Portuguese as Campos, and the narrator has told us that such translations were not uncommon.

Here the genders are more than simply the reverse of those in "The Bride from Odessa"; they are inverted and queered. In "The Bride from Odessa" it is the woman who assumes a false identity to marry and emigrate. In "Émigré Hotel" the narrator guesses that the man who leaves assumes the Jewish identity of his friend, a man who had, perhaps, been his lover. With this transfer of identity, the Gentile Anne becomes, in the eyes of her family, contaminated by the Jewishness of a husband who himself assumes the Jewishness of another. Jewishness is, in this text, all about performance and ascription. The characters touch down in a range of Jewish spaces: Lisbon during the war, New York, Buenos Aires, and Tel Aviv. The grandchild winds up in Argentina, in a kind of roundabout way, and then back in Europe. Part of the pleasure of the story is the mystery and the fact that Cozarinsky drops clues but doesn't wrap it up with a ribbon. The reader is left believing, not without a touch of uncertainty, that the original (if not necessarily the "real") Felder is Campos, and the narrator his grandson.

Jewishness in these narratives is about a shared history and a geography of movement, as well as a connection to a sacred narrative. It is also about practice—religious, cultural, culinary, sumptuary, economic. In Argentina, it includes deliberately acquiring land to carve out a space for survival in the face of European hostility. The body of Jewish-authored texts produces the reality of Argentine Jewishness as surely as the presence of actual Jews in the JCA colonies, and on the streets of Buenos Aires, Rosario, and la Plata, making claims on national memory as they indulge in, or wreak havoc on, nostalgia. Jewish writers stake claim to their territory by writing themselves into it, whether or not their texts are autobiographical. To the extent that their works are about Jewish Argentina, they function as a structure, a house of books and celluloid whose shape and presence mark Argentina as also Jewish.

CHAPTER FOUR
# FAMILY STORIES AND THE INVENTION OF MEMORY

In *Zakhor*, his masterful study of the Jewish approach to the past, historian Yosef Hayim Yerushalmi examines the shift in the modern era from a tradition of remembrance to an embrace of historiography.[1] For Yerushalmi, this change from the intimacy of storytelling and ritual to the more detached gathering and presentation of evidence represents something of a loss. In its own way, Mario Muchnik's very personal history of the Jewish people attempts to reconcile these two modes of access to the Jewish past. The book's title, *Mundo judío: Crónica personal* (Jewish world: A personal chronicle), suggests as much. Muchnik presents the thousands of years of Jewish history in a chatty tone, interspersing jokes and inserting imagined conversations with his presumably Gentile interlocutor into his broad-brush narrative. Muchnik calls his book a "personal chronicle," but it is not an autobiography; rather he assumes the mantle of Jewishness to authorize the telling of a larger tale. Muchnik avoids the personal memory that is prerequisite for understanding the self, Jewish or otherwise, and that avoidance distinguishes him from the majority of Argentine Jews who write about their people's past. These other writers take Yerushalmi's admonition to remember in a deeply personal way. Their remembrance, which is not only Jewish but also Argentine, is largely made, not incidentally, through the media of fiction and memoir.

The classic story of Jewish immigration and assimilation in Argentina is the turn-of-the-century Jewish gaucho narrative, proposed by Gerchunoff's novel and confirmed by his father's gravestone in the Moisés Ville cemetery. A narrative of integration, both audacious and aspirational, it has achieved the patina of nostalgia. Gerchunoff's ur-text of Jewish Argentineity is subsequently reworked in an urban setting by Ana María Shua and Alicia Steimberg in their vignettes of, in Steimberg's words, musicians and watchmakers, as well as overprotective aunts and warm kitchen aromas in crowded apartments. The family story of the Jewish peddler who eventually works his way up the economic ladder as a respectable merchant is the urban counterpart to the Jewish gaucho. The desire for preservation of Jewishness simultaneous with assimilation, solemnly represented in the early texts of Jewish Argentine writers, is rendered as nostalgia and loss in second-generation writers like Shua, and sometimes satirized as in Steimberg and Mario Szichman, who lampoons not only the desire to forge a Jewish Argentine memory, but also the desire to leave Jewishness behind altogether. When women become protagonists of these stories the result is often somewhat less comfortable: they may be the woman who works her way out of prostitution into a reputable marriage (in Glickman), or the ancestor who may not have been Jewish herself (in Cozarinsky), or the angry and betrayed runaway wife and mother (in Gorodischer).

The second novel in Mario Szichman's Pechof family trilogy, *Los judíos del Mar Dulce* (The Jews of the sweetwater sea), opens with Berele Pechof quite literally constructing the past, making a movie about his family.[2] Here Szichman engages with two quintessentially modern modes of storytelling: film and the self-referential narrative. In his effort to locate the family within history, Berele intersperses documentary footage with actors playing the family and still photographs that interrupt the flow of both history and the motion picture. Language is both necessary and excessive in the Pechof family film, for in order to understand the relationship between the big events of history and the family story, between documentary footage of the First World War and the Russian Revolution, performances by actors, and photographs of family members, there must be some sort of narration. Since Berele is filming without sound, language does not emerge artlessly as voiceover or dialogue; rather it is written on title cards over which the camera lingers long enough to allow them to be read. As they discuss the difficulty of making the visual elements seem part of a seamless whole, Berele and the editor overtly address the challenge of memory making. The process of making memory and making history thus becomes a part of the story.[3]

As Berele has the editor stop the film and rewind, he causes history to move backward and forward, suggesting its very malleability, especially once it is both subjected to modern technology and turned into story. The family's intimate history, the film suggests, can fully be understood only with reference to the external events that push the Pechofs out of

Europe and pull them into Argentina. The stillness of the stills interrupts the smooth flow of Jewish macrohistory. The images that encapsulate the family's small history do not move; instead they capture specific moments and enshrine ancestors, holding them motionless to preserve them for their descendants. They suggest a longing for permanence and foundation in the face of movement and change.

The inclusion of family photos in the Pechof film, and by extension in the novel, points to the centrality of photography in the production of modern memory. Indeed, photography plays a critical role in Jewish Argentine memory narratives, many of which include family photographs as illustration. Cristina Zuker's novelized family memoir, *El tren de la victoria* (Victory train), relies on the visual evidence of family photos to enhance the reader's knowledge and to draw us into the text. The hairstyles, clothing, furnishings, and setting immediately available in a photograph evoke the particular time, place, and people who populate the memoir. More complicated are the photographs in *Los judíos del Mar Dulce* and Ricardo Feierstein's *Mestizo: A Novel* (*Mestizo*). Both these books are novels, but the photographs that accompany the written text in both are of real families. In *Mestizo*, the photographs are primarily of the generation of the narrator's grandparents, prior to their move to Argentina, who exist in the fiction as memory. The photographs, by their very nature, make a truth claim, even as their inclusion in a novel undercuts that claim. Feierstein's narrator describes the photographs, but he does not always give complete or reliable information about them. The photographs provide immediate but insufficient access to a past in which photography itself was a new technology. In Szichman's novel the photographs of the family are postimmigration; they depict the family in the Jewish colonies: vast stretches of pampas, the family cow, a small dwelling, the family dressed in the garb of Eastern European Jews. These quintessentially Jewish Argentine images are interspersed within historical photographs that feature the geopolitical reality of the era, frequently in the person of Lenin, creating a visual connection between family memory and world historical events.

In addition to serving to illustrate and complicate novels and memoirs, photography emerges as a recurrent trope in family history narratives as it reclaims, documents, and falsifies the past. If, as John Berger reminds us, "[t]he most popular use of the photograph is as a memento of the absent" (180), photographs are as important when they are suppressed as when they are displayed. Photographs are variously mutilated and hidden; characters may refuse to let them be made at all or stage them in ways that obscure reality and place falsified visual evidence in its place. In Edgardo Cozarinsky's story "Real Estate" (*Bienes raíces*) the mother's face is cut out of the family photograph when she runs away. Similarly, in Angélica Gorodischer's "Camera Obscura" (La cámara oscura) the family has hidden away a family portrait that includes Gertrudis, the grandmother who absconded with the photographer her husband brought home to take the picture.

The photograph in "Camera Obscura" attests to its own production as an object laden with meaning. The story of a happy family that the image purports to tell is belied by the story of its making, and the contestation over those events is the core of Gorodischer's narrative. When the wife of Gertrudis's grandson displays the photograph on the mantel, restoring the grandmother to the family, her husband is appalled. For him, suppressing the image of the grandmother who ran off, leaving her husband and children, is necessary if the family is to make a claim to respectable Argentineity. As far as his wife is concerned, Gertrudis was more than justified in leaving a husband and children who treated her like a servant, making a new life with the photographer who finally really saw her, both literally and figuratively.

The excised photograph of the runaway mother is similarly revalued in Cozarinsky's "Real Estate." The mother's transgression initially places the narrator and his father, who cuts her out of the family pictures, in the tale's moral center—abandoned, harmed, humiliated. Her motives are never examined; she is simply the woman who wronged them. The last sentence of the story, however, shifts that moral center to the mother's second son, who remains with her, returning to the Jewish space of the colonies to stay by the side of his now-institutionalized mother. The narrator, having once acquiesced to his father's version of the family tragedy, now lives with his own sense of guilt, recognizing his half-brother as the good son who stayed by his mother's side, while he had never questioned his father's excision of the mother from the visible manifestation of family memory, the photographs. The mother, literally cut out of the family picture, returns, maimed, to her now-abandoned home, accompanied by her true (i.e., loyal) child, revising the family story.

The portrait on the mantelpiece also plays a significant role in Nora Glickman's play *Una tal Raquel* (Some woman named Raquel). In this case the picture of the grandmother is not hidden, but her story is. Like the photographer in "Camera Obscura" who both made the image that makes memory possible and instigated the act that has made the family suppress that memory, Raquel Liberman defied the conventions of shame by telling the story of her own prostitution and denouncing to the police the Jewish prostitution ring that victimized her and many others. When her granddaughter sees the picture, she identifies her grandmother as a prostitute but also as a hero. The photographs in both Gorodischer and Glickman undergo severe, gender-specific resignification by women in both texts who insist on rereading them.

Gertrudis's grandson hides his grandmother's image and the Liberman family studiously avoids talking about theirs in order to suppress evidence of a past that the characters find shameful. More to the point is that theirs is the shame of the debased mother. The photographs, when they were taken, were of young women, whose scandalous sexuality is troubling enough. The passage of time, however, has turned these young women into the mothers, grandmothers, and aunts of subsequent generations, the very figures entrusted with preserving tradition and guarding morality. That they are the ones who have transgressed, whether as prostitutes or runaway wives, is bad enough; that they are the progenitors of subsequent generations, whose precarious claim to national belonging is precisely the claim to respectability, is unthinkable—at least to their sons and grandsons. Their daughters, nieces, and daughters-in-law are far more forgiving. They see in these women a struggle for survival, a complex morality that encompasses transgression with loyalty, and victimization with a determination to survive.

The story of these women, told in the form of their photographic image, undergoes two revisions. In the first the image of the transgressive woman, whose behavior casts doubt on the respectability of the family, is excised or hidden. The second revision brings the woman's picture back, now telling the family story to include the woman herself, her point of view, and the circumstances of her transgression. The photographs in *Una tal Raquel* and "Camera Obscura" seem to capture a simple reality, but they are open to a variety of readings. Szichman's characters in *At 8:25 Evita Became Immortal* (the best known of the Pechof novels, and the only one to have been translated into English) believe that photographs themselves have the power to create reality. In it, the slightly loony Itzik Pechof refuses to be photographed as a way to forestall death. If there is no photograph to put on his tombstone, he reasons, he cannot possibly die. His brother Jaime, determined to leave Jewishness behind and pass as the scion of an old Argentine Christian family, not only appropriates the photographs of a "rancid oligarchical family," he stages a photo of his brothers and sisters posed as their descendants. In all these texts photography's relationship to remembrance and truth is put to the test.

Memory and truth are also at the fraught center of Feierstein's *Mestizo*, in which a trove of family photographs functions as an *aide-memoir* to the protagonist, David Schnaiderman. *Mestizo* takes the trope of reclaiming memory literally as Schnaiderman wakes from unconsciousness with partial amnesia and spends much of the rest of the novel struggling to piece together clues to figure out who he is. His name is fitting: *schnaider* means tailor, and like a tailor he searches for a pattern that will allow him to create a useful garment from the scraps of material he gathers, including the photographs of his grandfather's family. Schnaiderman's search for himself is linked to his apparent witnessing of a murder, so his success will not only return his identity to him; it promises to lead to finding a killer as well. In his search for the killer and for himself, Schnaiderman carries around pictures of the victim to show to people and photographs of his family in his attempt to simultaneously solve the crime and regain a sense of self. He hopes truth will follow remembering. *Mestizo*'s struggle to claim Jewishness as constitutive of Argentineity occurs against a backdrop of antisemitism, and it is the brave Jews of the past, Schnaiderman's grandfather among them, who make Jewishness a viable component of the modern *mestizo* nation. The grandfather is "one of the firm legs upon which you can base your mestizaje" (144). Memory, here the memory of the grandfather, relegates identity as purity to the past, but in a way that keeps it available as a resource for the present.

The solution to the crime in Ricardo Feierstein's *Mestizo* is relatively banal; the more profound story that the novel tells is that of the recovery of memory and the mending of the self within a nation just emerging from more than a decade of state violence. The underlying national crisis, produced by a state determined to homogenize the nation under the banner of patriarchal, nationalist, Catholic authoritarianism, and that terrorized its way into acquiescence and compliant obliviousness, is reflected in and refracted by the amnesiac protagonist of *Mestizo*. Just as Schnaiderman has information about himself that nevertheless is insufficient to supply him with a deep sense of who he is, the nation needs to face its recent past and take responsibility for it. It must make a living memory to replace the willed obliviousness to the state-sanctioned kidnapping, torture, and murder in which thirty thousand lives were taken. Recuperating the memory of what he witnessed personally at the crime scene is insufficient. Schnaiderman, like the nation, needs to plumb his own history to learn the causes and consequences of the crime in order to recover—in the sense of both healing and retrieving—the self.

Schnaiderman's father narrates a family history that associates Argentine disappearances with Polish state terror in the early twentieth century. The link between the two, characterized by his sense of Jewish vulnerability, is

# FAMILY STORIES AND THE INVENTION OF MEMORY 73

reinforced by his recollection of the pogroms of the Tragic Week in Buenos Aires and the arrest of the real-life journalist Pinie Wald:

> Yes, life was hard in Poland. Here they say it is dangerous to get involved in politics, with this killing that the military has done lately, they say that they have made thousands of kids disappear, a terrible thing. There in Poland they sent you to a prison in the city, and *chau, pinela*, no one returned. They tortured them and they killed them, that happened to anyone who got involved in politics.
>
> The people in the *Bund* were Jewish socialists. Here in Argentina, there was one man named Pinie Wald, who published in the daily *Die Presse*; in 1919 they accused him of wanting to create a soviet here during "La Semana Trágica." There were *pogroms* and many dead, it was something terrible. (63–64)

The murder mystery of *Mestizo* makes a wonderful allegorical frame for the narrative of identity-making in a multicultural society, but it is the family memoir, often converted into fiction, that stands out as a dominant mode of memory production in a wide range of postdictatorship Jewish Argentinean texts. Like Feierstein's *Mestizo*, these texts refuse a simple Jewish otherness that would set Jews and Jewishness apart from Argentine history, culture, and society. Also like *Mestizo*, they take on the play between the recovery of memory and its production. Some of these narratives hew closely to what might be called fact, (as) if their authors were truly able to sort out what really happened to their parents and grandparents from what has been embellished or outright invented. These are the stories that are passed down through the generations, like Luisa Futoransky's *El Formosa* (The Formosa) and Cristina Zuker's *El tren de la memoria* (The train of memory), or that are rediscovered after coming close to being lost, such as Andrés Neuman's *Una vez Argentina* (Once Argentina). Some, like Alicia Dujovne Ortiz's *El árbol de la gitana* (The Gypsy woman's tree), begin with the outlines of family history and invent a deeper past; others, including Manuela Fingueret's *Daughter of Silence* (*Hija del silencio*), imagine a deliberately withheld story. Narratives of the crossing from Europe to Argentina map the geography of displacement and migration, and the stories they tell are often of forgetting and uncertainty, thus chronicling both the making and the breaking of silence. Novelized family memoirs such as Neuman's and Futoransky's, like the vignettes of Alicia Steimberg's *Musicians and Watchmakers* (*Músicos y relojeros*) and Ana María Shua's *The Book of Memories* (*El libro de los recuerdos*), begin with the urgent need to leave the Eastern Europe of the pogroms, and all include silence and forgetting, as well as memory.

*The Book of Memories* is in many respects Shua's loving evocation of a Jewish family's experience of immigration and assimilation, but its title is deeply ironic. It is a book of forgetfulness and contradiction as much as memory. The first loss is of language itself: Yiddish is never even named but rather evoked as "the Other Language." Once Yiddish is lost as a Jewish language we are left wondering to what extent Spanish can take its place. The memory book to which the title refers is a text that the novel's characters consult in a dialogue among those remembering, who in turn invoke the memory of others. These memories do not quite coincide, but from them a history emerges.

The three aunts in Luisa Futoransky's *El Formosa*, whose title refers to the ship on which the family sailed to Argentina, also remember a shared past differently. In this version of contested memory the three elderly women, all born in the same place, cannot agree even on the name of the country they lived in (61). Their different memories, however, are explained by historical circumstances:

> What country are you talking about if one time the *shtetl* changed masters three times in the same day; one group came, killed, and said we were the Czar's Russians; then some more showed up and said we belonged to Podolia Gubernia; and at night we were Ukrainians, Poles, or something, and it was slaughter all day long. (my translation)

> [De qué país me hablás si una vez el *shtetl* cambió de dueño tres veces el mismo día, vinieron unos mataron y dijeron que éramos rusos del zar, después vienieron otros y dijeron que éramos de Podolia Gubern y a la noche éramos polacos, ucranianos o algo así y mataron todo el día. (61)]

Geography and history must be agreed upon for the family story to cohere, but here the political map on which that story plays out is itself contested. The only constant in the aunts' old village is the determination of a variety of attackers to kill its Jewish inhabitants. Even though the three women carry uncertainty with them, they never lose sight of the constant that is their own Jewishness.

The crisis of memory reaches its peak when Jewishness seems about to be forgotten altogether. Andrés Neuman's autobiographical novel, *Una vez Argentina*, narrates a Jewish family history long and vast enough to include most of the tropes of Jewish immigration to Argentina, but its pivotal moment is the protagonist's discovery, rather late in childhood, that he is, in fact, Jewish. Nor is Jewishness particularly legible in Andrés Neuman's fiction more generally. *Una vez Argentina* is nestled in a body of work otherwise set in a globalized, anodyne present. In contrast to Neuman's largely ethnicity-free novels, stories, and poetry is this one surprising, very Argentine Jewish text.

When the preadolescent Andrés is uprooted from Argentina by parents fleeing dictatorship and state terror, he knows himself to be simply an Argentine.[4] The utter secularization and assimilation narrated in the novel is refuted by what we go on to read as the recuperation of the narrator's family's history and cultural identity. What was just family for the child, with entry into adulthood became Jewish family, newly marked as different and worthy of remembering, shaping, and archiving. Neuman isolates the moment when being Jewish goes from being unnamed and unnoticed, just another way of being Argentine, and of being ambiguously foreign in Andalusia, to its being crucial, in need of note and notation. Yet Neuman's narrator-cum–alter ego never completely identifies himself as Jewish: "I've never felt Jewish; and, if I was, I never found out about it." [Nunca me he sentido judío; y, si lo fui, no llegué a enterarme (100. All translations from this text are my own.).]

Beginning with its title, *Una vez Argentina* is so deeply historicized and mythologized that it can pretty much stand as a prototype for the Jewish Argentine family saga. Its referential touchpoints include the sea voyage from Eastern Europe to Argentina; settlement in the countryside by the Jewish Colonization Association followed by rural-to-urban migration; family members who immigrated and settled immediately in the Jewish neighborhoods of Buenos Aires; the first generation's economic struggle leading to solid middle-class economic stability; deep strains of music, music-making, and art; political commitment and activism; heartfelt patriotism for a country that provided refuge; secularization and intermarriage; all culminating, in Neuman's immediate family, in still another exile.[5] The chronological narrative of Andrés's childhood, from his birth to the family's boarding the plane that will take them from Argentina to Spain, includes his memories of the dictatorship, as well as the stories he heard of his parents, aunts, uncles, and cousins who had to go into hiding or leave the country.

The narrator, Andrés, born in 1977, tells the story of being a child of both the military dictatorship and of Jewish parents. The story of the nation before the protagonist's birth is told through the lapidary memories of the earlier generations, whom the narrator knows only through the stories his parents and grandparents have told him. That story moves back and forth in time, creating thematic links with the more recent, and personally lived, story of the young Andrés, with his childhood memories of school. Andrés gathers his family's history as best he can, acknowledging the difficulty of piecing together the shards of memory bequeathed to him. When he imagines the life of one of his uncles, whom he never knew and whose story has been reduced to a few barely recalled moments, the reader is left with the sense that what is most important is what is most missing. Similarly, the story of Andrés's paternal great-grandfather's life before he came to Argentina is lost in the fog of what has escaped memory. Such stories may be partially recovered, but their greater value is their availability for the constitution of a mythical past. Once their setting changes from Europe to Argentina, however, they take on the material consistency of history. Their protagonists marry, establish businesses and families, and their story intersects with national history.

Andrés narrates his own story chronologically, interspersing it with stories of his parents, grandparents, great-grandparents, aunts, and uncles. His family remembers many of its most important moments as they relate to Argentine history: a key event occurs "one year after General Uriburu's fascist revolution" (95), and great-grandfather Jacobo is remembered to have died at around the time Perón did. The family history touches on virtually every familiar moment of Jewish Argentine history. Jonas, for example, recalls the Tragic Week of 1919. Read in the context of other Jewish Argentine family stories, we can see how very representative it is. Yet Neuman takes this canonical Jewish story and tells it from the point of view of the inheritor of that story who only learns that it is a Jewish story as it unfolds. Andrés is slow in learning that his family memories were specifically Jewish ones because the family's Jewishness was so thoroughly folded into Argentineity. After several generations of assimilation and secularization, any consciousness of its Jewishness has disappeared, only to reappear when Jewish otherness once again surfaces in the wider culture that has repressed, not eliminated, it. His recounting of the AMIA bombing and the Argentine state's complex response to it, in contrast to the public's more thoroughgoing sense of horror, is a case in point. Neuman's text is a quintessentially Argentine story in which Jewishness is both unremarkable enough that the narrator was not aware of it himself and at the same time absolutely fundamental to it.

Rediscovered Jewishness in *Una vez Argentina* is pervasive, with the paternal, Jewish family heavily represented at the beginning, lending a Jewish tone and texture to the narrative as a whole. We eventually learn that Blanca, the maternal grandmother who leaves a written narrative for her grandchildren, and who is the very first character introduced in the novel, is the daughter of a Gentile French mother. Nevertheless, Andrés claims a form of Jewishness for his mother, who almost literally performs Jewishness when her prospective violin teacher, after telling her that having a Spanish surname means that she will never be able to truly play well, since only Germans and Jews can be thus gifted, decides to take her on as a student—and she learns to play and becomes a professional violinist. Marrying the Jewish Victor Neuman and giving birth to babies of Jewish ancestry is not nearly as Judaifying an action. When asked by his Jewish classmates what his mother "is," the child Andrés replies, "a violinist." Unaware that he is linking her to Jewishness by virtue of her musicianship, his answer underscores the cultural meaning of Jewishness, in contrast to an essentialist notion of identity. The Jewish history of this family is so palpable that it is shocking to read that when Andrés encounters two practicing Jews among his classmates, he is confronted with the possibility of his own Jewishness for the first time, and he does not know what it means. Unlike him, these boys are real "Jews, the kind you could tell knew what they were" [judíos, de los que se notaba que sabían que lo eran (90)].

It is striking that among the many family sagas in which Jewishness is a powerful component in the lives of the characters and the themes of the texts, there are so many that are also stories of intermarriage and its resulting multiple pulls on identity. *Una vez Argentina*, *El Formosa*, *La crítica de las armas*, *El árbol de la gitana*, *The Book of Memories*, and Daniel Burman's suite of Ariel films all explore what seems like an almost inevitable link between assimilation and intermarriage. Cristina Zuker's *El tren de la victoria* (Victory train) also tells a history of Jewishness and intermarriage. Zuker's father was a well-known Jewish actor and her mother a Catholic from Andalucía. After a first chapter that takes place more or less in the present, the immigrant narrative begins, weaving back and forth between the two sides of the family and the present, with key historical events as the nodal points of the chapters. The story of the Jewish branch of the family flows along a familiar path: cousins marry, make the difficult journey to America, and have their children who in turn become Argentines as Jews. As Zuker begins with those who came to Argentina, Jewishness and Argentineity are developed together.

The most remarkable difference between *El tren de la victoria* and most other Jewish Argentine origin stories is its utter lack of nostalgia. The Jewish branch of Cristina Zuker's family is deeply unhappy: her Jewish grandfather beat his children, and he and his wife never accepted their son's marriage to a non-Jew. Although they seem to have some affection for the narrator's brother Ricardo, who joined the *montoneros* to become an urban guerrilla, they never accept either their daughter-in-law or the narrator.

Moreover, Cristina's famous father was a womanizer and a gambler who left the family on its own for long stretches of time and ultimately abandoned them. He was, not surprisingly, emotionally distant from his children as well. He might have brought his daughter candy and books to read, but she feels so alienated from him that she never refers to him as father, instead using his (and her) last name, "Zuker." The Jewish side of the family is acknowledged and their story is told, but Cristina and her brother revere their mother and resent their father, and the memories of love and warmth are all bound up with their mother's family, not his. In contrast to the Jewish family memoirs of writers like Shua, Steimberg, and even Neuman, in Zuker's text there is no warm memory linked to Jewishness. When Cristina remembers her grandmothers, she describes the terse bitterness of her Jewish *bubbe* in contrast to the effusive warmth of her Catholic *abuela*.

The figure of the warm, nurturing grandmother is so deeply ingrained in Jewish culture that the appearance of an embittered, mean old woman in the role is very nearly cataclysmic in its effect. In contrast to the Jewish mother, who is often scorned for smothering her children with love, inducing their guilt, and controlling their lives, the Jewish grandmother is typically cherished, not least because the perceived power of the mother is either appropriately channeled or strictly attenuated in the grandmother. The ancestral grandmother, whose memory has been burnished to a high luster over the generations, is typically admired for her brave resourcefulness as an immigrant and her ability to assure her own survival and her family's. The living grandmother, in contrast, is more likely portrayed as a gentle woman, a little anachronistic, and the object of affectionate humor.[6]

In those stories in which the matriarch is more than a cipher, like Edgardo Cozarinsky's "The Bride from Odessa," Angelica Gorodischer's "Camera Obscura," and Nora Glickman's *Una tal Raquel*, the immigrant woman's courage may be somewhat unconventional. Cozarinsky's Odessa bride appropriates the identity of her husband's original Jewish fiancée, calling into question the very legitimacy as Jews of the family of which she is the progenitor. The power of Gorodischer's story lies in the contestation over the meaning of the grandmother's decision to leave the husband and family for whom she had sacrificed herself for years. The narrator cannot understand why his wife wants to remember the woman who he thinks shamed his family; she is appalled by his lack of sympathy for her. Glickman's play recuperates the story of the prostitute who is neither simply calculating woman nor abject victim, but rather a combination of the two and more. The matriarch in these narratives typically holds a shameful or dangerous secret. She troubles the identity of the family; her actions constitute its original sin, the compelling soft, sore spot that endangers the family's identity, respectability, and standing. These texts necessarily recover the half-hidden figure of the grandmother; her story drives the family narrative. Moreover, these narratives implicitly argue that the women whose lives they recount are worthy of being the family matriarch.

In Alicia Dujovne Ortiz's *El árbol de la gitana*, the story of the biological mother and grandmother recedes in favor of a maternal figure who transmits the family's stories. Like Neuman (who also credits his grandmother with writing a family narrative), Zuker, and others, Dujovne Ortiz writes a family history that is also a political history, a tale of immigration and exile, and a story of Jewishness inscribed into a family marked by multiple diasporas.[7] The expatriate child of intermarriage, Dujovne Ortiz lays claim to Jewish Argentineity in two self-recuperating narratives, *El árbol de la gitana* and, later, *Las perlas rojas* (The red beads). In these narratives Dujovne Ortiz assembles an autobiographical fiction from the diverse elements of her own lineage. The writer's identity is both nationally grounded in Argentina and predicated on uprootedness, providing a kind of stability that is nevertheless loosely anchored to place. Hers is an identity in exile, one that must be stable for survival, but that cannot be entirely fixed. This sort of loosely anchored identity is something like a linear narrative, in which the end is unlikely to be identical to the beginning, but in which beginning and end are connected as new matter accrues to it. In exile, identity is disrupted and its performance can be recuperative. Dujovne Ortiz juxtaposes the fragile, individual shards of ancestral and national identity to make a usable past, a mosaic gathered in exile and wandering, an identity in flux, flexible enough to claim some grounding but not be utterly tied to it.

The Gypsy of the first volume's title animates the maternal aspect of storytelling. She appears to the fictionalized Alicia to tell her family stories and to guide her actions. A projection of the protagonist's future, aged, self, she is one of the many ghosts who haunt the women of the family; Dujovne Ortiz puts into her mouth the family stories that her own mother told her.[8] At the end of the novel the Gypsy woman and the mother resolve into a single figure:

> As the Gypsy turns ever so slowly, I fear that she will hurl in my face my theft of her tree of stories.
> 
> When at last we are face to face, my mother Scheherazade does not have the black goat's face nor the gray-green eyes with which I adorned her, or kept vigil over her, but instead her Indian conquistador marrano Genovese Irish black sparkling eyes, with straight lashes bending toward her forehead, and great melancholy eyebrows, wise and tender with all the still water.
> . . .
> Not only does she not reproach me for Gypsying her stories, she tells me another tale. (All translations from this text are my own.)
>
> [Mientras la Gitana se de vuelta con extremada lentitud, temo que me eche en la cara el hurto de su árbol de cuentos.
> 
> Cuando al fin quedamos frente a frente, mi madre Sheherezade no tiene la cara de cabra negra ni los ojos pardoverdosos conque yo le adornara, o la velara, sino sus ojos indios, conquistadores, marranos, genoveses, irlandeses, negros, relucientes, de pestañas derechas, caídos hacia las sienes, con grandes cejas melancólicas, sabios y tiernos con toda el agua quieta.
> . . .
> No sólo no me reprocha que le haya agitanado la historia, sino que me cuenta otro cuento. (292–93)][9]

In *El árbol de la gitana* the narrator layers the story of her exile in France with tales of an arduously recuperated heritage that includes Eastern European Jews, Mozárabes from Toledo, Christians from Genoa, Iberian explorers, indigenous pampas dwellers, and even a conquistador who helped claim the Canary Islands for Spain. Each precarious thread is intertwined with all the others to form an intricate past of migration and exile. Astonishingly, and crucially, all these peripatetic figures, and the rivers of the lands from which they sprung, coincide in one remote place in Argentina:

Seen on the map, then, the Ortizes, the Oderigos, the Dujovnes, and several more dove in head first. What captures my attention most powerfully is the place they arrived: Entre Ríos—"between rivers." All of them, sooner or later, wound up in Entre Ríos, a tiny spot surrounded by rivers—the Paraná, the Uruguay, the Volga, the Guadalquivir.

[Mirados en el mapa, pues, los Ortiz, los Oderigo, los Dujovne y algunos más se zambulleron de cabeza. Lo que me llama poderosamente la atención es el lugar de llegada: Entre Ríos. Todos, tarde o temprano, fueron a dar a Entre Ríos, un puntitio rodeado por el Paraná, el Uruguay, el Volga, el Guadalquivir. (100)]

*El árbol de la gitana* is structured like a loosely woven fabric, with each chapter on the family's past followed by one about Alicia's peripatetic life in France. The story of her exile from Argentina under dictatorship, interlaced with the family saga, moves chronologically but along different scales of time. The latter recounts family legends about Columbus, her ancestor Akiva Dujovne's encounter with Gypsies, great-grandmother Teodora's madness, and ancestral memory of Indian wars. The narrator struggles to create an adequate genealogy based on the different kinds of loss and absence sustained by her family.

A fraught Jewishness threads through this saga, from Columbus's purported Jewishness to the conflicting stories of bloodlines that call into question the purity of the Jewish branch of the family and suggest the subterranean Jewishness of the narrator's Catholic ancestors.[10] Although Alicia's father is the obviously Jewish parent, her Catholic mother's history is shot through with Jewishness. A subterranean stream of *conversos*, Marranos, and Judaizers runs through the maternal line. Ironically, her father's family may have originated as Chazars, seventh- or eighth-century converts to Judaism.

I wondered, fixing my gaze on their faces:
The Chazars were converts? The Spaniards were Marranos? So much the better. It's all the same to me if I'm Jewish on one side or the other.
"So you want to be Jewish no matter what?" asked the Little Voice, that disapproving presence we have inside, and who always plays Devil's Advocate.

"And it isn't obvious?" I answered, annoyed. "How many more moves do I have to subject myself to for my intention to be clear?"

[Yo meditaba mirando fijamente las caras:
—Los jázaros eran conversos? ¿Los españoles eran marranos? Tanto mejor. Me da lo mismo ser judía por la derecha o por la izquierda.
—Así que querés a toda costa ser judía?—me preguntó la Vocecita, esa presencia criticona que uno tiene en su interior, y que siempre hace de abogado del Diablo.
—¿Y no se me nota?—le contesté irritada—. ¿A cuántas mudanzas más tendré que someterme para que mi intención resulte clara? (155–56)]

Like Feierstein, Dujovne Ortiz enjoys the complexity of impurity.[11] Her ancestors were a mix of Jews who may have been Christians and Christians who had once been Jews. After the death of both her parents, the narrator travels to Israel, where she imagines her Spanish mother, not her Jewish father, in the Dead Sea. Blending their two histories, joining their bodies and their stories to hers, Alicia refuses to indulge in separation: "At that spot in the chest where the sternum ends, we are all together" [En ese punto del pecho donde termina el esternón, estamos todos juntos (293)].

The protagonist's peregrinations reinforce her Jewish identity, and they establish her link to the trope of the wandering Jew. The memory of the persecution that impelled those moves forms a crucial part of family memory, so that the pampas storms the first Dujovne settlers weathered are reminiscent of the "night of the feathers," the pogrom during which Cossacks tore open pillows looking for money, and also tore open people. Nevertheless, as the Gypsy woman of the title points out, "it is not only Jews who move from place to place" [No sólo a los judíos se les da por mudarse (156)]. The narrator comes to realize that although her ancestors' migrations were the result of persecution, her family contains some who were persecuted and others who perpetuated persecutions on others:

But perhaps the most surprising thing is the motive for their journeys. Why did they travel?
I looked from right to left before answering myself:

Some because they were persecuted, others in order to persecute. Perhaps because I am the result of both sides I wound up with this balancing act. I am not always the victim.

[Pero acaso lo más sorprendente sea el motivo de sus viajes. ¿Por qué viajaron?
Miré a derecha y a izquierda, antes de responderme a mí misma:
—Unos por perseguidos, otros para perseguir. Quizás por ser el resultado de unos y otros me haya quedado el balanceo. No siempre soy la víctima. (110)]

The complexity of Alicia's lineage obviates any claim to blameless victimhood; no pure identity is possible once the messy details of the past emerge.

Once the two branches of her family arrive in Argentina, the stories of Alicia's paternal side predominate. The men are the ones who seem most altered by Argentina, even as they carry with them powerful memories of their past. Alicia's father, born in 1903, was to have been named Akiva, for the medieval rabbi who, as a young man, was one of three sons who went into the Kingdom of Shadows and the only one to return alive and sane. But Akiva, the narrator tells us, is too hard a name to carry in Argentina, and so he was called Carlos, comfortably Hispanic and inadvertently prescient of his commitment to Marxism. As a founding member of the Argentine Communist Party, Carlos Dujovne returns to Russia bearing his Jewishness as well as his communism. Once educated he returns, first to Uruguay and then to Argentina, where he founds a publishing house dedicated to Marxist texts.[12] It is left to the reader to decide which land—Argentina or Russia—is Carlos Dujovne's Kingdom of Shadows.

The novel proper ends with the father's death, although both the narrative apparatus (in the form of an epilogue) and its structure, which foretells early on the death of both parents, privilege the telling of story over its content, thereby honoring the maternal line. For if the fathers are the narrator's link to Alicia's Jewish-Argentine-Marxist history, it is the mothers who tell the stories. In many Jewish families, and in many Jewish texts, women transmit the culture through the food they prepare. Novelist Silvia Plager invokes Jewish food in both fiction and nonfiction. One of her novels, echoing the Mexican *Like Water for Chocolate* in its title, *Como papas para varenikes* (Like potatoes for *verenekes*), intertwines sex and food. But Plager has also written a cookbook, *Mi cocina judía* (My Jewish kitchen), which is a kind of culinary family memoir that includes anecdotes and photographs alongside the Plager family recipes. These are supplemented by recipes and stories contributed by close to thirty Argentine Jewish writers, artists, and intellectuals. Dujovne Ortiz, in contrast, refuses the role of culinary tradition-bearer. The grandmothers and mother in Dujovne's family do not cook; they tell stories.[13]

Dujovne Ortiz's mother, a translator (i.e., someone who makes a coherent text out of someone else's stories), wanted to write a novel about her ancestors; the daughter takes up that task and writes this book. Most importantly, the mother joins the narrator in the three mythic faces of womanhood—grandmother, mother, daughter—as they continue through the generations. Exile has separated the daughter from her mother; her journey back brings her back to both her homeland and her mother: "this return to Buenos Aires was, above all, a pilgrimage to my mother" [Pero ese regreso a Buenos Aires era, sobre todo, una peregrinación a mi madre (288)]. The daughter's return is the moment in which she and her mother become one, as their faces, and even their ages, fuse. Unlike sons in exile, for whom the mother is radically other, symbolically the lost homeland that has both borne them and cast them out, daughters, especially if they are mothers themselves, find themselves in a chain of maternity in which they themselves are both mother and child:[14]

> My mother seemed to be my age. Our separation had joined our temporalities. We spent two months revolving around each other like gentle, agreeable planets. If ever we grazed each other we produced a crystalline sound of the music of the spheres.
>
> [Mi madre parecía tener mi edad. La separación había ensamblado nuestros tiempos. Nos pasamos dos meses girando la una alrededor de la otra como planetas suaves y bien acordados. Si alguna vez tuvimos un roce produjimos un sonido cristalino de música de esferas. (288)]

The separation of the exiled daughter from the mother disturbs the cosmic order; their reunion both restores that order and makes the mother's death possible. The daughter comes back to a symbolic disarray made manifest in the off-kilter maternal home: "The house is lovely, but it lacks symmetry" [La casa es preciosa, pero le falta simetría], Alicia notes (288). Together she and her mother restore the equilibrium of the house, which is both self and cosmos: mother and daughter as "gentle, agreeable planets," enabling the passage of one generation to the next.

> And the two of us, as if all the future were ours, set about rehanging the pictures according to rational criteria imported from France [. . .]. When it was time to leave, several little old ladies came to cry, saying that this was it, that we'd never see each other again, but mine bid me goodbye radiantly, in her now, finally, symmetrical apartment in Flores.
>
> Two months later, in Cali, I learned that she had died suddenly, despite the fervor and the hope with which we had straightened out all that was bent.
>
> [Y las dos, ardientemente, como si todo el futuro fuera nuestro, nos dedicamos a reclavar los cuadros según criterios racionales importados de Francia [. . .]. Cuando llegó el momento de partir, varias viejitas vinieron a llorar diciendo que esta vez era la vencida, que no volveríamos a vernos más, pero la mía me despidió radiante en su departamento de Flores, ahora finalmente simétrico.
>
> Dos meses más tarde, en Cali, supe que había muerto de repente pese al fervor y la esperanza con que habíamos enderezado lo torcido. (289)]

The protagonist's journeys do not stop with the mother's death; Alicia does not take her mother's place in Argentina. Instead, she carries on the essence of the mother, returning to Paris, where she can write, and to Cali, where her daughter lives and gives birth to another daughter in this line.[15]

In his discussion of Latin American Jewish exile writing, "La nación imaginaria" (The imaginary nation), Leonardo Senkman argues that the political exile of Jewish subjects as a result of the 1976–1983 Argentine dictatorship cut them off from not only the land but also the history of the nation. Exiled Argentine Jews' former sense of belonging to the nation's collective past and future is disrupted when they are cast out of what they had taken to be their homeland. They turn, as a result, to a Jewish past as historical exiles, reigniting questions of identity, a realignment from national identity to cultural/religious identity. For Senkman, *El árbol de la gitana* is a profound example of this national deracination: in it exile is complete; the connection to nation is reduced to fragments and the roots of the family tree are planted in the air. He contrasts this with the sense of reconciliation, or Jewish hybridity, in Feierstein's *Mestizo*, in which the newly redemocratized nation opens a space for the protagonist's sense of participation in the national whole. Senkman does not note the masculinized context of *Mestizo*; he does not mention that this (re)conciliation happens in the hypermasculine space of the soccer stadium: the team as nation, the majority's joy at winning are fulfilled as masculine pursuits. In what we might characterize as a feminine version of exile, Dujovne Ortiz's Alicia is not physically reconciled with the lost maternal line or the lost nation. Alicia's reunion with her mother, a reconciliation in which mother and daughter literally put their house in order, ends with the mother's death. Alicia's daughter, on the other hand, follows her male lover to Colombia where he can discover his roots (notably, more than she can establish herself as part of the Latin American continent).

The Gypsy woman, nomad par excellence, is Alicia's touchstone. Only language-made-narrative can make memory or history. The title of Dujovne Ortiz's novel gestures benignly to the familiar image of the family tree, but the author takes the trope to a terrifying logical conclusion: its conversion into heat, flame, and, eventually self-consummation in the logs of a fire tended by God.

> Well, don't worry, because—end of story—there's nothing. He Who Dreams Us tries things out, tests them, experiments. He is seated before the hearth of life and throws in different logs.
> 
>   Let's see, what happens, he thinks, if I throw in this piece of thicker and drier wood, or this greener and slimmer one? And every new story is like a log, that, when it burns, changes the destiny of the others, because the one on the top, that is, the one most recently laid on the pile, absorbs the flames of those below and they, in turn, when they feel its presence, stretch anxiously, extending their tongues in their attempt to trap it.
> 
> [Bueno, no te preocupes porque último no hay nada. El Que Nos Sueña prueba, ensaya, experimenta. Está sentado frente a la chimenea de la vida y echa leños distintos. ¿A ver qué pasa—piensa—si arrojo al fuego este madero más seco y más gordo, o este más verde y más fintio? Y cada nueva historia es como un leño, que, al quemarse, cambia el destino de los otros, porque el de más arriba, o sea, el más recientemente colocado,

absorbe las llamaradas de los de abajo y éstos, al sentir su presencia, se estiran con ansiedad, sacando la lengua en el intento de atraparlo. (185)]

The narrative reconstruction of the family tree, where each branch is a log that feeds the family fire, some old and some young, some thick, some thin, the more recent ones absorbing the smoke and flames from those below, the ones below reaching for those above. Although the grandfather's voice assures her that this consummation is not about any endings, but rather the story of a family's life, the paternal story is this ultimately nihilistic story of life as a passage to oblivion: one of the author's grandfathers kills himself because the pampas are simply too vast. Rootedness and migration are recurring tropes. The family tree is a similarly powerful and fraught image in other family memory texts. The psychiatrist in *Mestizo* berates Schnaiderman, because the family tree he talks about is selective, fragmented, and insubstantial. Whole sections of the novel, many of which include family history but exceed it, appear under the title "The Family Tree," and the visual image of the tree itself eventually emerges in full toward the end of the novel (224). The illustration that becomes the tree evolves throughout Feierstein's novel. It begins as the frontispiece, a line drawing of a sturdy male body as the trunk of a tree, with a halo of branches emerging from its bowed head. This drawing appears at the start of each of the novel's four numbered sections and at the very end. The same image appears again in a nonfiction book by Feierstein, *Contraexilio y mestizaje* (Counterexile and hybridity). In that book, the image contains an explanatory chart: the three roots of the tree are indigenous, Spanish colonial, and immigrant; the trunk is "the spirit of the land"; and the branches and foliage modern and contemporary history. Feierstein's tree is rooted metaphorically in histories whose geographies overlap; the immigrant root is oxymoronic. This powerful, suggestive image contrasts powerfully with the more prosaic, conventional family tree in Feierstein's *La logia del umbral* (The lodge of the threshold, 71). Its lines and boxes in descending order provide a conventional but utterly necessary *aide-memoir* that is utterly unlike the real-tree-as-metaphor for a past that goes beyond family genealogy in *Mestizo*.

In the realm of visual art, Mirta Kupferminc has taken the tree as one of her most powerful images. Some of her more abstract images include prints of a large tree stump she found and brought back to her studio; the tree may be truncated, but it still bears its rings of history. Her displaced wanderers in *En camino* (*On the Way*) bear uprooted trees, roots and all, from place to place as they traverse the space of the image.

Figure 4.1. Mirta Kupferminc, *On the Way* (*En camino*), 2001. Etching, 15.75 in. × 25.20 in. *Source*: Reprinted by permission of the artist.

Kupferminc's trees are bigger than the figures that carry them along, yet these wanderers seem to bear their burden with a kind of determined ease. Two of them are pushed back, as if by a wind, as they move forward; one, carrying the most massive of the trees, is not walking at all, but rather standing firmly on the ground, facing backward with wide eyes and a serious face. The two figures in the front of the procession hold their trees in such a way that the roots precede them, as if the roots were pulling them forward. Like Feierstein, Kupferminc embraces the oxymoron of the migratory root. For Kupferminc, it is not that one of the roots of Jewish Argentineity is the very fact of migration, but rather that the wanderers carry their deepest roots with them as they travel through their diaspora. Kupferminc returns to this powerful image in 2018, this time imagining not only the uprooted trees her wanderers bear, but, in one image, the continuing power of the machinery that, it is implied, cast them into exile but hold them fast psychically. In still another work, her wanderers travel, trees and all, on a rickety boat sailing on an impossibly turquoise-blue sea with Lodz behind them and the port of Buenos Aires ahead.

The image is fractured, and one of the tree-bearing wanderers leans forward, thigh-deep in the water ahead of the little boat; he is perhaps the

Figure 4.2. Mirta Kuperminc, *Arqueology of the Journey* (*Arqueología de un trayecto*), 2018. Etching, gold leaf, inkjet print, 23.6 in. × 33.5 in. *Source*: Reprinted by permission of the artist.

ghostly presence of one washed overboard. Nevertheless, he is borne up and connected to the port ahead of him and the city behind him by the gold leaf that fills the cracks of the broken image. Kuperminc's very technique is an affirmation of strength and survival. Using the Japanese practice of kintsugi, in which broken pottery is painstakingly mended, usually with molten gold or silver, she creates beauty and a story of resilience out of the repair itself.

The story of the crossing from Europe to Argentina that Kuperminc captures in her visual art is a fundamental trope in Argentine Jewish history. The sea voyage itself is echoed in Luisa Futoransky's family memoir, and it is vividly depicted in the first episode of Juan José Campanella's immigrant television miniseries *Vientos de agua* (Winds of water). It is also central to entry into manhood via sexual initiation in *Ydel, el judío pampa* (Ydel, the pampas Jew), as well as to the cruel history of human trafficking. Children's murals of the *Weser* on the walls outside the Moisés Ville museum reimagine the voyagers' joy on their arrival and depict a Jewishness subsequently integrated fully into Argentina by intertwining national and Jewish visual iconography. And, in Angélica Gorodischer's "Camera Obscura," the voyage culminates with the birth of the problematic daughter of migration at the moment of disembarcation, on the gangplank, in the liminal space that is no longer quite the ship and not yet quite Argentine soil.

CHAPTER FIVE
# JEWISH LEGIBILITY AND ARGENTINE SELF-FASHIONING

In the early part of the twentieth century a young Walter Benjamin wrote, in an innocently prescient letter, "It would be bad for Europe if the cultural energies of the Jews were to leave it" (qtd. in Sznaider 1). Argentina may never have crossed Benjamin's mind, but that nation, too, would be the lesser without the cultural energies of its Jews. Yet in Argentina Jews are not always legible as such. Nor are all readers of literary texts, consumers of films, and viewers of paintings, prints, and photographs equally receptive to details that mark the embedded presence of Jews and Jewishness in the nation; for the fibers of Jewishness woven into the fabric of Argentine society are sometimes close to invisible. From a distance, by which I mean the affective, likely disengaged distance of someone who is neither a Jew nor an antisemite, the warp and woof of Argentine Jewishness may not be readily discernible to the eye. Other times the threads of Jewishness stand in stark contrast to those that lie beside them or cross over and under them. For the most part, Jewishness is barely a trace in the dominant discourse of Argentina, though it is a trace that, from certain angles, takes on substance. Visibility is prerequisite to legibility: Jewishness needs to been seen and perceived as such before it can be read and interpreted.

Alberto Gerchunoff's strategic move in *The Jewish Gauchos of the Pampas* was to make Jewishness visible by writing about Jewish experience in Spanish for a primarily Gentile readership.[1] Not only did he write in Spanish rather than Yiddish, he also made his Jewish characters both familiar enough for comfort and exotic enough to be interesting to his non-Jewish Argentine audience. At the same time, his goal was to make Jewishness legible as Argentineity. By reconciling being Jewish with being Argentine, he claims Jews' rightful place in the nation. A century later, in a quartet of films released between 2000 and 2016, filmmaker Daniel Burman portrays a Jewishness already woven into Argentineity, with varying degrees of visibility, and not entirely without resistance. Nevertheless, Burman's are gentle stories; in them Argentineity and Jewishness mesh with increasingly minimal friction.

Set firmly and explicitly in a Jewish milieu, rife with Jewish references, Burman's four Ariel films are all concerned with the relationship between Jewishness and Argentineity. Each movie, *Waiting for the Messiah* (*Esperando al Mesías*), *Lost Embrace* (*El abrazo partido*), *Family Law* (*Derecho de familia*), and *The Tenth Man* (*El rey del Once*), is set in a different circumstance, but because their protagonists share a given name, and in the first three films are played by the same actor, together they suggest a Jewish Argentine everyman.

The amateurish videos that the first Ariel makes in *Waiting for the Messiah* both enmesh the character in his Jewish neighborhood and give him the opportunity to escape it. Ariel Goldstein is young, coltish, unformed, sweetly ambitious, and a bit of a schlemiel. Disarming and charming, he is still a child of the Jewish community. Ariel is both a member and chronicler of the Once neighborhood with its Jewish landmarks, including the synagogue that, after the attacks on the AMIA, are protected by pylons to keep cars—which could be car bombs—from coming too near. He documents Jewish rituals as family keepsakes but also as pedagogical devices: his pitch for a bar mitzvah video begins with an explanation of the meaning of the ritual, which works both diegetically—to convince prospective clients that they need to have a document of this important moment—and extradiegetically, to teach the mostly Gentile Argentine audience about Jewish life and culture. Ariel also documents his own family, videotaping his mother as she shops for shoes; the same medium that shows the public face of Jewishness records the private moments of the Jewish mother and her son.

To watch Burman's *Waiting for the Messiah*, *Lost Embrace*, and *Family Law* in the order of their making is to trace the decreasing visibility of Jewishness as Argentine Jews assimilate and move into the professional class. The fourth, *The Tenth Man*, charts its protagonist's return and reassimilation into Jewish Buenos Aires. The Ariel films, like the novels and memoirs discussed in the previous chapter, locates the drama of Jewish Argentineity in the family. Unlike those texts, however, Burman's Ariel quartet leaves the immigration story behind to focus on the way the family grounds Jewish Argentineity in the twenty-first century.

The death of the mother in *Waiting for the Messiah* triggers the son's journey to adulthood. At the beginning of the film the adolescent Ariel is still very much his mother's adored child. She patiently teaches him that a stolen purse means little; she is playful with him as she tries on shoes, and calmly straightforward as she explains to him that she has inoperable cancer. When she tells Ariel that she will soon die he says that she cannot possibly: he still needs her to take care of him. After her death, we begin to see Ariel in the company of his father, most sweetly and sadly as they ride away from the mother's grave, on the back of a kind of golf cart, facing the camera but receding into the distance. Burman quotes that shot in *Family Law*, but this time an older Ariel is leaving the grave of his father. In the second film, *Lost Embrace*, the son is unable to find his way into a productive adulthood until he is released from his sense of duty to his mother, whom he has seen as the sad victim of his father's abandonment. The film quartet traces a journey from the rejection of the father's world (the first Ariel struggles to escape the bubble of the small Jewish world in which he grew up, and he is especially keen not to take over his father's small café; i.e., to become his father) to a deeper understanding of the father's behavior in the second, in which Ariel Makaroff comes to understand that his father did not simply abandon the family but left in the wake of his wife's infidelity and became a war hero to boot, to the third Ariel, whose ambivalent feelings about his father are finally resolved. The fourth film explores the conundrum of the son whose loving, nurturing father nevertheless always puts the needs of others before those of his family.

The Ariel of *Family Law* is older and more assimilated than the first two, and his class position is different as well. The son of a lawyer, Ariel Perelman's world begins outside the bounds of the Jewish neighborhood that constrict Ariel Goldstein, in which Ariel Makaroff wanders about trying to figure out what he wants to do with his life, and to which the fourth Ariel returns after his New York sojourn. The first and youngest Ariel of *Waiting for the Messiah* struggles to escape his constricted Jewish world in part by abandoning his Jewish childhood sweetheart and getting involved with a non-Jewish woman, but everyone around him insists on his Jewishness. The third Ariel has left the neighborhood behind and has already become a lawyer, like and unlike his father. Everyone refers to them both by their last name, Perelman; one barely discerns that he is in fact another of Burman's Ariels. Perelman senior is a compassionate public defender, while the son is a law professor. The traces of the immigrant's deep connection to his community, still apparent in the father, are gone in the son. Neither of them is a particularly observant Jew. A brief glimpse of a book about Passover in an early scene in the father's office is the only visible sign of Jewish observance in the film until the moment of his funeral. The film lingers on the Jewish burial service, beginning with a long shot that gives the viewer a global, but distanced, view. This long shot stands in stark contrast to the medium, highly personalized, shots that dominate in the film and give us access to domestic intimacy. The burial ritual brings both father and son back to Jewishness; Ariel, like all the other men in the cemetery, even the Gentiles, wears a kippah.

In *Waiting for the Messiah* Burman thematizes the representation of Jewish ritual, even as that ritual may be intrinsic to the plot, as is the case of the mother's funeral. Later, a Jewish wedding is the occasion for an investigation of both desire and identity as Ariel hands over the means of representation—the video camera—to his Gentile colleague and lover, so that he can participate in the celebration as a member of the Jewish community, and not just as its chronicler.[2] The self-referential opening scenes of *Waiting for the Messiah*, in which the young Ariel narrates a travelogue of his neighborhood as he records it, overtly place Jewishness in the visual frame and explicate it with the voice-over not just for Ariel's hoped-for audience, but for Burman's. *The Tenth Man*, shot in the historically Jewish neighborhood of El Once, largely with a handheld camera, echoes the documentary feel of the first Ariel's videos. His video camera now seems antiquated; the fourth Ariel echoes its use as he employs a smartphone to show his fiancée, still in New York, around the old neighborhood, pointing out some of the same landmarks. Both films are intent on making Argentine Jewish space legible to their audience.

Whereas a Jewish wedding ceremony is the site of a complex scene surrounding desire and identity in *Waiting for the Messiah*, in *Family Law* Burman elides the marriage ceremony altogether, sequencing directly from courtship to married life and parenthood. Unlike the adolescent Ariel of *Waiting for the Messiah*, Ariel Perelman has no visible ties to a traditional Jewish neighborhood, and his decision to court and marry Sandra, a Gentile, is not fraught. Their marriage is loving, and she is clearly the sensible adult in the relationship. For the most part, Ariel Perelman seems easy with a restrained, nearly invisible Jewishness. Nevertheless, his discovery that his child's school emblem is a cross (his wife tells him it's not a symbol of Christianity, but rather of Switzerland, which rather misses the point) is a moment of anxiety that the filmmaker dilutes with wry humor. Ariel frames his Jewishness as utterly—and amusingly—incorporated into Argentineity. "Your parents are Spaniards, mine are Poles. We're a typical Judeo-Christian Argentine family," he says to Sandra. "What do we have to do with the Swiss?" But he also wonders aloud, "What were they doing during the Holocaust?" Sandra does not share her husband's Jewish unease with Swiss neutrality. For her the Swiss signify differently and unproblematically: they are very neat, and anyway the school is close by and their child has a partial scholarship.

The fourth Ariel comes full circle, returning from a US sojourn to a full commitment to the Jewish community in the Once neighborhood that young Ariel Goldstein struggled to leave. If the first and third Ariel films follow the pattern of increasing assimilation among Argentine Jews, the fourth sends its Ariel far outside the bubble of the Argentine Jewish world, raising the question of return and recovery of the Argentine Jewish past via the son's search for the father.

Other texts make a greater claim on reshaping the Argentine national narrative to highlight events that are salient for Jews in particular. Like the story of Jewish immigration, which found its way into public discourse via Gerchunoff's tales of the Jewish settlements, such moments can make their way into national consciousness by way of inclusion in cultural texts produced by Jews. *La Semana Trágica*, the Tragic Week of January 1919, for example, is the subject of novels by David Viñas and Andrés Rivera, two novelists whose work is often excluded from studies of Argentine Jewish literature, since it rarely focuses on specifically Jewish subject matter. In mainstream Argentine history, the Tragic Week refers to the brutal suppression of strikers demanding an eight-hour workday, worker safety, and better wages. Viñas, Rivera, and the documentarian Herman Szwarcbart, however, focus on the weeklong pillaging of a Jewish neighborhood in Buenos Aires in the wake of that strike. The army and police both participated in the attacks, first on the strikers, and then, along with large numbers of well-to-do Catholic youths, on Jewish homes and businesses. Estimates of the dead range from slightly more than a hundred to well over a thousand, and thousands more were injured.[3] Some commentators have called it the only pogrom ever to take place in the Americas. For families who were barely a generation away from similar mob violence against Jews in Russia and Poland, the complicity of the authorities as well as the actions of the mob were all too familiar.

Both Viñas and Rivera frame the events of the Tragic Week in the large context of Porteño society. In Viñas's *En la semana trágica* (During the Tragic Week, 1966) the focus shifts back and forth between the events in the streets, narrated in a journalistic style, and the story of Camilo Pizarro, a young student attracted both to the military and to securing his place among the fashionable social set. Camilo's antisemitism is of a piece with his belief in class superiority and a sense of entitlement that is tinged with a certain disquiet. His anxiety about being accepted into the upper echelons of society comes to a head when he is called a *guacho* (a stray, a bastard) by a cross-dresser. Coming from this character, whom Camilo disdains, the epithet is especially painful. The abject space from which the cross-dressing figure speaks makes the accusation unquestionable, both as a truth in and of itself and as coming from someone whom Camilo is helpless to confront, lest he tarnish himself by condescending to acknowledge him.

Insofar as there is little individuation of the Jews whose presence underlies the events signaled by the novel's title, they are not the central figures of Viñas's novel. The Jewish presence is that of the mass of workers. Viñas's protagonist, the egocentric Camilo, embodies the mindlessly militaristic, fundamentally insecure hegemonic class that Viñas implicitly skewers in the novel. The author relies on his readers' compassion for the workers, developed without recourse to conventional literary technologies of creating sympathetic characters or personalized vignettes, and on the fundamentally unpleasant Camilo, to carry the critique of the novel and to ensure that a moment laden with meaning for Argentine Jews takes its rightful place in the Argentine cultural consciousness. Only at the very end of the novel, when Camilo and his classmate enter a pool hall and humiliate and then murder a middle-aged Jewish man, does the narrative open up to include the perspective of a Jewish immigrant. In the face of Camilo's disrespectful address—he calls the man "Moishe"—the man tells him his name is not Moses, but Aaron. Given that in the Biblical Exodus, Aaron is Moses's brother, and he is the one to lead the Israelites into the Promised Land, the conflation of Moses/Moishe (as antisemitic slur) and Aaron can only be seen as deeply ironic. Viñas's Aaron dies in what was still another promised land that did not fulfill its promise. In other words, he both resignifies what was hurled as an antisemitic slur and insists on his own personhood, encapsulated in his name. By insisting that Camilo see him as a person, Aaron demands both legibility and respect.

Thirty-three years later, in 1999, Andrés Rivera reinforces Viñas's situating of this moment of Argentine history in *El profundo Sur* (The deep South). In that novel, Rivera quickly establishes the connection between Jews and Bolsheviks in the mind of the vigilante who opens fire during the Tragic Week:

Roberti Bertini aimed at a short, blond guy—he might have been young—who was running close to the long wall at the corner. He'd taken his time choosing his target from the back of the pickup truck that had stopped on that street in Buenos Aires, filled with Jewish stores. Filled they told them, with Jews and Bolsheviks. With Bolshevik Jews, said the man with a narrow smile, who yelled "Fire, fire" as if his life depended upon their shooting.

"Do you know of any Bolshevik who isn't a Jew?" the man with the sharp, unsteady smile asked them.

"Aren't they actually the same thing?" asked the man with the sharp, unsteady smile. And he went pale.

"Aren't they the ones who took over the city?" asked the man with the sharp, unsteady smile, and he laughed, as if he were gasping for breath, as if he couldn't breathe. And the pallor went down into his hands. (my translation)

[Roberto Bertini apuntó a un tipo bajo y rubio, joven tal vez, que corría pegado a la larga pared de un esquina. Había elegido su blanco, sin apuro, desde la caja del camión descubierto que se detuvo en esa calle de Buenos Aires, poblada de negocios judíos. Poblada, les dijeron, de judíos y de bolcheviques. De bolcheviques judíos, les dijo, con una sonrisa filosa, el hombre que gritaba *tiren tiren*, como si le fuera algo más que la vida si ellos no tiraban.

—¿Conocen, acaso, un bolchevique que no sea judío?—les preguntó el hombre de la tenue sonrisa filosa.

—¿Acaso no son la misma cosa?—preguntó el hombre de la tenue sonrisa filosa. Y empalideció.

—¿Acaso no son ellos los que ocuparon la ciudad?—preguntó el hombre de la sonrisa filosa, y se rió, como si jadease, como si se quedara sin aire. Y la palidez le llegó hasta las manos. (11)]

The novel, an oblique narrative of the Tragic Week, opens with this passage, yet the conflation of Jews and Bolsheviks is phantasmagoric in the text: neither the intended victim of the shooting nor the elderly poet who is actually killed is Jewish, and Jewishness itself disappears from its pages, as, in fact, do the events that precipitated the killing. Moreover, observers like Marta Inés Waldegaray can write about Rivera as a socially conscious writer without mentioning ethnicity, Jewish or otherwise. Herman Szwarcbart's film *Un pogrom en Buenos Aires* (A pogrom in Buenos Aires) has a similar hole where its center might have been. Szwarcbart barely makes it in time to interview his own ninety-five-year-old grandfather for his documentary about the Tragic Week, filmed in 2007, but his grandfather said he knew nothing about it.[4]

If Szwarcbart and Rivera look back at a moment in the past that neither of them lived and that seems to melt between their fingers, other narrators hew closer to their own present. Journalist Pinie Wald, who was jailed during the Tragic Week, published his autobiographical novel about the events in 1929, in Yiddish, calling it *Koschmar* (Nightmare). Wald's account was not translated into Spanish until 1987, and in 1988 it came out as *Pesadilla: Novela crónica de la semana trágica* (Nightmare: A chronicle-novel of the Tragic Week).[5] The publication history of Wald's text may be taken as an object lesson in the vicissitudes of Jewish visibility, no less legibility, in Argentina. In 1929, when Wald published *Koschmar* in Yiddish and the book began to make its way through the Jewish world, it remained unknown in Argentina beyond the Jewish community. Written in Yiddish, it was not accessible to the non-Jewish majority; moreover, it circulated more or less clandestinely for the first ten years of its existence. The demise of Yiddish as a world language as a result of the Holocaust made *Koschmar* even less accessible, even among Jews. In 1987, in the aftermath of the dictatorship, novelist Simja Sneh translated the book into Spanish as part of an anthology of Yiddish literature, which was published by Editorial Milá, an imprint of the Asociación Mutual Israelita Argentina (AMIA). That publication venue also helped limit its readership largely to Jews. In 1998 another Jewish novelist, Pedro Orgambide, prepared a new edition of Wald's book for the independent Editorial Ameghino. Orgambide compares the book to the new journalism of writers like Rodolfo Walsh and Truman Capote, and David Viñas likens Wald to Kafka. Viñas and Orgambide thus claim Wald as a precursor of the globalized modernity of Capote and Kafka, and reinforce Argentina's place in that modernity by invoking Walsh as well. The Tragic Week is a crucial moment in Argentine Jewish history, but—as the odyssey of Wald's *Koschmar* suggests—it is the efforts of Jewish writers, filmmakers, and scholars who have made it legible as such to the larger society.

Like Pinie Wald, who wrote close to the events he narrates, Luis Saslavsky, one of Argentina's earliest film directors, addressed the plight of

Jewish refugees from Nazi Europe in his 1942 film *Ashes to the Wind* (*Ceniza al viento*). The film follows several narrative strands, but important among them is the decision of a liberal newspaper owner to stop publishing his paper in order to keep his son, who is being blackmailed, from inserting right-wing propaganda into it. The particular event that triggers the shutdown is the government's refusal to allow a group of Jewish refugees asylum in Argentina. This episode refers to an historical event, in which the Argentine government had initially given permission for a ship carrying refugees to enter Argentina but subsequently changed its mind. The film depicts an interview with the press that appeals both intellectually and emotionally to the viewer. The speaker for the refugees is a highly respected scientist. As he speaks eloquently, the camera pans to the people—largely women and children—who are seeking asylum. The filmmaker strikes a balance between the absolute othering of the pathetic refugees, whose connection to the feminine reinforces both their vulnerability and the fact that the group poses no threat, and the desirable familiarity of the cosmopolitan, implicitly productive man whose presence will only enhance Argentine society.[6] The film's point of view is utterly clear: it is wrong to deny these people entry into the country. The father/newspaper owner is, like the refugee's spokesperson, a man of integrity. His son, on the other hand, is underhanded, weak, and subject to coercion. Saslavsky brings this episode of Argentine history to the screen as a way to make it visible and to persuade his audience at a time when the situation of European Jews was dire.

Similarly, more recent narratives, both in film and print, inscribe a more recent attack on the nation's Jews into national consciousness. Jewish responses to the 1994 bombing of the Buenos Aires headquarters of the AMIA often contain the implicit message that the attack, which killed eighty-five people, was perpetrated not on Jews as outsiders to the nation, but rather on Argentines who happen to be Jews.[7] Although this position is perhaps a bit disingenuous, it does serve to incorporate Jews fully into Argentina's citizenry, and it stands in contrast to the relatively quiet response to the bombing of the Israeli embassy in Buenos Aires two years earlier. That attack was perceived as an attack on a foreign entity, not on Argentina, even though the majority of its victims were Argentines.[8]

Gustavo Efron and Darío Brenman speak directly to the way a consideration of the attack on the AMIA affects the construction of Argentine and Jewish identities. They trouble the insistence on Jewish versus non-Jewish victims, Jewish versus non-Jewish names, typical of both Jewish and Gentile commentators, and they suggest that absolute incorporation of Jewishness into Argentineity is the optimal way to consider the attack. Why mention Jewishness at all, especially in a postmodern era when the very notion of identity is so utterly outmoded? The discussion of antisemitism, national identity, and belonging in this article is fraught with tension and anguish. The anxiety that permeates Efron and Brenman's analysis illustrates just how Jewish legibility both exacerbates Jewish otherness and makes it possible to elude cultural genocide.

Just as surely as Gerchunoff, Tavosnanska, Rivera, and Viñas each in their own way deliberately write Jewishness into Argentineity, and Efron and Brenman question their efforts, other writers have written opaquely about Jewishness. The Jewishness of Edgardo Dobry's poems, for example, lies largely beneath the surface. Only Dobry's assertion that there is "something Jewish" in his work attests to that fact.[9] Still, Jewishness can only have meaning if it is perceived. Its significance as a presence in and an element of Argentine culture requires that it be noticed and acknowledged. While the importance of maintaining a sense of identity for a discernible sense of self is undeniable for Argentine Jews themselves, the very presence of Jewishness for Argentina's sense of itself as a modern nation is predicated on the conscious intervention in the elaboration of a national discourse.

As readers of texts and of their surroundings, Jews, like other minorities, are sensitive to signs of Jewishness that others might ignore or simply not understand. The tango quintet La Camorra, for example, is legible as a specifically Jewish Argentine group pretty much only in Jewish (and perhaps in antisemitic) contexts. Their music is fully part of post-Piazzola composition and performance, and in the venues they play in, both nationally and internationally, they perform as Argentines pure and simple. La Camorra differs from many Jewish tango performers of earlier eras, who changed their names in order to fit into a music scene that in fact already included many of them. Jews who wanted to sing tangos were advised to change their names:

> If you want to sing tango you can't be called "Leon" or "Zuker," Celedonio Flores advised Marcos Zuker's older brother, who then renamed himself Roberto Beltrán. Every Abraham became Alberto; every Israel, Raúl. Noiej Scolnic chose to be Juan Pueblito. Isaac Rosofsky reinvented himself as Julio Jorge Nelson. The tango embraced Jews gladly and without prejudice on the condition that they fake their background a little. (my translation)

[Si querés cantar tango no podés llamarte León ni Zuker, le aconsejó Celedonio Flores al hermano mayor de Marcos Zuker, que entonces se rebautizó Roberto Beltrán. Cada Abraham se puso Alberto, cada Israel Raúl. Noiej Scolnic eligió ser Juan Pueblito. Isaac Rosofsky se reinventó como Julio Jorge Nelson. El tango acogía con gran disposición y desprejuicio al judío, a condición de que disimulara un poco su origen. ("Tango que me hiciste goy," *Página 12*, n.d.)]

The archness of the last sentence both affirms and denies Jews' right to Argentine culture, and the article's title somewhat theatrically (and therefore perhaps ironically) denounces the demands of absolute deracination. Together they turn the Jewish *tanguero* into his own other and suggest why and how Jewishness is an attribute that emerges and recedes depending on the circumstance.

Unlike the former Abrahams, Isaacs, and Israels of the early and mid-twentieth century, the members of La Camorra have kept their Jewish-sounding names. Not that the idea never passed through their minds. In order to appear sufficiently authentic as tango musicians, the group once considered but discarded it. Buried in the press kit that Spain's Latin American cultural center, Casa de América, helpfully attaches to its announcement of the concert is an interview in which one of the group's members mentions that they once considered changing their Jewish-sounding names. The comment emerges as a sign of the repressed: that Jewishness is in fact aligned with Argentineity, but uneasily. The masking of Jewishness is simultaneously conjured and erased in this one utterance: it was something they did not do. Yet the mention itself suggests that, to be *tangueros*, making the music is necessary but insufficient. Even musing on the possibility of a name change is a recognition of the pressure to do so. To be *tangueros*, even prissy *tangueros* who demand the silence of the concert hall and complain of the noise and inattention of the *milonga*, one must be truly Argentine, and Jews would appear to be Argentine only if they are not too Jewish. Jewishness is uneasily aligned with the deep Argentineity of the tango. The fact, amply documented by Nudler and Judkovski, that the tango has Jewish roots, does not suffice, however embedded the strains of Eastern European Jewish music are in it. The desire for such documentation, to claim a Jewish connection, is another example of Jewish anxiety about being sufficiently Argentine— even as, or perhaps because—it stakes a claim to Argentineity. Although the specificity of Jewishness for a tango group is no longer overtly denied by means of a name change, the members' Jewishness is not salient either. The announcement of La Camorra's 2009 concert in Casa de América identifies the group, generationally and musically, as post-Piazzola tango players with classical and jazz backgrounds. The Centro Sefarad, a sister institution of Casa de América promoting Jewish culture in Spain and a cosponsor of the concert, on the other hand, took care to introduce the group as Jewish Argentine on its website and in its publicity magazine. Given its scope of interest, the only reason for its sponsorship was the very Jewishness that had been rendered nearly invisible elsewhere. Jewishness is an attribute that emerges and recedes depending on the circumstance.

La Camorra may be representative of the ways the grandchildren and great-grandchildren of Jewish immigrants appear more seamlessly Argentine as the very visible Jewishness of the first and second generations dissipates. We might call this assimilation, but I would like to nuance it. In some cases second-, third-, and fourth-generation Argentine Jews are unrecognizable as such to non-Jews. Their dress, bearing, speech, and formal (usually public) education is no different from that of non-Jews. They develop the interests of their non-Jewish compatriots. They root for the local soccer team, get involved in local and national politics. They adopt the dominant norms of beauty. They learn to perform gender as the larger culture does. At the same time, many undergo two socialization processes—one that shapes them for Argentineity and one that shapes them for the Jewish version of that national identity. In Daniel Burman's film *The Empty Nest* (*El nido vacío*), for example, Martha, the character played by Cecilia Roth, is completely legible as a middle-class woman who decides to return to the university to get her degree now that her children are growing independent. Her conversation, gestures, style, and her mode of interaction with both her husband and her children are all recognizable within the conventions of middle-class, middle-aged urban Argentine femininity. There is nothing overtly Jewish about her. She does not pepper her conversation with Yiddish, and her accent is pure Porteño. Her clothes are stylish; her hair is fashionably blond. There are no signs of Jewish observance in her behavior or in the objects that decorate her home. Nevertheless, when she needs to prove her Jewishness in order to pass through security to board an airplane to Israel, she dances a hora and speaks Hebrew.

Such compartmentalized Jewishness should, I think, be understood not as a public repudiation of Jewish identity but rather as an ease with all aspects of a Jewish Argentineity that neither hides nor displays itself in any self-conscious way. Another way to understand this phenomenon is to look at the ways Jewishness has dissolved into Argentineity. Martha's original decision to give up her studies in favor of marriage and raising a family, her subsequent intellectual pursuits, and her sense of self-worth within the family are all perfectly coherent with traditional Jewish womanhood. The fact that these characteristics are also part of middle-class intellectual Argentineity suggests the extent to which Jewish ways of being overlap with, and have been productive of, those traits. Commitment to both women's education and traditional gender roles within the family, the uneasy subordination of women's own intellectual, economic, and creative development to expectations of them as wives and mothers are to be found in Jewish—but not only Jewish—families.

One telling moment in the postproduction of *The Empty Nest*, one, presumably, that the director did not oversee, occurs in the English and Spanish subtitles. Leonardo has written a novel called, to my ears, *La familia Ros(s)*, which the English titles render as *The Rice family*, thus deethnicizing the family. Betsy notwithstanding, "Ross" is a version of "Roth" and a common Jewish name. "Rice," though recognizable enough as an English surname, does not sound that much like "Ross." The Spanish subtitles, for their part, render the line as "La familia Arroz," which is phonologically almost identical to "La familia Ross." Curious, I checked to see if Arroz is indeed a surname (I had never heard it, but I am a foreigner), and it does not turn up in lists of Spanish surnames or genealogies. In other words, an oblique but still fairly noticeable Jewish reference was not received as such by the surrogate listener/viewer. If we read subtitles as an instance of film reception—and we all know that these renderings are sometimes utterly bizarre—this one is very interesting for the way it cannot hear a Jewish reference as real, but as subtle, as the strains of klezmer in tango. On the other hand, sound film makes national otherness evident. Cecilia Roth, who plays Leonardo's wife in *The Empty Nest*, has had a successful career as a film actress in Spain, where her Argentine accent lays bare another kind of alterity. In films like *All About My Mother* (*Todo sobre mi madre*) by Spanish director Pedro Almodóvar and *Martín H* by Argentine expatriate Adolfo Aristarain, Roth has been cast as an Argentine in Spain, which accounts for her audible difference. Any Jewish alterity she might bring along to those roles is subsumed into that more perceptible difference.

The limited legibility of Jews in literature, film, and the plastic arts is often the effect of a small detail, which may be peripheral to the plot or major themes, that resonates with the reader or viewer, grabs their attention, and recalibrates the meaning of the text as a whole. Such details share some properties with Roland Barthes's punctum, that apparently superfluous element in a photograph that pierces the viewer's consciousness and floods the image with meaning. For Barthes, looking at a photograph of his dead mother, the punctum is necessarily deeply personal and in that sense idiosyncratic. Unlike the punctum, caught by accident by a photographer intent on capturing something else, the Jewish moment in a literary text or in a carefully scripted film is not inadvertent. Nevertheless, it is possible to conceive of something analogous to the punctum, a detail that is both intentional and available to a specific subset of viewers who share a common frame of reference. The deliberately placed detail might function either as a code for insiders or as a way of marking a certain kind of presence. Jewish legibility is often a matter of seeing this sort of punctum, the detail that marks the visual space or the text as Jewish to those for whom it opens up to a larger meaning not directly referred to in the image itself.[10] Martha's exuberant performance of Jewishness for El Al security is a comic version of the punctum; it punctures the decorum of international travel and stands in stark contrast to her husband's fraught concern with his dignity and the subdued Jewishness that serves as protective coloration in Argentine society but that will not do at all in assuaging the concerns of Israeli airline security. Whether the hora scene represents the film's "reality" or functions as a burst of surrealist projection from Leonardo's overwrought mind is not the issue. After all, the bulk of the narrative turns out to be a movie script he feverishly writes in a burst of nocturnal creative anguish.

Another deliberate punctum occurs in Fabián Bielinsky's movie *Nine Queens* (*Nueve reinas*), a caper film in which the young and apparently naive con man, Juan, played by Gaston Pauls, notices a deed from the Jewish Colonization Association on the wall of an elderly woman's home and surmises that he can win the confidence of the woman by insinuating that his family shared this bit of Jewish Argentinean history with her. In this case the punctum is doubly deliberate. Juan exhibits his ability to win the old woman's trust by inventing a story of a Jewish past when he sees the Moisés Ville deed on the wall. In so doing, he demonstrates a familiarity with Jewish Argentine history, as well as a quickness of mind that impresses the older con man, Marcos, who has taken him under his wing. At this point in the film the audience does not know that the old woman is part of a larger scam, and that she is in cahoots with Juan. Until now, nothing in the film has suggested that Juan is Jewish, but in this moment he implies to the old woman and to the audience that he is. The twist, that she is in on the scam, means that the Jewish detail was deliberately planted so that Juan could do this bit of showing off. The moment in which the young con man plays at being Jewish may be just that—a performance for the benefit of his audience within the film and in the movie house.

The Jewish punctum may be more subtle than in these films by Burman and Bielinsky. Edgardo Cozarinsky's novel *La tercera mañana* (The third morning), for instance, contains a single, but slowly unfolded, detail that identifies its protagonist as Jewish. Late in the story the narrator remembers his great-aunt taking him to the Buenos Aires zoo as a child. The woman, who seems to the child immensely old, has an accent. He makes fun of the way she speaks, and although his parents reprimand him for it, they also find her Spanish a little risible, perhaps a bit embarrassing. The second reference to the great-aunt's accent specifies that it is from Kishinev. The text makes no further remarks on Kishinev, a town in Bessarabia that had a sizable Jewish community at the beginning of the twentieth century. Because this recollection occurs at the end of the novel, it is only in retrospect that the protagonist is obliquely identified as Jewish. Occurring as something like an afterthought, it also indicates that the narrator's Jewish background is not a particularly significant element in his own sense of self. Yet the detail is as deliberate as anything else in this slim novel, and its being broken down into two parts—first the accent and the child's reaction to it followed by his parents' ambivalence, and several pages later the revelation via metonymy that it is Jewish—is telling in a novel where story loops back on itself to modulate meaning. The passing reference to Kishinev calls up the history of a brutal pogrom, indelible for readers whose memory includes it.[11] The novel's implication is that the old aunt was a survivor of that attack; the woman's great age concentrates in her the narrator's connection to an ancestral past that is emblematized by the pogroms and the institutionalized violence against Jews. This part of the past, which the young boy's family bears, has nevertheless been destined to lose its power as the visceral memory of those who experienced it firsthand dissipates in subsequent generations. The aunt's accent, the embodied linguistic evidence of her history, has become an object of ridicule and discomfort. For the reader with no knowledge of the story of the pogroms, whose memory traces other paths, the reference is incidental, at most folkloric. Kishinev is just another Slavic-sounding, vaguely exotic, marginally humorous place-name.

The protagonist's Jewish background plays no significant role in the novel, but the detail evoking Kishinev has the wounding potential of the punctum to rechannel the emotional response of a particular set of readers.

These shared historical memories inject a minor character with a past, and they also stake a claim for a Jewish presence in an otherwise unmodified Argentine national culture. The textual presence of Jewishness at the periphery of the narrative opens the text up to a multiplicity of readings. It also reminds the reader that the subject unmarked for ethnicity is assumed to belong to the dominant culture. If the text does not bear a visible sign of Jewishness, most readers will automatically read the characters as members of the Catholic majority.

What is true for characters in a novel also holds for writers themselves. Alicia Dujovne Ortiz, the expatriate child of intermarriage, is best known for her biographies of Eva Perón and María Elena Walsh, and Andrés Neuman resists self-referentiality in the majority of his writing. In texts such as Dujovne's *El árbol de la gitana* (The Gypsy woman's tree) and Neuman's *Una vez argentina* (Once Argentina), in which Jewishness is overt, however, Esther Bendarhan, indirectly following Phillipe Lejeune, finds what she calls a "Jewish pact" that opens up all of the author's work to a reading for Jewishness.[12] The Jewish pact theory is problematic insofar as it encourages a scavenger hunt for overt Jewish references, to find evidence of the pact itself, at the same time that it promotes a reading of texts for traces of Jewishness that the pact promises. Moreover, it suggests an authorial intentionality that may well be absent. Conversely, any such pact may be intentionally avoided or undermined. Nevertheless, the idea of the pact offers a justification for reading texts through Jewishness that has enriched our understanding of writers who are identified as Jewish but whose work is generally read with no reference to that cultural context.

Edgardo Cozarinsky's "Émigré Hotel" (Hotel de emigrantes), discussed in chapter 3, takes the question of the Jewish pact itself as one of its themes. Although the narrator is not religious, and may not even be Jewish according to the law of maternal descent, the narrator makes the Jewish pact by his commitment to digging out the story of a Jewish past. "Émigré Hotel," then, may be read as a key to the suite of stories grouped together in *The Bride from Odessa* under the title "Dark Loves" (Oscuros amores) not least because the maternal grandfather's history remains obscure and ambiguous. These stories, which speak of lost and troubled love, have no overt Jewish content; but their placement within a collection whose title conspicuously names its Jewishness may provoke the reader to find Jewish resonances in its stories of ambiguity, abandonment, alienation, loss, and memory.

Juan Gelman's connection to Jewishness in the 2007 collection *Mundar* (Worlding) is similarly tenuous. The poems of *Mundar* range widely. They are not so much set in a place as a narrative would be, but rather voice a being in the world, and from time to time a specific place, signaled by language itself, as where a woman speaks in Nahautl to secure the poem to Mexico. The poem "Accidentes," however, gives a sense of time and change. Its space is the space of the world and the stars, seen from the speaker's vantage point, given to him by his mother. The mother's stories confer upon him his visage—the face that is his and that the world knows him by. The poem is about opening up and loss, a hope for change, and accidents that give and take. The open confidence radiates hope in the possibilities that the contingencies of the world offer; the final word, "goodbye," shuts that hope down.

The face bestowed upon the speaker by his mother is specifically Jewish and tragic. It is the story of the blood shed in the antisemitic violence of the pogroms. It is a litany, with all that suggests of shared knowledge, experience, and also representation of suffering.

> In the crumbs of your splendor,
> Mamma, I heard the recital
> of pogroms and blood
> that gave a face to my face. (my translation)
>
> [En las migas de tu esplendor,
>   mamá, recibí el recital
>   de pogroms y de sangre
>   que dio rostro a mi rostro. (25)]

This moment of Jewishness in the poetry is unique in *Mundar*. Skip this poem, and you skip the fact of Gelman's Jewishness. So the question is, how far does this autobiographical moment take the reader? Does it make the other poems read differently? It is possible to argue that the reference to Moscow in a subsequent poem, "El encuentro" (The encounter), could be read as a reference to Jewishness even without reference to "Accidentes"? What is certain is that "Accidentes" seals the reference as Jewish.

> How was it, how is it still?
>     Did you see my eyes upon her mouth and did she
> look at your silence or the roof
> that sheltered you in Moscow?
>     . . .

> In the questions of dawn/
> father/I see you heaping tongues
> of clear love/the lines of
> travels that you did not recount
> even to yourself. (my translation, backslashes in original)
>
> [¿Cómo fue, cómo es todavía?
> ¿Viste mis ojos en su boca y ella
> miró tu silencio o techo
> que te abrigaba en Moscú?
> . . .
> En las preguntas de la madrugada/
> padre/te veo montando lenguas
> del claro amor/las líneas
> de viajes que no contaste
> ni a vos mismo. (64)]

This is a version of the family narrative, a series of questions to the father about his life, his relationship to his wife, to his work, and to his displacement. Such themes are Jewish, of course, but they are also deeply Argentine, and perhaps deeply human. We learn in school that universality is best represented by the very local, the very personal. Jews have no monopoly on displacement, but Jewish displacement stands as a synecdoche for universal exile, diaspora, uprootedness. When poet Hugo Savino, recalling Celan, says "all writers are Jewish," he is both honoring and deracinating the specificity of Jewishness.[13]

In other cases, the Jewish pact is even less overt and may be largely a function of the desire of the reader. Alejandra Pizarnik, for example, is labeled Argentine, Jewish, and lesbian, but none of those identities exhausts her poetry. Still, Florinda Goldberg's complex reading of Pizarnik as a Jewish writer is compelling, and Evelyn Fishburn's subtle reading of Pizarnik and Jewishness leaves little doubt of the poet's real and conflicted connection to Jewishness. Fishburn identifies only four poems in Pizarnik's extensive oeuvre that refer to Jewishness, three of which (as Cristina Piña notes) were published posthumously. These might serve as Jewish puncta, but their scarcity, and the fact that the poet did not publish them during her lifetime, make an argument about a Jewish pact unsustainable. However, Fishburn also refers to "an extremely veiled" and "super-condensed, overdetermined joke" included in *La bucanera de Pernambuco, o Hilda la polígrafa* (The [woman] buccaneer of Pernambuco, or Hilda the polygraph) that "is obviously intended for a small, dedicated, and perhaps slightly obsessive Jewish readership" (Fishburn 2007, 55).

Nora Glickman uses the words of Alejandra Pizarnik in her epigraph to her play *Una tal Raquel* (Some woman named Raquel) about Raquel Liberman, on being an outsider. Alterity in Pizarnik's case no doubt came from many places, but for Glickman the Jewish resonance is inescapable, and juxtaposing Pizarnik's words to a story of Jewish outlaw sexuality, albeit with different emphases and different details, makes Glickman's reader see Pizarnik in a Jewish context. On the other hand, a recent paper on Pizarnik included in a conference panel on Jewish writers addressed nothing remotely connected to Jewishness, stripping the term of meaning entirely. Here the inclusion of Pizarnik remits to a simplistic notion of Jewish "being" that apparently gave the conference organizers an excuse to find a spot for a paper that in fact had nothing to do with Jewishness as a problematic.

Nora Catelli, in contrast, discusses Jewishness as one of several overarching themes in Pizarnik's diaries. Yet as Catelli presents it, Jewishness in the diaries is less an overt theme than a resonant absence, and, to a lesser extent, an example of what the critic terms the poet's "characteristic charge of ambivalence."[14] It is striking that the bulk of Catelli's discussion of Jewishness refers not to Pizarnik's writing in the diaries, but to her apparent lack of engagement with the traumatic memory of the Holocaust. Catelli's understanding of what makes a text "Jewish" is an engagement with the suffering of the Jewish people, or what Jewish historian Salo Wittmayer Baron termed—and criticized, albeit before the Second World War—as the lachrymose view of Jewish history. Catelli seems to have expected to find more Jewish substance of this sort in Pizarnik's diaries and seems surprised at the extent to which Jewishness is merely peripheral, even folkloric. Catelli characterizes Pizarnik's references to her family as "*costumbrista*," which typically suggests a superficial rendering of local color washed with exoticism. Whatever family references there are in the diaries are, in Catelli's own reading, wholly prosaic; she characterizes the tone of other Jewish references as both "offhand and moving" [casual y patético" (n.p.)]. More importantly, Catelli links Pizarnik's alterity to an alienation from language itself. Like Ben Bollig, she points out that as the child of Yiddish speakers, Pizarnik found Spanish always a little alien. That alienation from language, they imply, sharpened her poet's edge, but they differ in the extent to which they read this alienation as a particularly Jewish problem. Bollig puts this alienation from language in the context of other Jewish writers;

Catelli sees it as an issue for immigrants more generally, suggesting how idiosyncratic Jewish legibility can be. Paradoxically, Catelli announces that she is addressing Jewishness in her paper, while Bollig insinuates it much more subtly into his article.

Overwhelmingly, it is Jewish artists, filmmakers, writers, and thinkers who make and keep the Argentine Jewishness visible. Exceptions exist, of course. Eduardo Mignogna's 1996 film *Autumn Sun* (*Sol de otoño*) warmly develops the relationship between a Jewish woman and a Gentile man whom she schools in Judaism so she can pass him off as a Jew to her brother. Juan José Saer normalizes Jewishness with his characters Marcos and Clara Rosemberg, and Ernesto Sábato's overt philosemitism runs up against the stereotypes of Jewishness he sometimes falls into. As Leonardo Senkman notes, the inclusion of Jewish characters in Leopoldo Marechal's *Adán Buenosayres* gives life to the well-worn "some of my best friends are Jews" trope, as the characterization of Adán's Jewish confidante Tessler takes on antisemitic overtones. Among Gentile writers in Argentina, Jorge Luis Borges has most notably incorporated marks of Jewishness in his work.

As critics such as Jaime Alazraki, Saúl Sosnowski, Edna Aizenberg, Mario Satz, and Evelyn Fishburn have shown, Borges is drawn to Jewish mysticism and to the arcane practices of Judaism. "Death and the Compass" (La muerte y la brújula), for example, famously relies on the detective's knowledge of the workings of the Jewish calendar, but Borges also wrote contemporary Jewishness into his stories. The demure but modern Emma Zunz sacrifices her virginity to avenge her father, and Santiago Fischbein, the young Jewish gangster in "The Unworthy Friend" (El indigno), grows up to be a bookseller. Moreover, in "The Dead Man" (El muerto) Borges enmeshes Jewishness itself in hybridization: Azevedo Bandeira's face contains characteristics that mark him as Jewish, Black, and Indigenous (Borges 1971, 30). I remit you to the extraordinary scholarship on Borges and Jewishness for a thorough analysis of Borges's relationship to and representation of Jewishness. Here, I will merely invoke Fishburn by saying that Borges brings together the two elements fundamental to Jewish Argentineity: the particularity of Jewish experience and the richness of Jewishness as a signifier (1998). Ilan Stavans simply calls Borges "the Jew," a label also applied to him by an antisemitic government official, who meant it as a threat. Borges took it as a compliment.

If Borges flirts with Jewish identity, the legibility of Jewish writers' own Jewishness may be compromised by their use of pseudonyms, as if the writers themselves were playing with just what their readers would see.

Jewish writers have used pseudonyms whimsically: Israel Zeitlin translates himself almost literally as César Tiempo. Sometimes the choice is playfully erudite, hiding Jewishness in plain sight. Samuel Glusberg, cofounder of the influential literary journal *Martín Fierro* and, with Leopoldo Lugones, the Sociedad de Escritores Argentinos, published under the name of Enrique Espinoza. He also founded and directed the editorial house Babel and the literary journal of the same name. Glusberg took his pseudonym from Heinrich Heine and Baruch Spinoza (Espinoza in Spanish), thus giving himself a name with deep Jewish roots that nevertheless link to the Christian world in which modern Judaism is enmeshed. Heine, born Jewish and converted to Christianity during a time of increasing discrimination against Jews, was called Heinrich, the German form of Enrique. Glusberg makes the name his own via translation to Spanish, simultaneously laying claim to a German Jewish tradition and the language of Argentina. Espinoza, on the other hand, is an already-Spanish name, recognizably *converso* to those aware of such things, and Spinoza is a pillar of secular Jewish philosophy. Glusberg makes a complex cultural claim via the pseudonym, but in 1924, when he writes *La levita gris: Cuentos judíos de ambiente porteño* (The gray overcoat: Jewish stories of Buenos Aires), he does so under his own name.[15] Babel indeed.

Such legibility can help perpetuate difference. As Katherine Ostrom has shown, when Jews can't be easily identified, Gentiles can get nervous. Ostrom points out that marking Jewish difference allows Cristina Pineda's characters to hide their antisemitism in *Las viudas de los jueves* (The Thursday widows):

> In one episode, Virginia's friend and neighbor Lila Laforgue asks if a pair of potential buyers are "paisanos" and, when Virginia fails to take her meaning, has to clarify herself with a more common euphemism, "rusos" [Russians] (145). When Virginia tells her that the family's last name is Ferrere, Lila says, "Sefardíes. Yo conocí un Paz que era, un Varela que era. Te engañan con esos apellidos, y te terminan haciendo meter la pata." [Sephardic Jews. I knew a Paz who was one, a Varela who was. They fool you with those surnames, and you wind up sticking your foot in it.] (179–80).

Jewish art and writing in and about Argentina are most legible when they fit into the sphere of the modern. Legibility here takes a different turn, having to do with just what it is that people will pick up and look at. So despite his dazzling erudition and complexity as a writer, Mario Satz has barely been recognized by the critical establishment. His series of Kabbalistic novels on the solar system and the universe has merited the attention of a few brief references in books by historians like Senkman and literary critics like Sosnowski, and only handful of scholarly articles, one of which laments the fact that Satz is so little read.[16]

Unlike Satz, a prolific writer whose work has been virtually ignored by literary critics, Mirta Kuperminc's visual art has been widely acknowledged, but at times it has been, perhaps fruitfully, misread. Kuperminc's visual art, like Satz's fiction, is steeped in Jewish mysticism, but she is also an artist of Jewish Argentine modernity, and her engagement with Kabbalah has, in part, been routed through the abundantly visible and nourishing cultural torrent that is the work of Jorge Luis Borges.[17] Her work also includes such secular Jewish references as the Holocaust and the AMIA bombing. The secret pact between letters and numbers, the covert holy words written in the pelt of a tiger or scattered around the edges of a canvas, make their way into Kuperminc's images, but so do meditations on tattoos in the context of both the Holocaust and body art, explorations of exile and displacement, and commemoration of attacks on Jews in Eastern European ghettos and on Jewish institutions in Buenos Aires. Sometimes, however, viewers read modern materiality and political allegory where Kuperminc crafted spirituality.

Kuperminc's *To Be a Witness* (*Ser testigo*) is a mural-size piece that consists of a series of images of a young man looking downward with his hand covering his eyes. This image, in concert with the piece's title, Kuperminc says, was understood by one foreign viewer to be a response to dictatorship and the complicity of much of the Argentine populace, who resisted witnessing. The young man with the hand over his eyes seems, in this reading, to try to avoid seeing and therefore to avoid the responsibility of the witness to bear witness.

The formal layout of *To Be a Witness* may be part of the reason this viewer thought the installation was about the dictatorship. With its grid of individual images of a young man's face, it is reminiscent of the rows of photographs of the disappeared, all enlarged to the same size, arranged in rows and columns encircling the pyramid in the Plaza de Mayo, where the mothers of the disappeared have long walked in silent protest. These faces, each an individual, each pictured in a blowup of a school photograph or an official identity card, whatever most recent picture the family could find, each one a person, each one a life. Over time, these images have grown more like each other. As fashions in hairstyle, eyeglasses, makeup, and facial hair

# JEWISH LEGIBILITY AND ARGENTINE SELF-FASHIONING

Figure 5.1. Mirta Kuferminc, *To Be a Witness* (*Ser testigo*), 2006. Glass, paper, wood, 11.48 ft. × 16.40 ft. *Source*: Reprinted by permission of the artist.

change, these images from the 1970s and 1980s blend into each other for the contemporary viewer for whom the look of the era becomes less and less about individuals and more about a certain dated style.

Kupferminc's images, all of the same size, but of a single individual, a young man, seem to be answering the demands of the faces lining the obelisk in the Plaza de Mayo, or pinned onto the makeshift fence surrounding that monument. Will he bear witness or not? Will this one observer look into the eyes of those who are gone? That is, perhaps, what Kupferminc's observer saw in her piece. It is not, however, how the artist meant the piece to be understood. Kupferminc explains that it is about the praying of the Schm'a, the prayer that declares the unity of God. The covered eyes make this witness to the oneness of God possible. The subject in prayer does not refuse to see, but rather blocks out distraction. The work is about mystery and interiority, another kind of witnessing altogether. The reference to the prayer, and the abstracting of two of its letters to form the word "witness," is recognizable to those who know the Hebrew and Talmudic tradition.

Much of Kupferminc's work is laden with references to secular Jewishness, Jewish spirituality, and Jewish religious practice. She embraces a range of Jewish historical traditions, from the lachrymose with its focus on Jewish suffering, including images referring to the Holocaust, and to the wanderers scattered by the Jewish diaspora, to the sacred, with images suggesting Jewish liturgy and ritual, as well as the mysticism of Kabbalah. Kupferminc's work is often self-referential. The child of Holocaust survivors, she returns repeatedly to her parents'—and especially her mother's—experience in numerous canvases and installations. On the other hand, images like that of her gorgeous tiger, with the name of God hidden in its stripes, goes beyond tragic history to explore the realm of the sacred. They suggest, Kabbalistically, the importance of the word not as signifier alone, but as embodiment of the mystery itself. The sacred word becomes, in her work, the visceral image. Not all of Kupferminc's work deals with overtly Jewish themes, but enough of it does that she is often seen and shown as a Jewish artist. In contrast, Jewishness in the work of Guillermo Kuitca, a somewhat younger Argentine artist, is submerged and barely legible.

Kuitca's early work is referential, even anecdotal, and contains autobiographical elements as well as political and historical references. In his 2010 retrospective at the Walker Art Center in Minneapolis, the earliest piece, from 1980, squeezes the numbers 1 to 30,000 in a small rectangle of canvas, a reference to the number of people disappeared during the period of state terror often called the Dirty War. The canvas foreshadows Kuitca's fascination with enumeration, the meticulous counting-out—here with unspoken (and even unrepresented) reference to each individual victim, each particular death. A decade later, Kuitca's counting-out emerges in the ordered spaces of institutions: a school, a prison, and a cemetery, so that each structure itself is sketched out, grid-like, as in an architectural drawing, with each space in the grid painstakingly drawn and numbered. In these pieces, in the absence of represented human bodies, the numbers themselves count out the implied presence of people filling those spaces.

Kuitca names the institutional series *Tablada Suite* for one of those places, La Tablada, Argentina's largest Jewish cemetery. With this title, Kuitca not only infuses Jewishness into the mix of Argentine institutionality, he also highlights it by using the cemetery's grid as the point of reference for all of them. Of the ten images constituting the *Tablada Suite*, made between 1991 and 1993, the cemetery is one among many; only by naming the series after it does Kuitca suggest that it might be of particular importance in understanding the whole, a play of emphases between the verbal and the visual. In his decades-long exploration of enumerated and increasingly abstract spaces, the very particularity of La Tablada is startling, an instance of the presence of Jewishness just under the surface. It is the moment of visibility of that which seems to have been so casually hidden.

The artist's series of theater plans continues the theme, without the oppressive overlay suggested by school, prison, and cemetery, often beyond the borders of Argentina. Moreover, the use of color, the move toward abstraction in his collages of theater seating charts, in which the shape of the auditorium overtakes the now-obscured individual seats, and, finally, the melted-away, sinuous abstractions created by downloading seating plans and manipulating the images with water to soften them, undoes the orderly numbering. Until recently, Kuitca's general trajectory has been marked by the evacuation of anecdote. The emotionally laden, politically resonant references to the disappeared, and, shortly thereafter, the similarly freighted representational, if abstracted, floor plans of specifically Argentine institutions, gives way to a less burdened space of reference.

Kuitca's most recent work includes images that return to the narrative and representational. The motif of the bed returns, as does his play with scale: tiny human figures, minuscule beds and chairs, scattered about in vast rooms. The suite of paintings *The Family Idiot* (2019), for example, recalls some of Kuitca's earliest pieces containing human subjects, usually small figures nearly lost in the space of enormous canvases, apparently unaware of each other's presence. One large painting is part of a series called *El mar dulce*, a reference to Buenos Aires's Río de la Plata. Labeled, simply, "El mar dulce," it also carries a kind of title within the frame of the painting itself. The words "Yo quiero recordar aquel beso con el que me besabas en Odesa" [I want to remember that kiss with which you kissed me in Odessa] are scrawled across the bottom edge of the canvas, establishing a geographical tension and a space of memory between Odessa and Buenos Aires. The quotation itself echoes a line from Jorge Luis Borges's poem "Gunnar Thorgilsson," where the poet writes, "Yo quiero recordar aquel beso/con el que me besabas en Islandia" (I want to remember that kiss/with which you kissed me in Iceland). In Kuitca's variation, the Borgesian longed-for memory of a kiss in a foreign and somewhat exotic place is transformed into a kind of erotic nostalgia linked to an ancestral homeland.

Kuitca's canvas contains four separate groups of figures: two apparently heterosexual couples engaging in various forms of sexual activity, a sleeping

Figure 5.2. Guillermo Kuitca. *El mar dulce (The sweetwater sea)*, 1984. Acrylic on paper mounted on canvas, 67 in. × 122 in. *Source*: Reprinted by permission of the artist.

woman, and a line of three nude men who appear to be looking at themselves in a long, horizontal mirror. Connected by a bright red foreground, but separated by walls in some cases and by distance and isolation in others, these scenes of intimacy seem like depictions of anomie. Dominating one section of the canvas is a visual quotation from perhaps the most famous scene in Sergei Eisenstein's classic Soviet film, *The Battleship Potemkin*, in which a baby carriage bumps perilously down the steps leading to the Odessa harbor. This reference to Kuitca's heritage—his grandparents were from Odessa—is mediated by a cultural icon, immediately recognizable to the film-literate, evoking the terror and vulnerability that infuses Eisenstein's scene. Just off-center in this canvas, in which most of the figures are painted with large brushstrokes that are evocative rather than meticulous, creating an effect that is expressionist more than realist, and with a generally muted palate, is a carefully rendered table, colorfully covered with a patterned cloth, on which sits a menorah. The Jewish reference is unmistakable, just off-center in this busy, but at the same time uncrowded, canvas. Viewers are invited to linger over each section and to create their own narrative out of these disparate elements. We are not told precisely where to place the Jewishness of this image, but we know it must go somewhere. Somewhere near the center, somewhere clear, but somewhere also somehow detached from the rest.

The Odessa steps motif recurs in other pieces in the Walker retrospective as well, once in another in the *Mar dulce* series, where as a painting-within-a-painting it dominates the center of the canvas, hanging spotlighted on the rear wall in the room that also holds Kuitca's recurrent beds, chairs, and doors. It is also rendered all alone in a pen-and-ink drawing and, in a sculptural moment that Kuitca likens to the screen character stepping out of the frame in Woody Allen's *The Purple Rose of Cairo*, becomes the series of maps on mattresses that sit on platforms on the museum floor.

Kuitca addresses this oblique autobiographical reference to his ancestry in a similarly oblique way in the question-and-answer session following the opening-night artist's talk on the occasion of the Walker retrospective. I dwell on this moment because it seems to me emblematic of Jewish legibility (or illegibility) not only in Kuitca's work but elsewhere. The artist's talk was, in fact, conducted as an interview of Kuitca by the two curators of the show, Olga Viso, then director of the Walker, and Douglas Dreishpoon, the guest curator. It is most likely that before going on stage, the two interviewers discussed with Kuitca the general focus of their comments and questions, as well as the artworks from the exhibit that would be the center of discussion. The conversation among the three took as its central topic the fraught relationship between the artist and the very basics of painting (his attempt to liberate himself from paint itself, his shedding of anecdote, the banishing of the human figure from the image). It also gave the two experts a chance to demonstrate their knowledge of and insight into the work in the process of eliciting Kuitca's own reflections on his art. The discussion was deeply personal, insofar as it dealt with Kuitca's struggle with his art, but no other piece of autobiography made its way into that part of the event, and the vast majority of the pieces the curators chose to discuss were those with the least historical and autobiographical charge. They even discussed the deeply political *1-30,000*, an overt reference to the number of disappeared during the Argentine dictatorship's Dirty War against dissidents, solely with reference to its formal properties and how they presaged those of later works. (Viso discerned the outlines of the bed that would subsequently become one of Kuitca's leitmotifs, and Dreishpoon saw an early fascination with linearity and enumeration that emerges full-force a decade later.) In other words, the art experts held to what most resonated with them in the images, a living illustration of Kuitca's observation in the question-and-answer session that what happens in a work of art is the zone created between the image and the viewer (not "in the zone," but the zone itself). Kuitca himself offers an explanation of the piece that not only informs the audience of the historical reference, calling to mind the canvas's function as an overtly testimonial work, but also tells how he thinks the piece works as a visual paradox between what is discernible only if you look closely and what you can see from a distance, and how it works emotionally, forcing the viewer to struggle to separate the numbers, each one "tragically" (the artist's word) a person. Without letting go of questions of formalism and of how art functions, Kuitca shifts the audience's attention to the national-particular, away from the general-universal that Dreishpoon, especially, labors to confer upon him.

The audience, however, was eager to know about the links between biography and art. For many of the questioners, the zone between themselves and the image is enriched by a knowledge of the artist—his family history, his motives, his interests—and Kuitca himself responds to Dreishpoon's insistence on the artist's universality by saying that "we use the term global, universal as a kind of shield. There has to a be a moment of privacy between the viewer and the work; a story that's built between you and the work; that zone—what you bring and what you get might not happen."[18]

His work may be imbued with identity, Kuitca suggests, but that does not mean that identity can be isolated. When an audience member asks what, apart from *1-30,000*, is Argentine in his work, he replies, "Everything." Kuitca explains that his art must all be Argentine because he lives and works only in Buenos Aires, but he goes on to say that there is no way to recognize the Argentineity in his work. That play of presence and absence is just a little disingenuous, but it signals Kuitca's wariness of autobiography. Grids of Argentine institutions, variations on the Teatro Colón seating plan, even brief references to tango, and certainly the *Mar dulce* series refer overtly to the space he works in. References to Jewishness are highly mediated, but present as well.

When questioned on the references present in the Odessa steps quotations in his work, Kuitca only slowly comes to their autobiographical charge. First he mentions the artistic genealogy of the image, noting the frame in the film immediately previous to the one he depicts, detoured through the influential work of Francis Bacon: the nursemaid guiding the carriage is shot; blood runs down her face. When Kuitca eventually gets around to mentioning that his grandparents were from Odessa and suggesting that the carriage, about to travel wildly and dangerously, connected metonymically to the boat that gives the film its title, his reference to Russian immigration to Argentina elides Jewishness. For the Argentine Kuitca, "Russian" may connote "Jewish," but his Minnesota audience would not likely assume so.

Eventually Kuitca actually mentions being Jewish, raised in a secular family, the child of a psychoanalyst.[19]

Like Kupferminc, Kuitca takes displacement and transnational movement, nowhereness imbued with angst, as one of his central themes. Whereas Kupferminc employs a recurring group of rather endearing human and semihuman figures endlessly traveling, sometimes weighted down with their belongings or their past, sometimes apparently unburdened, much of Kuitca's work evacuates the human figure, leaving objects imbued with human meaning. His remark that all his work is deeply Argentine because he lives and works nowhere else suggests a rootedness that gives meaning to the displacement of his maps and the empty baggage carousel, which Kuitca characterizes as perhaps the most bereft of spaces. Not only are you neither here nor there at the empty baggage claim, you are in a state of dispossession; the paraphernalia of your life, which you entrusted to another, may never be seen again. His child-size mattresses soaked in black so that the underlying pattern of sweet flowers is ominously stained, are the ground on which Kuitca paints his maps of Europe. Other images recombine the elements of US roadmaps, creating a world in which patterns brightly repeat but whose roads lead nowhere. Finding one's own town named and almost-correctly located is disconcerting—an effect of the Midwestern location of the exhibit. Kuitca was certainly not painting for a Minnesota public, and the gallery notes point out that for him the names of Minnesota towns were exotic. The sense of self-recognition among the visitors to this is exhibit was inevitable, and the curators warn us not to make too much of it. Yet the pull of recognition fills the zone between viewer and painting with a complex sense of being displaced in one's own space by its utter meaninglessness to the artist who put it there. A viewer from Coon Rapids is hailed into the work only to discover that Coon Rapids is no more than a sign of the exotic mundane, another name on another map of a place that has no meaning. The sense of self-recognition among Jewish viewers of Kuitca's work, however, is of another order, because Kuitca's own autobiography is clearly among the references in his work (*yo* quiero . . .). The sense of being hailed into the work, and thus of being spoken to directly, is heightened for the Jewish viewer who sees a version of her or his own history inscribed on the canvas.

Kuitca's response to the audience member who asks about finding Argentina in his work speaks directly to the question of legibility in the artwork. Argentineity is constitutive of his art, but it cannot necessarily be read there. ("How can we see [it]?" "You can't." That "you" is telling—it is the "you" of the viewer from outside; the "you" who must ask how to discern Argentineity who cannot.) The tension between Kuitca's entrenched Argentineity (on which he insists when Dreishpoon wants to exalt him with universality) and the undermined emplacement of labyrinthian maps, brightly misleading in their cheerfully messed-up realism or stained with wretchedness and vulnerability onto mattresses, suggests the extent to which not only legibility but also the paradox of belonging/not belonging permeates Kuitca's work.

If the political message of *1-30,000* makes it into this show because it also presages Kuitca's fascination with lines and numbering, a piece like *Kristallnacht*, which—while echoing the grids in other work—appears to derive from the history of stained-glass windows, and refers directly to Jewish history, is absent not only from the Walker retrospective, but also from discussion of Kuitca's work more generally. The point here is not to claim Kuitca for Jewish art or Argentine culture, but to get a sense of how Jewishness is constitutive of his Argentineity and how both are constitutive of his art. Dreishpoon would evacuate these particularities from our reading of Kuitca's art; I believe that they enrich our experience of it.

Kuitca's art is one example of Jewishness as a trace in the dominant discourse that takes on substance only from certain angles. (In the dominant discourse of the art world, his Argentineity is similarly marginalized and similarly disappeared.) This now-you-barely-see-it-now-it-comes-into-view suggests that Jewish visibility is a kind of iridescence. Depending as it does on the relationship of the surface to the light, and especially the angle from which the light hits the surface, iridescence relies on the viewer's place in relation to the object.

Iridescence is characterized by sheen and changing colors; it is not fixed. But non-Jews can see Jewishness if they are able to move in and out of the stance of otherness, of assuming the perspective of the other as they move through a space that they share with others similarly and differently located. Where you stand affects the colors you see. The shiny colors of Jewishness, even the most overt references to Jewish history, practice, culture, and language, often depend for visibility on the amount of light (in the form of critical attention among other things) that hits them. The confluence of a text's Jewish theme, its author's Jewish biography, and the Jewish reader's desire for a "Jewish text" make for high iridescence. More subtle signs, as well as different social locations, require a deliberate shift in perspective, so that what viewers see depends not only on where they stand, but how they move.[20] The visibility of the nondominant hinges entirely on this kind of movement, and the ability to see depends on not maintaining a single stance, and on the willing and attentive travel from one spot to another in the presence of a multifaceted object. Our ability to move in and out of the stance of otherness, of assuming (or even merely trying on) the perspective of the other as we move through a space that we share with others similarly and differently located, makes legibility possible.

CHAPTER SIX

# INCIDENTAL JEWISHNESS

In 1940, Gisele Freund set sail for Buenos Aires, escaping the threat of Hitler's death camps, thanks to Victoria Ocampo, whom she had met over a decade earlier. Freund, who shot memorable portraits of Walter Benjamin, James Joyce, and Virginia Woolf, and who would go on to make the damning photograph of Eva Perón resplendently dressed and gazing at her jewels for *Life* magazine, was one of many Jews who took refuge in Argentina, not all artists and writers, certainly. Freund, however, reminds us of the notable Jewish refugees who didn't much act like refugees or reinforce conventional ideas about Jews perpetuated even by scholars, whose studies of Jewish cultural production in Argentina often center on the problematics of Jewish identity.

Jewishness is overdetermined by writers and others who identify as Jews and whose work is about being Jewish. But what of the writers and artists like Freund, whose Jewishness is not at the center of their work, those who in their creative lives were only incidentally Jewish? For Jews like Freund, who fled Nazi persecution, the question of Jewish identity must have been a very real, very personal issue. In her autobiography, *The World in My Camera*, Freund states that her parents thought of themselves as Germans, and that religion and race were never discussed in her house (5). In her account of her escape from Germany her only reference to Jewishness is to deny it when confronted by an SS officer, which undoubtedly saved her life (7). The plight of Jews, no less the larger question of Jewishness, is not overt in Freund's photography or her writing, although it may well have been subsumed into her anti-Fascist work as a young photographer, and the insistence on the absence of Jewishness in the first pages of her autobiography is a visible negative space that implies presence. Freund, we might say, was incidentally Jewish—which was quite enough to put her at risk in Nazi Germany.

The introduction of a handful of prominent Jews like Freund into the Argentine cultural elite via Ocampo and others no doubt played a subtle part in the establishment of Argentina's sense of itself as a modern, European nation. Ocampo, who commissioned the first modernist residence in Buenos Aires, and whose journal, *Sur*, introduced much contemporary European art, music, and writing to a Latin American readership, included numerous Jews in her modernizing project.[1] By the same token, the reaction in some quarters against Europhilic elitism may have been, in part, a response to the Jewish cast of characters whose presence made itself felt in Argentina in the 1930s and 1940s and beyond by antisemitic elements, for whom Jewishness is never simply incidental.

Incidental Jewishness is not just an attribute of some members of the intellectual and cultural elite, however. In recounting the history of his own family, Edgardo Cozarinsky explores incidental Jewishness from the angle of the seemingly unremarkable refugee families who settled in both the countryside and the city. Cozarinsky's paternal grandfather was the first child born in the Jewish Colonization Association's Santa Clara settlement. He was called Maurice Argentino, a name that sums up the story of the Jewish gaucho. Maurice, the Europeanized version of the Hebrew Moses or the Yiddish Moishe, carries the stamp of the baron, Maurice von Hirsch, who financed the Jewish agricultural settlements, and his middle name, as if in homage, lays claim to the national territory. For their part, Cozarinsky's mother's family were among the urban Jews who settled in the Once neighborhood of Buenos Aires. Neither family was religious, and neither was concerned with preserving Jewish traditions. Politically, they ranged from conservative to communist. The Cozarinskys never stopped identifying as Jewish, but they didn't much stop to think about it in their daily lives, either.[2] They were what Feierstein calls "Jews without Judaism" (1993, 376).

In the evolution, or devolution, into incidental Jewishness, it is as if the Jewish content of traditional Jews' lives has leached out of the individual and into the culture at large, where it is diluted and transformed, perhaps, but also transforms society in turn. Where Jewishness seems merely incidental, it often makes its mark quietly. In fact, the Jewishness of Feierstein's protagonist in *Mestizo* is both incidental to the plot and a crucial part of his own sense of alienation. Similarly, the fact that the victim is an Arab Argentine is meaningful but subordinated to her sexual history. The gender implications here are obvious: the male outsider recovers his sense of self and is, at least momentarily, integrated into society over the dead body of the sexualized outsider woman. Gender, sex, ethnicity, and politics also come together in the novel when a character named Chava (whose Hebrew name overdetermines her as a Jewish woman) is threatened with sexual violence for political activity that characterizes her Zionism as a form of Communism (134).

Chava's very legible Jewishness is far from incidental, but when Jewishness is incidental it may lead to or coincide with Jewish illegibility. Certainly the two overlap. It is unclear, for example, to what extent Jewish *tangueros* of the 1920s, 1930s, and 1940s gave up their own sense of themselves *as* Jews when they chose to change their names in order to be accepted in the world of tango.[3] Certainly, by hiding their Jewishness, they sought to be perceived as authentic to the world of tango. Nevertheless, their incorporation of Eastern European instruments and sounds to the music of tango, documented by both Nudler and Judkovski, makes an audible difference that might not be entirely intelligible. In the realm of the written word, the evidence of narrative fiction suggests that the Jewish diaspora in Argentina has woven its way into the nation's culture, but that it is often barely palpable. Incidental Jewishness stamps a subtle Jewish presence onto the text. It is like a watermark, visible if you look for it, or are aware of the likelihood of its presence. It asks for a minimal acknowledgment of Jewish presence in the national mix of cultures.

The uneasy assimilation characteristic of Jewishness in modernity is sometimes manifested in narratives whose characters are identifiable as Jews only by their names or associations; being Jewish seems peripheral to the performance of their daily lives. Mere traces of Jewishness in, for example, novels by Ernesto Sábato, Juan José Saer, and Vlady Kociancich and films by Julia Solomonoff and Fabián Bielinsky, which are peopled in part by such characters, map a quiet terrain of Jewish Argentina. The minor character who is a thoroughly assimilated Jew is more likely to find his or her way into books and movies by Jews than by non-Jews, though exceptions are not rare. Some of these narratives, like Sábato's, bear traces of antisemitism; others, like Saer's, include finely drawn, nonstereotypical Jews in their cast of characters.

Incidental Jewishness characterizes the individuals in these narratives, but it affects the entire culture as well. The mention of a Germanic or Eastern European–sounding name can call attention to the Jewish threads in the fabric of the world in which a story takes place. Sometimes an

Eastern European last name is the only sign of Jewishness in a text. When Humberto Costantini, for example, writes satirically of a group of quite bad poets pursued as political dissidents in *De dioses, hombrecitos y policías* (On gods, little men, and police), among them is a mélange of immigrants, including the probably, but only incidentally, Jewish "señorita Zimmerman" who stereotypically tries to raise money for the Communist Party.[4] Whether Jewishness is vestigial or simply normalized in these cases is a matter of perspective. Texts peopled by characters who are marked Jewish by their names or associations, but whose Jewish identity seems peripheral, map a quiet terrain of Jewish Argentina, as does the journal *Hispamérica*, which has unobtrusively showcased the work of Jews without announcing it as such. These cultural manifestations demonstrate that being Jewish can (not so) simply be another way of being Argentine.

In stark contrast to this subtle murmur of a deep connection to Jewishness is the visual and verbal overload of Jewish identity in Gabriel Lichtmann's 2014 film *How to Win Enemies* (*Cómo ganar enemigos*). The film opens with the ritual of the Jewish wedding, insistently highlighting its particularities: the canopy, the blessings in Hebrew, the breaking of the glass. Most of the main characters are Jewish, but the story of brotherly betrayal and retribution could be anyone's. The film is far too slight to claim biblical sources for the fraternal strife that is the motor of the plot.

Lichtmann's film is one variant of incidental Jewishness, in which displays of ritual mark as Jewish characters who in their daily lives are fully assimilated. In *How to Win Enemies* the wedding scene vividly establishes a Jewishness that is otherwise muted almost to the point of invisibility. Similarly, in Sebastián Dietsch and Ionantan Klajman's 2012 film *Mar del Plata* (named for the seaside resort), Jewishness is incidental to the film's slim plot, in which Joaquín Edelstein and his childhood friend David, both recently separated from their wives, take a weekend road trip to the resort. Joaquín reconnects with Elena, an old girlfriend; David meets a much younger local woman. For the purposes of the plot there is no particular reason for these childish and somewhat irritating men to be marked as Jewish, but the film is peppered with flashbacks that provide them with a Jewish background. Joaquín recounts his family's particularly Jewish immigration story, which includes a name change in Austria that allowed them to escape as Hitler was coming to power, and a flashback of Joaquin's wedding visually marks Jewishness with a traditional ceremony. Joaquín's Jewishness is made visible in a series of snapshots that in turn provoke the key memories that explain Joaquín's current emotional or psychological dilemma. Unlike the more expository memory sequences about his brief but intense relationship with Elena, however, the scenes that mark Jewishness provide, at best, a deep, albeit unstated, structure for understanding the character. The film's critics do not mention Jewishness in their reviews, and with good reason. Since Jewishness has nothing overtly to do with the plot, it seems gratuitous to mention it. Nevertheless, the writers deliberately mark Jewishness in the film, in which Joaquín has been displaced by a rival who is, apparently, not a Jew. The pompous, successful novelist Lautaro whom Elena has married has plagiarized a short story by a writer whose name marks him as Jewish: Eugenio Walter Valinsky. (In a meta-moment, Valinsky's name appears as the maker of the Vimeo version of the film's trailer.) The Gentile man thus establishes his dominance by succeeding where Jewish men fail: Lautaro gets both Elena and credit for Valinsky's work. The lesser masculinity attached to Jewishness that Daniel Boyarin writes about in *Unheroic Conduct* is a little embarrassing, and since the deliberately marked Jewishness of the protagonist is not overtly part of his present, public life, critics thoughtfully do not raise the delicate issue of what appears to be Jewish lesserness.

Jewishness in *Mar del Plata* is highly visible and completely legible, but it is still incidental. Similarly, Juan Carlos Kreimer's novel *Todos lo sabíamos* (We all knew) offers up a rich assortment of details of Jewishness that give color and texture to Kreimer's family saga about achieving and maintaining upper-middle-class status in Argentina. Still, at least one reviewer, Gabriel Lerman (whose own surname suggests that he is Jewish), finds the text bereft of what he calls "Jewish content." Lerman states adamantly that there is nothing particularly Jewish about this story, yet he goes on to note—in apparent self-contradiction—that it is sprinkled with Yiddishisms, tells the Jewish story of immigration, and dwells on the conventional Jewishness of key characters:

> The interesting thing about *We all knew*, the new novel by Juan Carlos Kreimer, is that the specificity of Jewishness, which is barely noticeable in the first chapters or in the ones that refer to his childhood and adolescence in Castelar, at no time recalls a kind of Jewish literature, nor does it try to situate the plot in a story about the Jewish community. Quite the opposite. Beyond very concrete references to Yiddish, to the traditional profile of his aunts, grandparents, and parents, almost all the characters, in particular those who were children and young people then and who are now adults, are set in the harshest and most corrosive

Argentine history, and they do no more than set the Millers, these Jews, on the path of a social class that got to the point of being able to buy 200 square meter apartments in the [prestigious] northern zone of the Capital and close to General Paz, when their grandparents counted lice in squalid and ill-smelling boats coming from Europe. (my translation)

[Lo interesante de *Todos lo sabíamos*, nueva novela de Juan Carlos Kreimer, es que esa especificidad de lo judío, que apenas puede rastrearse en los primeros capítulos o en los que refieren a la infancia y adolescencia en Castelar, en ningún momento envía a un tipo de literatura judía, ni intenta ubicar el relato en alguna trama cultural comunitaria. Por el contrario, más allá de referencias muy concretas al idish, al perfil tradicional de tías, abuelos y padres, casi todos los personajes, en particular los niños o jóvenes de entonces y los adultos de hoy, se engarzan plenamente sobre la más crujiente y ácida historia argentina, y no hacen más que instalar a los Miller, estos judíos, en el derrotero de una clase social que llegó a comprar departamentos de 200 metros cuadrados en zona norte de Capital y allende la General Paz, cuando sus abuelos se contaban las pulgas en barcos sórdidos y malolientes venidos de Europa. (n.p.)]

Lerman's point is that the story of the Kreimer family is deeply Argentine and only incidentally Jewish, even if their Jewishness is overt and obvious. Here Jewishness is decidedly legible, but it remains incidental, perhaps the best evidence of Jewishness as simply another mode of Argentineity.

For Lerman, the novel's Jewish ambiance is a minor detail precisely because the central problem of the novel is not Jewishness but Argentineity. It does not worry about the health or nature of the Jewish community or question the meaning of Jewish identity. These are taken for granted in this saga of a Jewish family in Argentina. The significant community here is the Argentine community, of which the Jewish family is a part. This is an immigrant story, universal in its applicability while specific in its details. Kreimer's novel is, then, an Argentine family story about a family that just happens to be Jewish. That "just happens to be" is not innocent, however. If on one level this family's Jewishness is simply one way among many of being Argentine, the novel can also be read as a Gerchunoffian challenge to dominant Argentineity, in which Jewishness is naturalized as a modality of

Argentineity. Kreimer paints a far bleaker picture than Gerchunoff, however. The material success of the assimilated family is inexorably marked by its spiritual poverty.

Daniel Birmajer's novel *La despedida* (The farewell) takes place in a similarly Jewish milieu, and the protagonist, Dreidel, as well as most of the other characters are Jewish. Like *Todos lo sabíamos*, the text makes little or nothing of the narrative of immigration, problems of assimilation, or the recording of a specifically Jewish Argentineity. In both texts, Jewishness is an attribute that emerges or recedes depending on the reader's own subject position. Jewishness is seamlessly folded into Dreidel's very Argentine idiosyncrasies. His preoccupation with aging, death, impotence, and lack of meaning are those of the modern subject, and his preoccupation with the loss of his friend Kler, who has withdrawn his friendship for reasons Dreidel cannot understand, is universal, especially when he discovers that the reason his old friend stopped talking to him was because Kler believed his wife was in love with Dreidel. Dreidel's work as a scriptwriter for video games, especially one into which he recycles the plots of classic Spanish literature and blends them with contemporary global politics, resonates with postmodernity's flattening out of culture. The response to this very successful game by political pundits and scholars who take its underlying politics very seriously is a very deft critique of postmodernism's solemnity and of conventional leftist politics.

*La despedida*, like *Todos lo sabíamos*, normalizes Jewishness. Nevertheless, there are signs of stress between Argentine society and the Jewishness the novel would have it embrace. When Dreidel begins to explain the meaning of *kippa* to a young Gentile woman she informs him that he need not bother—she has had Jewish boyfriends so she knows very well what the traditional male head-covering is. The Jewish character learns from the Gentile that Jewishness is not so strange to her after all. Yet Jewishness has apparently not permeated Argentine society to such an extent that Birmajer feels thoroughly at ease sprinkling his text with Yiddishisms, instead interrupting his story with footnotes explaining these terms to his readers.[5]

Then again, some of *La despedida*'s Jewish linguistic references remain untranslated. They are puns on names: Dreidel is the Hanukkah toy, a top that spins and falls—a good icon for this off-balance protagonist. His dead friend Kler's name means "clergy" in Polish, and a mysterious old woman who is something of a shaman turns out to be named Minián Rusha—a combination of the term denoting the quorum of men necessary for prayer (*minyan*), by extension the Jewish people (with the irony that it is a woman who carries the name of the ten-man minimum) and a cognate of *rusa*, colloquial Argentine for a Jewish woman. None of these names—Dreidel, Kler, Minián, Rusha—is a conventional name, Jewish or otherwise. Birmajer's onomastic wordplay appears to be directed toward a particular set of knowledgeable readers: Jews who will get the joke.

Much of *La despedida* is written in the minor key of Jewish humor, the humor of the self-deprecating underdog. As a protagonist Dreidel is wildly idiosyncratic and neurotic, nobody's idea of a hero. His penchant for announcing his impotence to any woman who shows the slightest interest in him forestalls both later embarrassment and any possibility of establishing a sexual relationship. It certainly plays on the trope of feeble Jewish masculinity. The novel is wryly humorous with a deep undertone of sadness for the loss of the friend and his friendship, and an overlay of fear of, tinged with a certain degree of contempt for, those who might have been implicated in disappearance and torture in the recent Argentine past but who live freely and with impunity. This mix of insight, anxiety, off-center perspective, and irony might easily be characterized as Jewish, but it is a Jewishness that is very much part and parcel of the modern, and specifically Argentine, condition. Birmajer, like Kreimer, attests to the notion that writers are not necessarily the most true to Jewishness when they represent the Jew as that which is most "other." The lesson of their novels is that Jewishness needs to be seen not just when it is obvious and different, but also when it is part of the flow and content of the norm. Andrés Neuman puts his finger on it when he speaks of his great-grandfather, whose very Jewishness is rendered as Argentine:

> That great-grandfather of mine, Sara Resnik's father, brought together certain contradictions that made him a perfect Argentine: a good conversationalist, funny but authoritarian, not entirely Jewish, twice an immigrant and host to immigrants. (my translation)
>
> [Aquel tatarabuelo mío, el padre de Sara Resnik, reunía determinadas contradicciones que hacía de él un perfecto argentino: buen conversador, cómico pero autoritario, no del todo judío, dos veces emigrado y anfitrión de inmigrantes. (91)]

Here is the modern Argentine: his Jewishness is foregrounded, but only to rescind its importance. To say that he is "not entirely Jewish" is to draw attention to that identity, only to set it aside, rendering it simultaneously present and absent. The old man's very use of language, his sardonic ("funny but authoritarian") sense of humor, his place among immigrants and as one himself, all supersede, but are also part of, his being Jewish. As the narrator makes clear, these are all quintessentially Argentinean traits; the overlaps are not only characteristic of each separately, but also emerge as Argentina becomes Jewish, and vice versa.

In contrast, overt signs of Jewishness are sparse in the world of assimilated Jews in Julia Solomonoff's 2009 film *El último verano de la Boyita*, released in English as *The Last Summer of La Boyita*. The rural setting of the movie is the province of Entre Ríos, one of the places where the Jewish agricultural colonies were established. When a nearby village's annual horseracing competition occurs, the soundtrack resonates as klezmer, but the music remains unremarked and very much in the background. Jewishness in the film emerges overtly only in a few specific moments of high contrast between the normalized Christianity of hegemonic Argentina and some deeply held Jewish belief or practice that it interrupts. Whereas the Jewish surname of the family in Solomonoff's earlier film, *Sisters* (*Hermanas*), serves only to enmesh the family wholly in the nondenominational Argentine problematic of a family split apart by state terror, *The Last Summer of la Boyita* establishes the family's incidental Jewishness in an early scene in which the child protagonist's mother finds an icon of the Virgin Mary as she is tucking her daughter into bed. Although the mother seems to pay little attention to the figure of the Virgin and regards with utter calm Jorgelina's explanation that the family's maid has given it to her so that she can learn to pray, she suggests that the child not mention it to her grandmother Sarah, whose very name underscores the fact that the family is Jewish. The little girl returns to the figurine later in the film, clutching at it and praying at the moment of her deepest distress.[6] This scene takes place at night, and the absence of the mother this time implies that the child is turning to the figure of the Virgin as a surrogate. The suggestion that Jorgelina not mention the Virgin icon to her grandmother displaces the mother's anxiety over assimilation onto an earlier generation, now superseded by a Jewish modernity in which a child's flirtation with Catholicism is regarded as best ignored. In a later scene, Jorgelina matter-of-factly affirms her Jewishness when, after asking what she is being given to eat and learning that it is pork, says she cannot eat it. For the child, Jewishness and Argentineity coincide perfectly naturally.

Curiously, the moment in which the assimilated mother is faced with the daughter's exposure to uninvited Catholic proselytizing occurs in another film set in the Argentine periphery, Paula Markovitch's *The Prize* (*El premio*), where Jewishness is also presumably incidental.[7] The film takes place during the dictatorship; the mother and daughter have left Buenos Aires in the wake of the disappearance of the child's father and his cousin. The only thing that marks the child protagonist as Jewish is her name: Cecilia Edelstein. Since the teacher calls the children by their surnames, the non-Hispanic (and to a lesser extent, non-Italian) Edelstein is repeated over and over. The name is never remarked upon, but its constant repetition reinforces Cecilia's difference in the small seaside town. The only other reference to Jewishness is Cecilia's learning how to say a Catholic prayer and cross herself, a skill she learns from her newfound best friend, Lucía, a classmate with whom she shares a school bench. When she comes home with this new ritual, which she practices over and over in bed next to her mother, the traumatized mother says nothing and registers a kind of dazed blankness. It is not that being Jewish is important in a religious way, but it is part of a web of family connections that dangerously distinguish Cecilia and her mother from the others in the provincial seaside town. They are urban and middle class, value reading and writing; they are articulate. In all these ways they are different from the other children in Cecilia's class, and presumably from their families. None of these traits is overtly Jewish, but they are all linked to a Jewish modernity that in the context of the dictatorship puts their lives at risk.

In *The Prize* and *The Last Summer of La Boyita*, the Jewish daughters of assimilated mothers confronted with the appeal of the dominant culture are both innocent and curious. The little girls in both these films are introduced to those aspects of Catholic practice that may be most appealing to a child—a personal relationship with the deity, the physical representation of a sacred mother figure—by caring, if ignorant, Catholics, in one case a child and in the other a domestic servant. In both films it is the mother who discovers her young daughter's newly learned Catholic practice; in both the daughter is curious about that practice, and Jorgelina especially is somewhat surreptitious in her repetition of the ritual, as though she knows it is illicit. The lure of Catholic ritual occurs at nighttime, in the intimacy of the child's bed. In both films the mother registers unease but decides that it is better not to make too much of the daughter's explorations, a sign of the mother's own assimilation and, simultaneously, her discomfort with too complete an embrace of the Gentile world. Being assimilated—or agnostic—does not mean embracing Catholicism, with its history of persecution and defamation of Jews, of which the child, presumably, knows nothing.

How to permit the child to explore, how to protect the child from all that knowledge of what it has often meant to be a Jew among Christians?

These modern, assimilated Jewish mothers are not outwardly devout, yet they still must deal with the moment of overt Catholic hegemony. Neither child is much altered by her brush with Catholicism, despite the scenes of them practicing these prayers and grasping the little figures of the Virgin. Each mother registers some level of discomfort with the daughter's flirtation with the dominant religion but decides that it is better to let the child work through it. The children also are a little unsure of what to do with this new knowledge that everyone but them seems to have. For them it is a moment of needing to figure out who they are and where they stand in relation to the dominant culture.[8] Pointing to these Jewish puncta makes them stand out, but in fact they are minor, almost imperceptible moments in these two films. They do not call attention to themselves, but they are there, normalizing and troubling Jewishness in the Argentine national imaginary. Both little girls are growing up to be incidentally Jewish, but the films suggest that they must learn to negotiate the interstitial space of acceptable alterity.

Ana Piterbarg's first feature film, *Everybody Has a Plan* (*Todos tenemos un plan*), set in the islands and canals of the Tigre Delta and in the cityscapes of Buenos Aires, is deeply Argentine not only in its settings, but also in its consideration of civilization and barbarism.[9] Within this world, none of the film's characters is marked Jewish, yet in the conversation between the twin brothers Pedro and Agustín, played by Viggo Mortensen, the one person they remember with fondness is "Old Rosenthal." All we know of this figure is that he was quite a character ("un personaje"). The Jewish-sounding name is mentioned more than once, but the moments are fleeting, and there are no details that might explain who he was or why the brothers remember him. It is a moment that notes the assimilation of Jews, and of whatever they might bring of Jewishness, into the Argentine landscape. Old Rosenthal is part of the Argentine, rural past of these two men. He is, by extension, part of what is most primeval about the nation—attached to the telluric and the violent, but in a way we do not ever learn. He is part of what pulls these brothers back together momentarily, what ties them to each other as family within the nation, in the moments before one murders the other and takes his identity.

The film was written by Piterbarg, but a number of her collaborators bear Jewish names (cowriter Ana Cohan; executive producer Mariela Besuievski; coproducers Christoph Friedel, Axel Kuschevatzky, and Julia

Solomonoff; and composer Federico Jusid). Whatever it is that might be Jewish about Piterbarg's colleagues is not overtly present in the film, and the fact of Jewishness as part of Argentine reality is no more central to the film than is the fact of the director's being a woman. The focus of the film is the male character, and although the film displays sympathy for them, the women characters have little meaning outside their relationships to the men. In other words, the identity of the filmmaker is subordinated here. The film treads the familiar heart-of-darkness plot and landscape (here the delta of El Tigre), but politics (sexual, ethnic, or national) don't enter into the film. Even Old Rosenthal may not have been Jewish at all.[10]

Another narrative of incidental, barely whispered Jewishness is Martín Kohan's novel *School for Patriots* (*Ciencias morales*), an examination of internalized repression and acquiescence to the abuse of state power, whose protagonist is a sexually repressed young Catholic woman working as a preceptor in a venerable Buenos Aires school.[11] The space in which the protagonist moves is overdetermined as national: the school is close to the Plaza de Mayo and the Cabildo, and its history is the history of Argentina, founded by the fathers of the nation. The students' inner lives are absent; we get a sense of their class position but little else. Still, early on the narrator notes that an element of disorder was injected into the school when girls were admitted. The inclusion of Italian and Jewish names in the roster of faceless students suggests another element of disorder that is nevertheless integrated into the school, and therefore the nation. Whereas the male student whose possible transgressions disturb the protagonist has an Italian surname, the Jewish family names are no more than the trace of a Jewish presence in Argentina. What is notable is that it is there at all. In other texts in which Jews are minor characters, their Jewishness tends to carry meaning. Here it is significant that it does not.

Similarly, Bebe Kamin's 1984 feature film *The Children of the War* (*Los chicos de la guerra*), which follows four adolescents conscripted to fight as it lays bare the brutality of the dictatorship and the irresponsible futility of the Falklands/Malvinas War it instigated, is the very incidentally but also discernibly Jewish Marcelo Rubín, the best friend of the film's protagonist. The only time Marcelo's Jewishness is salient is when the paramilitary find him and his friend Fabián breaking curfew and call him "ruso" ("Jew") as they kick the two terrified adolescents and threaten them with death. Kamin thus marks the character as Jewish and comments subtly on the dictatorship's entrenched antisemitism, but Marcelo is depicted primarily as an ordinary middle-class Argentine teenager who, like the other three young men in the film, is conscripted to fight in a war designed only to shore up a corrupt and brutal military government. Their antisemitism is of a piece with their overall brutality, but Marcelo's daily life is much the same as that of his Gentile best friend. This moment of antisemitic brutality, however, both underscores the state violence that is so close to the surface in the everyday world of Argentina under the junta and marks the particularity of Jewishness within that regime of violence.

Daniel Burman gets under the surface of incidental Jewishness in his 2008 film *The Empty Nest* (*El nido vacío*) to reveal a deep and ambivalent connection to Jewishness, particularly in its central male character, the middle-aged writer Leonardo. The film explores Leonardo's underlying connection with a deeper sense of Jewish loss and belonging masked by apparently incidental Jewishness, plowing another rich furrow in Argentine soil. In *The Empty Nest* Burman departs from his Ariel trilogy (which only much later became a quartet), in which his trio of young men named Ariel negotiates a passage from the bubble of Jewish Buenos Aires to, eventually, marriage with a Gentile woman, tracing a path that leads to an increasingly incidental Jewishness. *The Empty Nest*, the movie Burman made following the first three Ariel films, breaks with them: its protagonist is much older than the director himself is, is not played by Daniel Hendler, and is not called Ariel. As in the films by Solomonoff, Markovitch, and Kamin, nothing in the daily lives of *The Empty Nest*'s main characters suggests Jewish practice or a concern with Jewish identity. Jewishness is discernible only in the interstices—a family name, a tradition of naming a child for a dead relative, a menorah on a shelf.

Early in the film Leonardo, an uncomfortable outsider at his wife's class reunion, is asked by a woman how he defines himself. In response, Leonardo neglects to mention either ethnicity or nationality. His wife Martha tries to clarify his vague reply, but her answer is a bundle of negatives; she defines Leonardo by what he is not. Leonardo's somewhat shaky sense of himself is tied up, in the first instance, with his writing and his reputation, not his Jewishness. Leonardo has been a reasonably successful writer and the dominant figure in his family's life, but everything is beginning to shift around him. He has not been able to write for a while, his wife is returning to school and making new friends, and he is losing his starring role in his daughter's life. On the way home from the reunion, Martha informs him that their daughter has gone to a party and should not be expected home until the next morning. Leonardo's sense that he is neither quite successful enough nor really necessary to his family any longer is a pretty typical midlife-crisis moment, but to the extent that it also constitutes a feeling of being marginal in his world, it is also a subtle sign of both his Argentineity and his Jewishness. His fame as a writer is modest: his work is known in Argentina, but not beyond.

As we learn at the end of the film, the opening scenes in the restaurant, the car ride home, and Leonardo's declaration that he will wait up for his daughter and write are just the prelude to the fiction-within-the-film that makes up the bulk of the movie. As Leonardo's screenplay, the film-within-the-film can be read as an autobiographical projection of his own anxieties, in which the Jewishness that is suppressed in his everyday life returns with a vengeance. *The Empty Nest* quite literally enters Jewish territory when Leonardo imagines himself into a fully Jewish landscape, visiting his daughter, who is now married to an Israeli. Leonardo's middle-age identity crisis exposes one dilemma of Jewish identity in Argentina. The man who displaces him as the most important male figure in his daughter's life wears his Jewishness with ease and has achieved the international literary acclaim that has eluded the older man. The young, vigorous, successful version of masculinity against whom Leonardo implicitly measures his own diminution is Israeli, suggesting that Leonardo's barely perceptible Jewishness may be of more consequence than is at first obvious, subtly linking his invisible, incidental Jewishness to his fear of his own mediocrity. Leonardo's sense that he has never achieved the success, level of literary greatness, or international recognition that he had hoped for is intensified when his son-in-law's book wins a major literary prize and is translated into seven languages: The full flowering of authorship is reserved for the fully Jewish son-in-law. The younger man's book manuscript itself is bound in bright blood red, and Leonardo carries it with him like a wound, not able to bring himself to read it and telling himself and others that his daughter's husband is relying on his comments, those of a wiser, more experienced writer. The revelation that the book has outdone anything he himself has ever written is very quietly devastating.

Leonardo's screenplay, emotionally resonant but counterfactual, is as materially present on the screen as the frame story, the "real-life" story of the writer who is drying up, the middle-aged man who has not achieved literary greatness, the man who is being displaced as the central figure in the life of the women in his family. The next, vigorous generation threatens his primacy, his masculinity, and his very being as a Jew. Leonardo's Jewish identity is established and explored within the frame of his screenplay; inside that fictive world he can both experience his alienation and give it resolution. Being Jewish plays a role in Leonardo's estrangement from his family and his sense of being past his creative prime that it does not seem to play in his real life, and his Jewishness is implicated in the way he works through these problems. Still, in Leonardo's screenplay Jewishness is largely borne by others. His daughter and son-in-law move to Israel, and his wife's knowledge of Israeli dance gets them through Israeli airport security. Leonardo cannot even muster enough Hebrew to pronounce his son-in-law's name.

As in Burman's earlier film *Waiting for the Messiah*, the women in *The Empty Nest* seem to have no trouble integrating Jewishness, modernity, and Argentineity. In *Waiting for the Messiah* Jewishness is far from incidental; rather it is at the crux of the young protagonist's struggle to reconcile Jewishness with Argentineity and to escape the claustrophobic Jewish life that has been mapped out for him. Ariel's goal seems to be to make his Jewishness incidental, but the world he enters will not let him do that. His long-suffering girlfriend, Estela, brings a modern touch to their Jewish neighborhood but remains fully within its boundaries. Her ease with her Jewishness is not unlike Martha's in *The Empty Nest*, whose exuberant performance of Jewishness at the airport contrasts with Leonardo's own reticence.

Estela, Leonardo, and Martha are not foreigners in Argentina; their diaspora is the diaspora of new roots, flowers, and tendrils. Raanan Rein (2010) notes the subtle shift in identity: when Jews are also Argentines are they Jewish Argentines or Argentine Jews? The relationship between adjective and noun denotes a change not only in emphasis, but in what is essential and what may modify that essence, and in posing the question he also suggests, paradoxically, that essence is not quite so permanently essential. In the Tel Aviv airport, Martha blithely performs her Jewishness: she is an Argentine Jew for the purposes of Israeli airport security. But at home in Buenos Aires she is very much a Jewish Argentine, with the emphasis on the proper noun.

The family's visible lack of attachment to a Jewish identity in Buenos Aires, followed by a very Jewish emplacement in the second half of the film, suggests several possible readings. On the one hand, the film handily represents assimilated Jews who maintain a sense of being Jewish but who do not practice, or who practice minimally. The visual representation of Israel and its presence in the imagination of the writer indicate that even though his daily life in Buenos Aires is not outwardly Jewish, his sense of Jewishness is deeply felt. Nevertheless, the secular, assimilated way Leonardo lives his life is overridden by his subconscious and his anxiety about Jewishness. What he has left behind is what he imagines his beloved daughter is drawn to.

Burman's film-within-a-film can be understood as a manifestation of his protagonist's unconscious.[12] Written in a one-night jag after months of writer's block, Leonardo's screenplay gushes out like the return of the repressed it seems to be. The dreamlike bulk of the film even contains its own Jewish analyst in the person of Spivak, a paternal figure who not only observes and understands Leonardo's desire and his anxiety, but who offers a kind of talking cure for it. Spivak, a research neurologist, is a wise and detached observer. No one ever says that he is Jewish, but his aspect, his surname, his profession, and the fact that he eventually turns up on an Israeli beach strongly suggest it. Spivak functions as an embodied superego in the film, appearing at the most astounding moments and in the most unexpected places, including when Leonardo is flying his remote-control model airplane in a Buenos Aires park or sunning himself at the Dead Sea. In the frame story, he is the only one at Martha's reunion who notices Leonardo ogling the beautiful young woman who will metamorphose into the fantasy dentist Leonardo seduces. The neurologist's job is to get inside people's heads and figure out how they work, and Spivak's recurring presence is a manifestation of Leonardo's need for disentangling his feelings and desires. Like Leonardo, Spivak is not one of the former classmates but a tag-along husband, and therefore not quite an insider in this gathering. In this sense the two men occupy the symbolic place of the Jew in Argentina.

Leonardo's lack of overt attachment to a Jewish identity in Buenos Aires, followed by a very Jewish emplacement in the second half of the film, suggests that however incidental Jewishness may seem on the surface, it can hold a profound personal meaning. The visual representation of Israel and its presence in Leonardo's imagination indicate that even though his daily life in Buenos Aires is not outwardly Jewish, his sense of Jewishness is deeply felt. The fact that Jewishness can be incidental is a function of assimilation and a level of acceptance by the larger society. It is part and parcel of Jewishness as a mode of Argentineity.

Edgardo Cozarinsky's short story "Real Estate" (Bienes raíces) is a complex study of incidental Jewishness of a different sort, as it keeps in play both claims on, and refusals of, identity. The story shifts between first- and third-person narration, even as the point of view remains that of the first-person narrator, a figure whose Jewishness seems incidental until the end. The fact of Jewishness as an Argentine phenomenon appears at first only to account for the space in which the story takes place—a parcel of land in the old JCA colonies. It also provides the rationale for the narrator's visit: his desire to sell that plot of inherited land. This small quest, with its superficial and not emotionally compelling motive, brings him, however, to a complex realization about his identity and moral standing. He enters the situation contemptuous of and annoyed with his brother (upon whom he goes to great lengths to bestow that title, rather than "half brother"), a younger man who, despite his university education, has elected to spend his days unproductively in this primitive place, built of mud, with a dirt floor and a latrine out back. As the reader slowly learns that this land is the family inheritance as Argentine Jews, and that the worthlessness of the property is sealed by its being located at the wall of what was the local school and is now an insane asylum, the narrator discovers that the mother who abandoned him and his father, who ran away with a Gentile man, lived in Spain, and bore another son, is now inside the asylum, and that the brother has come to live in what is left of the family's hovel in order to be near her. The brother, identified at the end of the story as "the goy," the other, is, ironically, the one who closes the Jewish circle, who carries the Jewish mother with him, unlike the true Argentine, the legitimate—but abandoned—Jewish son. The story opens up the question of just who the true son is. Spain may be Argentina's mother country, but for the Spanish son, the ancestral homeland, imagined through the mother, is Argentina. He has lived his life as a Gentile and is known as "the goy" when he goes back to his mother's Jewish village in Argentina, but as the son of a Jewish woman, however lapsed, he can claim a Jewish identity. The last line of the story implies a depth of contradictory feeling about the mother, and about the narrator's sense of self, by newly describing the brother who had been the object of his disdain:

> What I could never have dreamt was that the only one to stay with her would be my brother, the only one, the good one, the Spaniard, the goy, the other half. (2004, 42)

> [Lo que no podía imaginar es que al final se la iba a guardar mi hermano, él solo, él, el buen hijo, el gallego, el goi, el otro. (2001, 58)]

This half-brother is the subject, against whom the narrator defines himself: the non-son, the bad son, the Argentine, the Jew, the half of the pair that is "other." Until this moment, the narrator has never described himself as a Jew, although his family history makes it clear that he is Jewish. His sense of being yanked from the center—of the story, of moral rectitude, of sensible behavior—is the climax of the narrative and is inextricably bound up with Jewishness. As in *The Empty Nest*, incidental Jewishness turns out to be the real life that is also a screen. Both Cozarinsky's narrator and Burman's screenwriter are fully assimilated and seem to wear their Jewishness lightly. Nevertheless, at a critical moment their Jewishness comes crashing down on them, not as a stable identity but rather as a complex of ethical, emotional, and relational challenges. Both "Real Estate" and *The Empty Nest* serve to demonstrate that although incidentality is by definition subsidiary, incidental Jewishness is not trivial. On the contrary, its presence suggests underground currents and connections that remain knotted, tangled, and contained.

CHAPTER SEVEN

# EMBEDDED JEWISHNESS

Memory and the State in Times of Terror

Jews in Argentina, like their counterparts in the United States, have shed much of their Oriental otherness. Assimilated Jews go about their daily lives virtually invisible as such to the larger society, incidentally Jewish. This incidental Jewishness is largely a property of individuals, for, clearly, observant Jews hardly wear their Jewish identity lightly. Incidentality, for its part, is an effect of a deeper cultural phenomenon, what I am calling "embedded Jewishness." Jewishness is embedded in Western history and culture generally and in the specifically Argentine version of that history and culture. Embeddedness implies both the difference between that which is embedded and its host and the breach of boundaries between two things so closely integrated. Embedded Jewishness can tool along unnoticed, modifying the larger society even as it is modified in turn. It is also, however, available for extirpation, demonization, and reinsertion in the space of otherness. Christians in the United States, for example, often conscript Jews into a common project when they announce their "Judeo-Christian" tradition and values. The adjective-noun construction, however, subsumes Jewishness into Christianity, which in turn supersedes it. At moments embedded Jewishness can be perceived, but unlike incidental Jewishness (to which it is related), it is always deeply meaningful, even though unspoken, whereas the point of incidental Jewishness is its apparent insignificance.

Embeddedness understood this way can explain why the integration of Jews and Jewishness into Argentina and Argentineity is real but not absolute. Moreover, embedded Jewishness is not equally benign from one historical moment to another. In times of state terror, the stakes are especially high and the challenges considerable in maintaining the both/and of Jewish Argentineity in the face of anti-Jewish sentiment that is embedded along with Jewishness itself. The precarious nature of Jewish belonging became particularly clear during the military junta of 1976–1983, with its symbolic and historical links to the Holocaust, but Jews' shaky hold on Argentineity was presaged in an earlier time of right-wing political repression. As Santiago Kovadloff argues, after a period of more or less benign acceptance in Argentina, Jews were reinserted into the constricting space of otherness with the military coup of 1930, when (coincident with the rise of Fascism and Nazism that he does not mention, perhaps because it is so obvious) Catholicism became a precondition for truly belonging to the nation. Adherence to the Church was not only a requirement for the presidency, it was a virtual prerequisite for serving in the military as well. Such exclusionary requirements for those aspects of citizenship linked to governance and maintaining order were encoded and justified in Virgilio Filippo's antisemitic text *Los judíos* (*The Jews*), published in the critical year of 1939. Filippo's screed, in turn, finds an echo in the suspicion cast on psychoanalysis as corrupt and corrupting during the military dictatorship of the 1970s and 1980s. Federico Finchelstein (2007) shows how Filippo's antisemitic rhetoric conflates sexual and physical degeneracy both with the Jewish body and with psychoanalysis as a potential contaminant of Argentine Catholic purity that ought to be excluded from the body politic. Presaging Finchelstein, Kovadloff maintains that the squeezing out of Jews from full citizenship during the series of on-again-off-again military governments between 1930 and 1976 laid the groundwork for the extreme othering of Jews during the near-decade of dictatorship that began in 1976. The incremental marginalization of Jews beginning in 1930 set the stage for their (discursive, but also actual) extirpation in 1976, as the Jew/outlaw became identified with the subversive/outlaw.

The focus of Kovadloff's discussion shifts from "the Jew" to civil society in general, which (so the dominant narrative argues) permitted the rise of the *guerrilla*—the armed opposition to the repressive state. This discursive shift, in which the marginalization of Jews gives way to the marginalization of civil society, which itself must be punished for fostering subversion (i.e., that the *guerrilla* emerges from civil society), retains its underlying connection to Jewishness; both are enmeshed in the opposition to the state that had, earlier, not only embraced them but was constituted by them. The actual confluence of Jews and the *guerrilla*, where it took place, was the occasion for especially severe, and often markedly antisemitic, punishment. The embedded Jew is elided into the embedded subversive, to be excised from the body politic.¹

The mechanization of death, the use of modern record-keeping techniques for the purposes of state terror, and the industrial precision of concentration camps constitute the horrific side of the modern that characterized Nazi Germany. In Argentina, Jewish writers and artists in particular signal the ways that the campaign against so-called subversives during the military dictatorship of 1976–1983 incorporated these practices in pursuing what the junta itself called its "dirty war." During the dictatorial regime, the state named an internal other that it endeavored to extirpate, one that mapped easily onto the historic trope of the Jew as other in Western culture. That made actual Jews more likely suspects in a nation whose right wing had in the past embraced the Nazi ideology associated with the horrific modern, to say nothing of its harboring of actual Nazis. There may have been no direct targeting of Jews *as* Jews under the dictatorship, but Jews, always and forever linked to subversion in the mind of the antisemitic right, were overrepresented as targets of state terror. Quite simply, the apparatus of state violence in Argentina deliberately took on the methods, trappings, and vocabulary of Nazi Germany and singled out Jews in ways that deliberately invoked Nazi practice. As a result, Jews appeared among their victims in disproportionate numbers. "Jew" was code for "subversive," even as the regime denied that Jewishness mattered at all. Alicia Dujovne Ortiz captures this deliberate, menacing paradox in her fictionalized memoir, *Las perlas rojas* (The red beads). As her protagonist is preparing to leave Argentina for Paris, just as left-leaning journalists are beginning to be disappeared, she is interviewed by an official who holds a dossier on her.² Among the intimidating questions he asks is, "Are you Jewish?" which he immediately follows with, "that's okay; it doesn't matter to me."³ The very claim of indifference to Jewishness serves here as a threat.

It is not so much *being* a Jew as it is *representing* the Jewish link to the left that puts Dujovne Ortiz's protagonist in jeopardy. In teasing out a distinction between traditional and ideological antisemitism in Argentina's right-wing political organizations throughout the twentieth century, historian Sandra McGee Deutsch illuminates the difference. Deutsch argues that traditional antisemitism, whose basis is religious, stands in contrast to ideological antisemitism, which tends to attach Jews to those aspects of modernity that the radical right rejects: democratic reform, syndicalism, socialism, internationalism. Whereas traditional antisemitism is largely a phenomenon of the masses, Deutsch argues, ideological antisemitism tends to be found among the elites (1986).

The Delegation of Argentine Jewish Organizations (*Delegación de Asociaciones Israelitas Argentinas*), known by its acronym, DAIA, was established in part to help Argentine Jews negotiate the underlying hostility of Argentine Christian society, but it did little to intervene on behalf of its constituents caught up in the machinery of state terror. The DAIA eventually released a meaningful report whose contents made clear the brutality of Argentina's 1976–1983 dictatorship and its effect on the Jewish community, but during the years of state terror the DAIA's leadership was hardly heroic.[4] As the official liaison between the Jewish community and the government, the organization was at least passively complicit with the military junta during its time in power. The DAIA leadership pointed out that Jewish institutions were not under attack, and they responded to the petitions of parents of disappeared children with little sympathy as well as with some of the junta's own cruel and hypocritical admonitions concerning wayward offspring and parental responsibility. Sara Rosenberg's novel *Un hilo rojo* (A red thread, 2000), depicts this fracture at the level of the family itself. When leftist activist Julia Berenstein is detained by government forces, her cousin Marcos, now the head of the engineering firm founded by Julia's father, collaborates with them instead of intervening on behalf of his own family member. The military is the company's main client, and Marcos is not about to jeopardize that relationship. Their grandfather, himself a radical in his day, does not forgive him this betrayal.

As a mainstream organization, the DAIA behaved with the same mix of complacency, self-interest, and fear that afflicted society as a whole, exacerbated by the underlying threat of antisemitism lurking just beneath the surface of the junta's language and practices.[5] The DAIA's *Special Report on Jewish Detained and Disappeared (1976–1983)*, which appeared at the beginning of 1984, is a study in self-justification. It underplays the dictatorship's brutality, grossly underestimates the number of Jewish disappeared, and implies that the disappeared were somehow responsible for their own victimization.

In the year 2007 the DAIA published a second study detailing the atrocities of the junta, *Report on the Situation of Jewish Detained and Disappeared During the Genocide Perpetrated in Argentina 1976–1983*, which not only characterizes the state terror of the period as genocide, but takes responsibility for the organization's weak response during the years of dictatorship. This DAIA report is an important source of information on the

Jewish targets of the repressive state and on the nature of the treatment they received (Braylan et al. 2007). Taken together, the DAIA reports work to establish the Nazi-junta parallel. At the same time, their juxtaposition reflects the complex relationship between Jewish and Argentine modernity in which Jews are simultaneously a part of and apart from the larger culture.

A panoply of films, artworks, novels, and *testimonios* make manifest the cultural presence of the junta-Nazi link using a range of methods, including journalistic reportage, historiography, and artistic creation separately and in conjunction with one another.[6] Alicia Partnoy, herself a survivor of one of the torture centers, wrote a testimonial text called *The Little School*, in whose introduction she notes that in the torture center the line between fact and storytelling is blurred. "Beware," she warns us, "in little schools the boundaries between story and history are so subtle that even I can hardly find them" (18). Similarly, Andrés Rivera weaves nonfictional texts into his novel *Kadish*:

> Arturo Reedson read, weeks before, in an issue of *Ñ*, that in the book *Zikaron-Memory: Jews and Soldiers during the Terror of Plan Condor*, whose author is the journalist Guillermo Lipis, are the following lines: "Declassified materials from the U.S. Department of State indicate that the leadership of the Argentina Jewish community organization, DAIA, affirmed that the dictatorships were not antisemitic in themselves, but that there were pockets of entrenched antisemitism consisting in individuals who exercised antisemitism in the Armed Forces; but this affirmation of the nonexistence of organic antisemitism does not jibe with the number of reported cases of kidnappings and disappearances, as well as kidnappings of Jewish entrepreneurs of the time." . . . "In this space of political laxity, between what was asserted and what actually happened, between 1,800 and 2,000 disappeared members of the Jewish community were slipped in." (my translation)

> [Arturo Reedson leyó, semanas atrás, en un número de *Ñ*, que en el libro, *Zicarón-Memoria. Judíos y militares bajo el terror del Plan Cóndor*, cuyo autor es el periodista Guillermo Lipis, se encuentran estas líneas: "Materiales desclasificados del Departamento de Estado de Estados Unidos indican que la dirigencia de la DAIA afirmaba que las dictaduras no fueron antisemitas en sí mismas,

sino que existían bolsones de antisemitismo enquistados que eran los que ejercían el antisemitismo en las Fuerzas Armadas, pero esa afirmación de la inexistencia de un antisemitismo orgánico no condice con la cantidad de casos denunciados de secuestros y desapariciones, así como secuestros de empresarios judíos de aquella época" . . . "En ese espacio de laxitud política, entre lo que se afirmaba y lo que efectivamente sucedía, se colaron entre 1.800 y 2.000 desparecidos de la colectividad." (59–60)]

It is not just the content of this passage that reveals the levels of subtlety between official and actual antisemitism, the apparent desire of the official, good-citizen Jewish organization to differentiate between the generals running the government and the colonels running the torture centers, but also the dense discursive fabric around Argentine antisemitism—the fictional alter ego of the author, the article in the magazine that quotes the book that quotes the official documents of the US State Department, that quotes the DAIA officials, and then loops back to report on the police reports filed, presumably by family members, on the disappeared Jews. Each of these has its own stake in the complex consisting of Argentina, dictatorship, Jewishness, and antisemitism.

As the DAIA reports and other sources show, Argentines were somewhat less utilitarian than the Germans in their campaign of state terror.[7] Rather than eliminating the weak and working the rest to death as slave labor, they tortured to intimidate and extract information, and they murdered, either in ways that they could exploit to promote their case to the rest of the populace (e.g., using newspaper accounts to argue that the dead had been killed as a result of an armed attack on the government by the victims themselves) or that kept those deaths secret (e.g., mass burials in remote parts of the country, or dropping drugged prisoners from airplanes into the sea). They were also less thorough in their purging: some clandestine prisoners resurfaced into official prisons, some were released and permitted to go into exile. Nevertheless, the imprint of Nazism on the Argentine regime was strong, particularly when Jews were its targets. As the second DAIA report shows, Jews were overrepresented among the detained and disappeared, numbering their presence in the ranks of the disappeared at least five times their proportion of the population, and likely higher (Braylan et al. 2007, 19). Other sources set their estimates of Jews among the disappeared somewhat lower, calculating the percentage to be between five and twelve, in a population that was only about one percent Jewish. Still, among the estimated thirty thousand detained and disappeared during the dictatorship, at least two thousand have been identified as Jews.

The Jewish otherness suspect during the dictatorship is that of the embedded other who is also the same, in that uncanny way that is so unsettling to an authoritarian regime that demands clarity and neat delineation. From the perspective of Argentina's dominant Catholic culture, the almost-familiar nature of modern Argentine Jewishness is a sort of perilous entryway, neither here nor there, into an imagined, more absolute, otherness. This liminal space separating and connecting one world to another is no neat dividing line, but rather the ample territory of what Gloria Anzaldúa, in another context, has called the borderlands. Ricardo Feierstein's 2001 novel *La logia del umbral* (The lodge of the threshold) embraces these borderlands as a Jewish space. The secret society of the title is a projection of the dominant culture, but it is one that has taken on a certain reality. When the protagonist's grandfather writes, "I belong to the Lodge of the Threshold. It is our destiny but also our choice," he is acknowledging that the meaning of Jewishness is produced by both Jews and the non-Jews among whom they dwell. [Pertenezco a la *logia del umbral*. Es nuestro destino, pero también nuestra elección (2001, 44–45, my translation).]

Samuel's family name, Schvel, translates as "threshold," so we might read him as the embodiment of the secret society that in turn is a metaphor for Judaism. Schvel's grandfather, a student of Kabbalah, links the family to the Lodge of the Threshold:

> Here, for example, he says: "the metaphor of Judaism, which defines us, is 'being somewhere else.'" We're here and we're not. That is why we are the manifestation of the "*threshold*," the borderline between parts, what connects and separates at the same time. That's us. (my translation)
>
> [—Acá, por ejemplo, dice: "la metáfora del judaismo, la que nos define, es 'estar en otra parte'. Estamos y no estamos. Por eso somos la manifestación del '*umbral*,' el límite entre partes, lo que comunica y separa a la vez. Eso somos." (44)]

The "being somewhere else" that is the family patriarch's definition of Judaism refers to an elsewhere from the original biblical homeland, the state of diaspora effected by the destruction of the Temple, but it plays out as not-quite-belonging in the modern nations of the world, including Argentina.[8]

Feierstein's protagonist, Samuel Schvel, is arrested and tortured in 1978, on suspicion that he knows something about the Lodge of the Threshold. Although all the details of Samuel's torture coincide with those undergone by people detained and disappeared by the junta, in the novel the cruelty he endures is framed in terms of his being a Jew, ever and always a member of the Lodge. The unmarked prison and the quasi-state that kidnaps and tortures suspected members of the Lodge of the Threshold are utterly intertwined with the clandestine war waged on the amorphous subversives; that is, anyone who roused the junta's suspicion of being insufficiently amenable to the tenets of the right wing, including non-Catholics and especially Jews.

It is not just literary texts, but the dictatorship's own use of antisemitic language and its targeted treatment of Jews, together with events like the bombings of the Israeli Embassy in 1989 and the Buenos Aires Jewish cultural center in 1993, that bring into sharp focus both the precarious place and the visibility of Argentine Jews and Jewishness. Three of the most compelling *testimonios*, firsthand accounts written by survivors of the junta's clandestine prisons, are those of Jacobo Timerman, Alicia Partnoy, and Sara Strejilevich. All three are Jews, and they all document these practices. Still, Timerman, Partnoy, and Strejilevich reflect, and reflect on, Jewishness in quite different ways, ranging from the marginal in Alicia Partnoy's *The Little School* (released many years later in Spanish as *La escuelita*), to acknowledged importance in Strejilevich's *A Single, Numberless Death* (*Una sola muerte numerosa*), to centrality in Timerman's *Prisoner without a Name, Cell without a Number* (*Preso sin nombre, celda sin número*).

Timerman's book was published in Spanish in 1980 and in English in 1981, several years before the dictatorship ended. An urgent and timely text, it was met with an enthusiastic reception in the international press and was soon made into a television movie starring Roy Scheider and Liv Ullmann. Timerman's position as a noted journalist before his imprisonment is perhaps another reason that his has been the most widely circulated of the three *testimonios*, and it still has great currency. Rereleased in both English and Spanish in 2015, it was named one of the twentieth century's most important books by *The New York Times*. In *Prisoner without a Name, Cell without a Number* and in his subsequent writing and statements, Timerman emphasizes the antisemitic treatment he received at the hands of his abductors and torturers.

At the other end of the spectrum, Partnoy, whose book *The Little School* first appeared in translation in 1986, published by a feminist press in the United States, was at first read primarily by women's rights activists, members of the human rights community, and academic feminists.[9] Now a respected scholar, poet, and human rights activist, Partnoy was, at the time of her imprisonment, just one more disappeared student whose Jewishness was, on her own account, incidental. She writes of her political engagement in left-wing Peronism that was at the center of her sense of identity as well as the immediate cause of her detention. Partnoy's being Jewish was of interest primarily to others, including her liberation-theology Catholic comrades, for whom a Christian commitment to social justice and the solace of religion were the bedrock of their activism. They wondered at the source of Partnoy's commitment, she who was not only a Jew but an atheist as well. Also interested in her Jewishness were Partnoy's captors, who taunted and threatened her in antisemitic terms that she responds to with derision. In fact, the humor that is one of the remarkable aspects of her *testimonio* coalesces in great part around her mockery of the would-be Nazism of her torturers. Scorning their Nazi-referenced threats to turn her into soap, for example, she remarks that they do not have sufficient technological skills for that (Partnoy 1986, 61).

Nora Strejilevich's testimonial novel *A Single, Numberless Death* (*Una sola muerte numerosa*), on the other hand, appeared in Spanish in 1997 and in English in 2002, when the world's attention had largely moved on from a dictatorship that had ended in 1983. The book won an international prize and has been translated into English, but it has not had the impact of either Timerman's account or Partnoy's. Nevertheless, it is a brilliant novel and has been the subject of a number of academic studies.[10] Strejilevich does not minimize Jewishness in her account; she details the antisemitic nature of her torture and, writing on the boundary between memoir and fiction, she adds affective weight to the drier historical accounts of the special treatment borne by Jews when they were in the hands of the junta's henchmen. Strejilevich recounts that when she was kidnapped she yelled out her name so that people would know who she was, but her captors accused her of sending secret messages in a foreign, Jewish language. They did not recognize her surname as a name at all, but rather heard its unfamiliar sound as a subversive statement.

Torturers who invoked the Holocaust in their treatment of Jews suspected of being dissidents emphasized the Jewishness of their victims, whose Jewishness was now clearly legible and far from incidental. Jews were targeted for special treatment, which the DAIA report breaks down into the following categories:

a) Antisemitic actions at the moment of abduction or detention;

b) Specific types of torture and humiliation inflicted on Jews during their stay in the concentration camps;

c) Usage of Nazi language, terminology or symbols;

d) 'Special' interrogations for the Jews;

e) Illegal appropriation of assets: extortion (2000, 12)

There are echoes of the Holocaust in all five categories. Yet because the Holocaust is so universally recognized as the paradigm case of state brutality, the resonances of the Holocaust in memories and representations of the dictatorship have become generalized. In Argentina, this assimilation of Jewish meaning into its own historical narrative may cause the particularity of Jewishness to fade. This oscillation between visibility and invisibility is at the heart of the discussion that follows. The salience of Jewishness in stories of the Holocaust by Jewish authors and filmmakers is inevitable—perhaps tautological, just as it is in Argentine Jewish family stories that begin with turn-of-the-century escape from the pogroms of Eastern Europe.

Diaspora narratives, which reimagine centuries-long stories of Jewish peregrination or midcentury immigration stories of Jews in Argentina, necessarily highlight Jewishness. Many Jews looked for refuge in Argentina because it was, for a time, open to Jewish refugees and because many had family there already. According to the *Holocaust Encyclopedia*, between 1933 and 1943 twenty-four thousand European Jews entered Argentina legally; another twenty thousand crossed the border without official government sanction. After the war, at least forty-eight hundred Holocaust survivors settled in Argentina.[11]

The cycle of narratively potent stories of displacement and migration rooted in the Holocaust was created by artists, filmmakers, and writers who stood in the same relationship to their stories as Alberto Gerchunoff stood to his. The memory of the Jewish past they recount is only a generation old. As the children of those who either survived the Holocaust or escaped Europe before it was too late, they feel intimately the resonances of the critical historical event that impelled their parents' move. The trauma of the Holocaust has engendered in them another kind of Jewish memory, transmitted through the body. The injunction to remember, "*Zakhor*," present in the "never again" of the Shoah, impels the struggle to verbalize what has been transmitted through the body itself.[12] Central to these post-Holocaust texts is the narrativization of silence itself. Marianne Hirsch calls it postmemory, and it is often characterized by the absence of verbal narrative.

Visual artist Guillermo Kuitca's installation of child-size mattresses makes oblique reference to the trajectory of Jews during World War II. Stained, as if bloody, they trace maps of Europe. His contemporary, Mirta Kuperminc, makes more overt reference to the Holocaust. The daughter of survivors who met and married after the war, Kuperminc's *Ghosts at the Lodz Ghetto* puts on canvas and paper her own family history and the long-delayed discovery of a half-brother who died at the hands of the Nazis. Like many survivors, Kuperminc's father did not speak of his first wife and family, all of whom were killed.

Haunted by the Holocaust, Kuperminc's canvases repeatedly examine her parents' trajectory from Europe to Argentina, sometimes stitched onto the very skin of the artist's hand. Her numerous images of the uprootedness of diaspora include paintings and prints of streams of fanciful refugees, some bearing their belongings, others unencumbered, and still others dragging symbolic trees, roots and all. Figures of Eastern European Jews haunt the corners of her canvases and hide under her sculptural chairs, and bleak landscapes of diaspora drop like oil blots onto the visual surface.

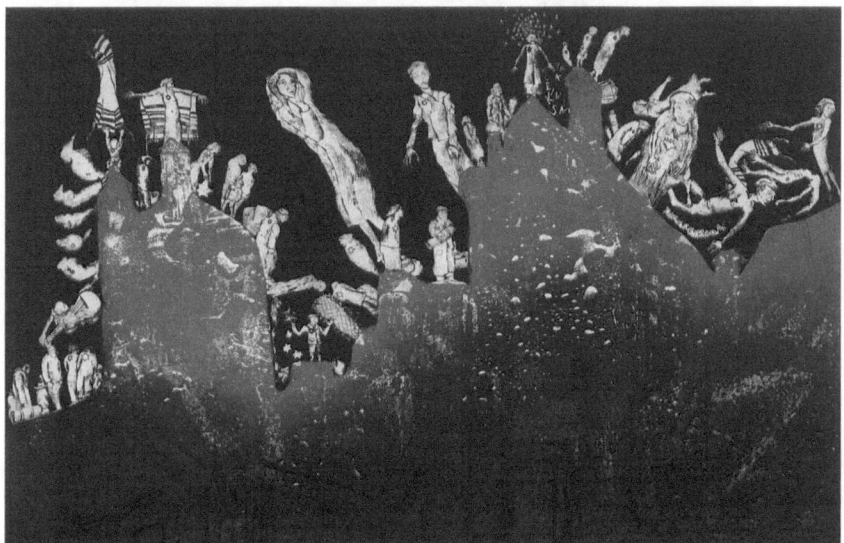

Figure 7.1. Mirta Kuperminc, *Ghosts at the Lodz Ghetto (In Daniel Kuperminc's memory)* [*Fantasmas en el ghetto de Lodz (En memoria de Daniel Kuperminc)*], 2000. Etching, 23.62 in. × 35.43 in. *Source*: Reprinted by permission of the artist.

Figure 7.2. Mirta Kupferminc, *That Place* (*Ese lugar*), 2007. Etching, 25.59 in. × 31.50 in. *Source*: Reprinted by permission of the artist.

Kupferminc turns the number tattooed on her mother's arm into a site of memory by virtue of repetition. It appears in multiple works, sometimes on its own, but at others (and to my mind most rivetingly), apparently casually observed as just one more physical aspect of her mother.

There are no images of Kupferminc's father's concentration camp number, however, because, the artist explains, he died before she began to create these pieces and she does not remember what it was. In other words, historical accuracy matters, and not everything can be passed on from generation to generation. Tattoos are an important motif in much of Kupferminc's work, most notably in her 2007 installation *The Skin of Memory*. Visitors to the exhibit, which was held at the Recoleta Cultural Center in Buenos Aires, were given temporary tattoos, randomly assigned.[13] Some had decorative designs stamped on their arms, while others got concentration camp numbers, so that the viewer's own body became the site of meaning production. Kupferminc's art of memory centers on the Holocaust, which directly marked the lives of her parents, rather than on Argentine state terror. When Kupferminc turns overtly to violence on Argentine soil it is to memorialize the victims of the AMIA bombing, with a sculpture that stands on the grounds of the site.

Kupferminc's joint installation with writer Manuela Fingueret, *La vida espuma* (Seafoam life), is much less overt in its reference to anti-Jewish violence than some of her earlier work. Her sculpture on the exhibit's poster combines the natural forms of trees with spikey, colorful wooden pencils arranged like cascading thorns; other images refer back to her embroidery, the motif of the artist's hands, to the colored pencils (now orderly). Fingueret's poems range over a variety of themes, including memory and forgetting, and a fleeting reference to the Holocaust. Fingueret's novel *Daughter of Silence* (*Hija del silencio*), on the other hand, delves mercilessly into it.

The novel confounds temporality itself, meshing past and present in its exploration of the precariousness of the subject under conditions of state terror. *Daughter of Silence* is particularly revealing when read in conjunction with Sergio Chejfec's *Lenta biografía* (Slow biography). Both novels recount traumatic history together with the impossibility of its full transmission, one through maternal lines and the other through the story of the father. Rita, the narrator of *Daughter of Silence*, tries to create a coherent account of her mother Tinkeleh's experience as a survivor of Terezin and Auschwitz as a way of trying to survive her own torture at the hands of the dictatorial state. Torture is meant to break its victim physically and mentally. By reconstructing Tinkeleh's story of trauma and survival, Rita struggles to withstand the brutality she is being subjected to, until at last she falls silent in a way that signals to the reader that her torturers have succeeded in killing her. Constructing a coherent narrative, particularly one that connects her to a maternal line of survivors, is Rita's only chance for maintaining her integrity and holding on to reality as she is being tortured. Elements of Rita's own story surge through periodically, but she is too enmeshed in her own pain to turn these moments into a coherent narrative. It is left to the reader to connect these narrative bursts to the mother's story, which, although viscerally felt, can still be held at enough distance for Rita to use it to make sense of a world outside of, but still connected to, her body. Rita's story can be understood as a Jewish story only insofar as it is a variation, in Argentina, of her mother's Holocaust experience. That "only" is substantial, however.[14]

Sergio Chejfec's *Lenta biografía*, also a novel of silence, loss, and the impossibility of memory, questions whether remembering is even desirable. The narrator's family memories in *Lenta biografía* are centered on two physical objects: his grandfather's art deco cigarette lighter and his father's telescope, neither of which carries a particularly Jewish significance. These objects, sites of memory writ small, are trappings of modernity and, in the case of the lighter's design, even of modernism.[15] They are not obviously accoutrements of Jewishness, except in a kind of metonymy in which modernity attaches in a string of associations to a lighter with an art deco design and an automatic mechanism; a small telescope (associated with both science and sight, and therefore with the shift from faith-based knowledge to an ocular epistemology); and Jewishness, especially as a sign and symbol of rootlessness and restless movement. The lighter and the telescope are, of course, also intimate signs of the narrator's particular patrilineal memory. Rita's reconstruction of Tinkeleh's memory travels along a maternal axis and is less about objects than it is about the affective connection between Tinkeleh's mother, Jasia, and her friend, Leie. The one concrete object that compels Rita is the yellow cloth star she finds hidden away in a box, about which her mother has never spoken. The star, a symbol of victimization, derision, and suffering, withheld by the mother from the daughter, stands in stark contrast to the deliberate patrilineal legacy of the beauty and utility of the lighter and the telescope.

Like *Daughter of Silence*, *Lenta biografía* reflects on time and memory. The present and the past are inseparable and, at the same time, utterly irreconcilable. In the novel's prologue Chejfec claims that *Lenta biografía* is "the lateral derivation" of a game of pool played in an unfamiliar, vaguely hostile bar. This perplexing spatial reference—the axis of derivation is typically vertical—suggests that the text is an offshoot, not a proper descendant of a game in which, in fact, a player strikes one ball to affect the trajectory of others. There is an odd coincidence in timing of the cue stick hitting the ball and the coffee cups in the bar hitting the saucers. One friend tells the other that his father is dying of liver cancer. It occurs to the listener (Chejfec calls him "the narrator," although he has yet to narrate anything), that time itself governs all these actions. The simultaneity of events during a conversation and a game of pool—the cue smacking the ball, a coffee cup coming down on its saucer, cancer eating away at the liver of one of the players' fathers—interferes oddly with the imperative of chronology and precipitates the meditation on time that underlies the novel.

> *Slow biography* perhaps derives from this sort of mental fatigue, which provokes reflection about *time as at once chronological and simultaneous*. The present is the space we occupy. How can we make the moment, in which history fades away and the future is its perpetuation, linger? (emphasis added, my translation)

> [De esa suerte de fatiga mental que provoca reflexionar acerca del tiempo como lo cronológico y lo simultáneo a la vez quizá derive *Lenta biografía*. El presente es el espacio que ocupamos. ¿cómo hacer perdurar el momento en el que la historia se desvanece y el futuro es su perpetuación? (1990, 10)]

The fraught temporality in the novel is expressed textually as Chejfec's narrator, in his attempt to parse time, repeatedly stumbles his way over the tenses of verbs as if they were small boulders. As he stutters over his verbs, past and present collide, and shades of the past will not easily resolve. The simple past is present in the present, and the imperfect is repeated as present tense.

This problem with time shadows the problem of the boundaries of the self in Chejfec's novel. The narrator states he will write his life, but his father's life presses in on his own; and the father's life, in turn, is haunted by the memory of his family of origin, all dead in the Holocaust. Time collapses in on itself as memory refuses to succumb to suppression, and the narrator comes early to the awareness that the very silence to which his father commends his past is the sign of its active presence in his memory and in his daily actions. The urge to remember and record the intimate history of the Holocaust grows as the father decides to write his own life, shortly after the narrator has made the decision to write his own.[16] In a passage that reads like a poem, *Lenta biografía* becomes a meditation on memory and postmemory:

> [The subtle past of dead things.] They remain alive, living on, in one's memory; and nevertheless they are no longer. They stopped being, were abandoned, and are only that pale, discolored stain left by recollections and feelings that seep into memory. Subtle pasts, that are no more and continue to be. My father's were not,

but rather had been, and I suppose that all he kept of them were those faded broad stains that remain in the memory like marks of reminiscence. Mine were not, but neither had they been; I did not possess, nor had I lived, those multiple pasts, and yet my father's many pasts were as if they had been mine: the subtle past, that was not and continues to be. (my translation, square brackets are in the original)

[(Sutil pretérito de las cosas muertas.) Siguen vivas, continuando, en la memoria de uno y sin embargo ya no son. Dejaron de ser, se abandonaron, y son sólo esa mancha leve y descolorida que deja en la memoria la exudación producida por los recuerdos y los sentimientos. Sutiles pretéritos, que ya no son y siguen siendo. Los de mi padre no eran, sino que habían sido, y yo suponía que sólo guardaba de ellos aquellos manchones desleídos que quedan en la memoria como marcas de los recuerdos. Los míos no eran, pero tampoco habían sido; no tenía ni había vivido aquellos pretéritos múltiples, y sin embargo los de mi padre eran como si fuesen míos: sutíl pretérito, que no fue y sigue siendo. (1990, 25)]

The narrator's father meets regularly with those of his own generation, friends with whom he speaks Yiddish. Lubricated with vodka and anisette they retell the stories of people they knew before they came to Argentina. The point of these retellings is not to settle on the truth of the past, but rather to be part of the community of storytellers itself (30). Any contradictions in the stories are welcomed as an occasion to keep on telling and listening (31). Soon the stories become one story, the story of a persecuted man who returns to his father's house, where he is engulfed by memories and a sense of once having being protected. There he finds his father slumped in a corner and is met by a person sweeping filth. This figure is only later revealed to be a woman, pregnant, decrepit, with dull hair described as "amorally blond"— amoral, perhaps, because it has no cause to be growing at all. Along with the dust and filth she is sweeping is the one nonutilitarian object in the house, an Elijah's cup for the Passover Seder. Deprived of humanity—"she jumped around like a monkey" (*brincaba como un mono*, 38)—the woman, who turns out to be the persecuted man's sister, exists only as a repository of his projections. The sister is a deracinated version of the utterly absent mother. Pregnant, she is a reminder of maternity; sweeping filth, including human excrement, she is linked to the lowest tasks of the body, all that the persecuted man is trying to escape. Coming home to this space connects the teller of the tale back to the body, and he sees the woman not as a subject in her own right, but as a sign of his own ruin.

Before long, however, this gendered tale is sucked into the vortex of Holocaust memory. This story, so painstaking in its introduction, is *the* story, but it refuses to stay still. In one version, the persecuted man comes home to find his father already dead; in another he may not be. Perhaps the persecuted man escaped (his last words may have been, "I am leaving. I don't know if I'll be back"); perhaps he died in the cellar among burlap bags filled with potatoes. Perhaps the sister died as well, either trying to escape, having escaped, or thinking the effort futile. The story is told and retold, obsessively, and after the multiple times that Yiddish is described as a language that sounds like it is being chewed, the story takes on the effect of having been chewed to a pulp as well. The possibility of biography, of a life in sequence, disintegrates in the obsessive retelling of the moment of the return of the persecuted man. Storytelling is caught in the whirlwind of the Holocaust, whipped around the eye of that storm, sucked into its vortex. The one constant of the story is the sister's statement, taken up by the persecuted man: "Now I want to know where in the world can I find a father like mine?" (Ahora quisiera saber en qué lugar del mundo podré encontrar un padre como el mío?) The loss of the father, and of his world, symbolized by the Passover cup cast to the floor and shattered, but also the recognition of the unique character of this particular man, is simultaneously reinforced and emptied of meaning with every repetition of the story and the refrain.

Chejfec's novel is an investigation into memory and into the incommensurability of language in the face of the Holocaust and its aftermath. Made of language, the novel spins language into the unraveled stuff of sound, taking the reader to the edge of representability. The man who repeatedly narrates the story of the persecuted man, and the woman who comments on it during the weekly gathering of a group of Holocaust survivors in Buenos Aires, make the story endlessly rich. The narrator's father, who keeps the silence of so many Holocaust survivors, savors the contradictions in the story. Resolution would diminish it and end the need for their evenings together. Storytelling is the occasion for community; it is not that the content is unimportant, but more important is the context, and the necessity of telling the story that contains all stories in order to shape and maintain the community of listeners. The weekly storytelling sessions are the skin and the skeleton that keep the body of the community from dissolving into an amorphous mass. In this, the weekly ritual of Chejfec's Holocaust survivors brings us back to Yerushalmi's characterization of traditional Jewish practices of remembrance. The core of the story is fixed but the details are ever in question, and its ultimate meaning is never quite achieved. It is a form of remembrance whose practice blends past and present, present and future, but that is unanchored in space and time.

Unlike the family sagas that fix a Jewish presence and a Jewish history in Argentina, Chejfec's *Lenta biografía* is a post-Holocaust narrative of unmooring. Fingueret's *Daughter of Silence*, which overtly links the Holocaust to the late twentieth-century Argentine dictatorship, tantalizes the reader with that fixed presence. Still, like the story of the return of the persecuted son in *Lenta biografía*, the reconstruction of the maternal line in *Daughter of Silence* is not powerful enough to assure survival: the Jewish family whose remembered story is its claim to both a Jewish and an Argentine identity is destroyed.[17] The obsessive storytelling of the father and his friends in Chejfec's novel contrasts fiercely with the determined silence of the mother in Fingueret's. One mangles the story through endless repetition and variation; the other wills it to oblivion by denying it the oxygen of words. The daughter's attempt to construct her mother's narrative out of the shards of memories and a handful of found objects is thwarted by the mother's refusal to speak in a grimly ironic attempt to save her daughter from the trauma she herself suffered. For Rita, the reconstruction of her mother's story is her one link to solace and sanity as she is subjected to torture at the hands of the terrorist state. Rita struggles to construct a narrative for Tinkeleh in order to place herself back into the ordinary temporality of the world. Her torturers interrupt the normal flow of time; the natural order of day and night are replaced by the bright lights of torture and the darkness of the blindfold, and the daily rhythm of ordinary life is at the utter mercy of her captors. The act of piecing together her mother's story offers Rita the possibility of recapturing the orderliness and comfort of chronology and causality. But Tinkeleh's trauma breeds silence, and Rita's attempts at making a coherent narrative of it fail. The trace of memory and the trace of history are all that is left.

In light of the tenuousness of memory that Chejfec and Fingueret speak to in these novels, the ease with which Jewishness itself might be lost emerges as a crucial question, and losing sight of Jewishness in a program of state terror whose stated purpose was to eradicate Jews is profoundly, disturbingly ironic. Although expunging Jews from the discourse around the Holocaust is not the same as demonizing, dehumanizing, and killing them, there are, inevitably, resonances between these practices.

Giorgio Agamben abstracts the Holocaust in a way that struggles to get to an ethics of representation and standing (who can speak for the dead? who can even speak of them?) at the same time as it threatens to empty the Shoah of Jewish meaning, and he has been followed by some of Chejfec's readers. Yet Chejfec's very postmodernity—what makes one reviewer proclaim the novel's fundamental importance in the construction of the new Argentine novel—lies precisely in its Jewishness. Reading *Lenta biografía*, it seems inevitable that Chejfec will be read as a Jewish writer, one whose existence as a Jew was made possible by his family's refuge in Argentina. Even so, Chejfec's attitude toward language and time, which seems so inextricably part of a Jewish past, is perfectly legible outside the Jewish frame, and Chejfec himself has said that he does not consider himself "a Jewish writer."[18] Kate Jenckes, for example, reads another of Chejfec's novels, *The Planets* (*Los planetas*), about the friendship of two young Jews, one of whom is disappeared, without any reference to either Jewishness or to a Jewish sense of history or time. Moreover, the "myopic witnessing" Jenckes sees in Chejfec also names precisely the obsessive re-viewing of the scene of the encounter with the dead or dying father and dehumanized sister that is the central motif of *Lenta biografía*. Not inconsequential is Jenckes's discussion of Chejfec's deployment of the myopic witness; the overlaps and resonances between what is Jewish, what is Argentine, and what is Judeo-Argentine is precisely the point here. Like Jenckes, Andrew Rajca ignores Jewishness in his study of memory of the dictatorship in *The Planets*, relegating the Jewish content of the novel to a footnote in which he nevertheless observes that

> this connection between the Holocaust and the "disappeared" is especially acute in *Los planetas*, as S and M are both Jewish, and there are multiple references to Yiddish, Orthodox Jews, religious ceremonies, and the Jewish neighborhoods they grew up [*sic*]. Multiple sections of the novel in fact explore the concept of Jewish identity (in its multiple iterations). (25, n. 8)

Rajca's one brief mention of the fact of S and M's Jewishness occurs in this footnote. He mentions Jewishness in the essay proper only once, tangentially, in a brief reference to the story-within-the-novel told by M:

> At the end of the story, both boys fall into a river and drown, and M explains that the moral of the story has to do with the insecurity of one's own identity, which M connects to a group of orthodox Jews that the boys saw on the street, saying that they too are unsure of the origins of their identity. (Rajca, n.p.)

The Orthodox Jews serve merely as an objective correlative here, one that is, moreover, oddly deployed. Whereas secular Jews often deliberate the nature of their identity, Orthodox Jews, who take the Hebrew Bible to be the word of God, are not in doubt about the origins of theirs.

It is not my intent to scold either Rajca or Jenckes for relegating the Jewish texture of *The Planets* to the margins. Rather, I am observing just how integrated into Argentineity and modernity Jewishness is in their analyses. But still. The antisemitism of the dictatorial regime, latent in Argentine culture, together with a military ethos that deeply admired Nazi practice, affected the prosecution of what the junta itself called its Dirty War in a way that was more pronounced when its victims were Jewish. What is at stake in the salience of Jewishness in these texts of Jewish incidentality is the risk that Jewishness might be integrated to the point of invisibility. A small library's worth of books has been written relating the Holocaust to contemporary thinking on memory, politics, language, and ethics, but to what extent can that cold-bloodedly intentional catastrophe be unlinked from antisemitism and therefore Jewishness without committing an ethical violation? Moreover, if the Jewishness of characters is incidental and normalized in these texts, especially as they are read by Rajca and Jenckes, the nondiegetic references to Jewishness that Florinda Goldberg so deftly explores rely precisely on the nonnormativity of both Jews as a group and the extreme violence and cruelty of the Holocaust as paradigm of Jewish history in its lachrymose mode.

A second, related, ethical question arises around the claim that the Holocaust is unique and that any attempt to make comparisons between it and other forms of state terror results in its banalization. For Jews outside Argentina, the comparison between the Holocaust and the dictatorship may at first seem unacceptable. One might observe that the purpose of the Nazi camps was genocide, and as brutal and deadly and even antisemitic as the Argentine prisons were, they did not have as their goal the eradication of a people and thus cannot be compared to Auschwitz and its kind. To enlist the Holocaust to describe another set of circumstances, according to this line of thinking, is to diminish its horror. Amalia Ran disputes this argument:

It is worth clarifying that the modification of Holocaust discourse does not imply the banalization of the original historical event; instead, on the contrary, it opens space for the representation of other silenced national and local traumas up to the present. Thus, the trope of the *Shoah* allows us to fulfill the demand to remember the past so as not to repeat it. (my translation)

[Cabe aclarar que la modificación el discurso del Holocausto no implica la conversión del evento histórico original en banal sino, en cambio abre espacio a representaciones de otros traumas nacionales y locales silenciados hasta el momento. Por ende, el tropo de la *Shoá* permite cumplir con la demanda de memorizar el pasado para no repetirlo. (2009, 17)]

As Ran points out, the Holocaust is a universal signifier and thus available to help explicate the ideology, language, and techniques of Argentine state terror. Taking this argument even further, Liliana Lukin asserts that the state terror practiced in Argentina during the dictatorship represents the *perfecting* of the Nazis' Final Solution (31, emphasis added). Lukin cites the visceral experience of reading itself as a path toward healing for her. Immersing herself for hours in novels, autobiographies, memoirs, documents, diaries, and letters about the Holocaust has shaped Lukin's very body, and reading the literature, *testimonios*, and documents written during and after the dictatorship in Argentina has done the same.

Faced with the failure of memory, the resurrection of the word. Standing out, in color, sentences take shape; they return my soul to my body, they are others, as I am another, again, for one single time. (my translation)

[Ante el fracaso del recuerdo, la resurrección de la letra. En color, resaltadas las frases toman cuerpo, me devuelven el alma al cuerpo, son otras, como yo soy otra, otra vez, por una única vez. (32)][19]

It is sobering to note that the 2000 DAIA document is titled "Report on the Situation of the Jewish Detainees-Disappeared during the *Genocide* Perpetrated in Argentina" [emphasis added]. I read this overt link between the Holocaust and the dictatorship as a marker of the organization's desire to distance itself from its own earlier acquiescence to the junta's characterization of its practices. The report goes on to defend the use of the term "genocide" by being explicit about its meaning. It is the right term to use, according to the authors of the report, because genocide is

> a practice, that proceeds to define a social subject as a 'negative other,' to its harassment and isolation within the social structure and to the setting of a whole group of actions destined to abduct him from the natural environment of his social existence and to annihilate him. (8)

The language surrounding the Holocaust has repeatedly been appropriated not just by critics talking about the Argentine dictatorship but by the dictatorship itself. The junta maligned, rounded up, and sequestered a class of people they perceived as a threat to the authoritarian state's notion of the proper citizen, with the express purpose of eliminating them. They used metaphors of contagion to justify this group's removal, and they coerced complicity of the rest of society by demonizing them on the one hand and demonstrating that anyone who seemed sympathetic to the marked group would also suffer their fate on the other. Marguerite Feitlowitz points out that the dictatorship's "lexicon of terror" (the title of her book) made deliberate use of Nazi vocabulary, and Florinda Goldberg speaks to the nation's observation that the Argentine generals adopted techniques of state terror perfected by the Nazis, despite their somewhat different technologies of death. Goldberg notes three broad similarities between Jewish experience under the Nazis and Argentina under the dictatorship and their aftermath: state violence itself, the experience of diaspora and exile, and

> (indignation toward) the indifference or passivity of the masses in the face of repression, a theme that in the case of Nazi persecution has breathed life into interminable (and insoluble) questions, interpretations, and apologies. (my translation)
>
> [la (indignación ante la) indiferencia o pasividad de la masa general ante la represión, tema que en el caso de la persecución nazi ha suscitado interminables (e insolubles) interrogantes, interpretaciones y apologías. (2000–2001, n.p.)]

For Goldberg and Ran, the junta's often overt embrace of the Nazi example has produced a rhetoric of othering on the one hand and a practice of denunciation on the other that emphasize the similarity between German and Argentinean state terror. Goldberg writes:

> The perception of a certain similarity between the persecution of Jews throughout history, especially during the Holocaust, and the action of state and para-state terror during the dictatorship of 1976–1983, has become part of the Argentine collective imaginary. (my translation)
>
> [La percepción de cierta semejanza entre la persecución de los judíos a lo largo de la historia, sobre todo en el Holocausto, y la acción del terrorismo estatal y para-estatal durante la dictadura de 1976–1983 se ha convertido en parte del imaginario colectivo argentino. (2000–2001, n.p.)]

Goldberg also notes predictatorship references in Borges, Silvina Ocampo, Piglia, Sábato, and others.

Moreover, Argentine cultural political observers carefully nurture the connection as a way, I believe, to maintain national and international awareness of the atrocities of the junta. I add my own link in a chain of citations beginning in 1984, just after the dictatorship had ended, with Osvaldo Bayer, and continuing through Reati and Goldberg herself, that points out the deliberate adoption of Nazi terminology by the regime, stressing the connection between the two, and that keeps the connection alive:

> Argentine discourse about/against the dictatorship adopted terms like "concentration camp," "ghetto," "final solution," and even "holocaust," together with place names turned into archetypes of a specific kind of horror: "the infamy of Auschwitz, of Bergen Belsen, of Oranienburg, and Dachau is reincarnated in the jails of Sierra Chica and Coronda, of the Chaco and the Pampa (Bayer 1984, qtd. in Reati 1992: 76–77)." (This and all subsequent translations of this text are my own.)
>
> [El discurso argentino sobre / contra la dictadura adoptó términos como 'campo de concentración,' 'ghetto,' 'genocidio,' 'solución final' y hasta 'holocausto' junto con topónimos convertidos en arquetipos de una forma específica del horror: "en las cárceles de Sierra Chica y Coronda, del Chaco y la Pampa se reencarna el oprobio de Auschwitz, de Bergen-Belsen, de Oranienburg y

Dachau (Bayer 1984, cit. por Reati 1992: 76–77)." (2000–2001, n.p.)]

If critics like Jenckes and Rajca minimize Jewishness in their readings of dictatorship narratives, others like Ran, Feitlowitz, and Goldberg maximize it. Goldberg notes a strategic deployment of Jewishness in novels, written during the dictatorship, which could not confront state terror head-on so instead invoked antisemitism and a more generalized anti-Jewish violence to challenge state terror indirectly. In her discussion of Enrique Medina's *Las muecas del miedo* (Fear grimaces, published in 1981), Goldberg argues that the author could refer only obliquely to the regime's brutality. The novel's references to Nazi-themed movies and the protagonist's memory of witnessing the verbal abuse of a Jewish man and confronting the men who are yelling antisemitic slurs at him allow the writer to do just that. Reflecting on this moment, his protagonist remembers a time when he forgot he had put on a yarmulke to take pictures at a Jewish wedding and was surprised by his own reflection. Argentina here is the metaphoric Jew/victim, surprised at its own link to Jewish experience.

Even more subtle is Goldberg's discussion of Abel Posse's futuristic *La Reina del Plata* (The queen of the River Plate, 1988), which, the critic argues, is sited in Jewish space and thoroughly immersed in the paradoxical structure of Jewish history. The paradox of Jewish history is that it simultaneously serves as a model and as evidence of the very impossibility of models. Goldberg calls this

> Jewish history in its double valence: as a paradigm of an inhuman persecution/destruction and as a paradigm of the collapse of all models.
>
> [la historia judía en su doble valencia: como paradigma de una persecución-destrucción inhumanas y como paradigma del colapso de todos los modelos. (2000–2001, n.p.)]

She goes on to point out that

> the social space in which the structure of *La Reina del Plata* is sustained, is taken from the imaginary of Jewish history, and particularly from the mechanism of segregation/exclusion/destruction.

[El paradigma central, el espacio social en el que se sustenta la estructura de *La Reina del Plata*, está tomado del imaginario de la historia judía, y particularmente del mecanismo segregación / exclusión / destrucción. (2000–2001, n.p.)]

Goldberg also argues that Posse's references to Jewish neighborhoods render Jewishness specifically Argentine. At the same time, *La Reina del Plata* posits a universal Jew, identified metonymically, with a description of clothing associated with the Orthodox. Both sorts of Jewish difference—the difference within Jewish neighborhoods and the difference from the culture *tout court* represented by the exotic figure of the Orthodox male—allow the writer to explore the extraordinary nature of Argentine state violence. Insofar as Jewishness stands for both difference and victimization in Posse's novel, it is an apt analogue for Argentina under dictatorship. The actual Jewish Argentine as subject, or even as victim, of the state apparatus of violence is subordinated, if not evacuated, in this use of the Jew as metaphor.

Textual practices that utilize Jewishness but mask the presence of Jews lead Goldberg to address the question of the ethics of linking Jewish experience, and especially the Holocaust, to other atrocities, without resolutely coming down on one side or the other. She writes:

> I do not pretend to evaluate here the similarities between the atrocities of the Holocaust and those of the dictatorships in the Southern Cone, but rather to note a problematic that has already been posed for much larger historical, cultural, and ethical fields.
>
> [No pretendo evaluar aquí las semejanzas entre las atrocidades del Holocausto y las de las dictaduras en el Cono Sur, sino dejar sentada una problemática que ya ha sido planteada para espacios históricos, culturales y éticos mucho más amplios. (2000–2001, n.p.)]

Photographer Marcelo Brodsky, on the other hand, bluntly links the two instances of state terror, likening the clandestine prisons into which the purported enemies of the Argentine state were disappeared, kidnapped, tortured, and often killed to the Nazi death camps. In his 2001 installation titled *NEXO 7: LOS CAMPOS* (NEXUS 7: THE CAMPS), displayed in the open-air walkway of the Recoleta Cultural Center in the middle of

Buenos Aires, Brodsky mounts a photograph of what looks like an ordinary railway sign at right angles to an actual sign nearly identical to the one in the photograph.

Both signs bear the heading "Places of Memory We Should Never Forget," the one in the photograph in German and the installation in Spanish. The photograph shows the sign outside a German railway station with its listing of a dozen concentration camps. The other, constructed to be its match, substitutes the names of the junta's clandestine prisons for those of Bergen Belsen, Auschwitz, and the like. Juxtaposed and identical in form, they make a powerful visual case for understanding the Argentine sites as Nazi-style death camps. Brodsky's photography installation, which sets the two reminders of state terror side by side, does not empty the Holocaust

Figure 7.3. Marcelo Brodsky, *NEXO 7: LOS CAMPOS* (*NEXUS 7: THE CAMPS*), 2001. Digital photograph and installation at the Recoleta Cultural Center, Buenos Aires. *Source*: Reproduced by permission of the artist. Photograph by Kenneth Kaminsky.

of its particularity. Instead, the overt link between the Nazi and Argentine concentration camps serves to shake the world into the need to remember both Argentina's disappeared and the victims of the Holocaust, making manifest the subterranean links between the junta and Nazi Germany.

In contrast to visual and verbal narratives that emphasize the fact of Jewishness in relation to the dictatorship, often via memory of the Holocaust, there exists a cluster of texts in which Jewishness is incidental to the testimonial narratives denouncing Argentine state terror. Brodsky, for example, is perhaps best known for his Good Memory (*Buena memoria*) series, in which a selection of annotated class pictures from the artist's high school tell stories of a future that includes disappearance, exile, and death. Red, yellow, and blue circles around some of the faces of his classmates connect to arrows that point to an abbreviated account of what happened to them. Included is the class photo of his brother, who was a victim of the junta. These annotated, drawn-upon photographs note the incidentally Jewish identity of a disproportionate number of the students, often solely by the fact of a last name.

As we saw in chapter 6, Jewishness that is incidental is not necessarily insignificant, particularly during the dictatorship. The child protagonist in Paula Markovitch's film *The Prize* (*El premio*) bears Jewishness as a dangerous form of difference of which she is barely aware. *The Prize* invokes, but then subdues, Jewishness as it reflects on state terror. Similarly, Graciela Fainstein's novelized memoir *Detrás de los ojos* (Behind the eyes); David Blaustein's documentary film *Spoils of War* (*Botín de guerra*, 2000); and Julia Solomonoff's *Sisters* (*Hermanas*, 2005) and Fabián Hofman's *I Miss You* (*Te extraño*, 2010), both feature films, all incorporate Jewishness into their tales of state terror and its consequences without turning them into stories about Jewishness. Before the titles in *Spoils of War*, the film reviews a story of cultural annihilation, with quotes from an 1879 newspaper, about indigenous children taken away from their distraught mothers as the lands were stolen from native peoples to make them available to foreign capital. The subsequent aerial shot over the titles situates the film's story transnationally. A view of the world narrows down over the ocean and the city of Buenos Aires and comes to rest on the streets of Buenos Aires, with what looks like documentary footage from the mid-1970s. This long black-and-white take dissolves into color and zooms in to capture interviews with a new generation of mothers whose children have been taken from them, among them those with Jewish names. Each tells a similar story of arrest, disappearance, and loss of a child. As the film settles into its locale, "Shuberoff" is one of the first names we hear—the mother of a disappeared child. Then overlapping voices of mothers name their missing children.

In these films, Jewishness is clearly marked but then apparently abandoned as a relevant signifier. Fabián Hofman's *I Miss You* begins with a single Yiddish word, "Bubbe" (Grandma), leaving no doubt as to the ethnic background of the characters, but the story of the family, in which one child is disappeared and the other is rushed out of the country in an attempt to save him, is not otherwise marked by Jewishness.[20] Similarly, Julia Solomonoff's film *Sisters*, about another family split apart by the events of the Dirty War, acknowledges Jewishness only to ignore it. The family's name, Levin, is Jewish, but there is nothing manifestly Jewish about their lives, nor do any artifacts or ritual objects mark their homes as such.

Many years after the publication of the *The Little School*, Alicia Partnoy reflects on the choice an artist or writer makes to center Jewishness in her work, or to make it peripheral. For Partnoy, it is not a matter of rejecting or hiding Jewishness, but a matter of emphasis. Whereas in *The Little School* Jewishness is present but peripheral, in her 2005 discussion of poetry as a means of resistance, Partnoy gives center stage to the Holocaust in relation to the dictatorship. She writes of her own grandfather's silence concerning the Holocaust, which he escaped as an immigrant to Argentina in the 1920s, but which took the lives of his entire family, and of her own poetry as a means of resistance as a disappeared person and as a political prisoner. Partnoy recognizes the centrality of Jewishness in her artist-mother's work, and in the writing of other poets, but for herself, without disavowing her Jewishness, she chooses to minimize its importance. Partnoy's is an incidental Jewishness as a chosen position, a way of registering and honoring a Jewishness that, nevertheless, does not feel like a determining factor in her own will as a political actor or as a poet.

> My mother, Raquel Partnoy, feels that those connections [to a family history of oppression and persecution as Jews] nurture her art and writings. Her series of paintings, "Surviving Genocide," comes to mind. She traces her cultural roots back to her Jewish identity. I, however, choose not to focus on my Jewishness.
>
> When feminist scholar Myrna Goldenberg befriended me and supported my writings fifteen years ago, she was doing pioneer work by finding relevant connections between my experiences in Argentina and those of Holocaust survivors. However, she did not

ask me to discuss my Jewish identity. It was not necessary. We all know that for the Nazis, for the perpetrators of the pogroms that destroyed my grandparents' families and forced the four of them into exile, my last name would have been enough to observe the way I lean on the trunk of my family tree, not with the anxiety the shipwrecked embraces a life board, but with the serene demeanor of she who knows that this tree is part and parcel of the woods she calls her history. (2005, 243)

Partnoy does not reject her family's Jewish identity; she honors it serenely. It is just not the whole story of who she is.

Acknowledging Jewishness is never a totally safe proposition, but Partnoy has never been one to worry about personal safety in the face of tyranny. The dictatorship that arrested and tortured her, and that killed many of her friends, had no campaign to eradicate Jews. But Jewish connections to early twentieth-century labor and anarchist movements, implicit contestation of forms of obedience and hierarchy rooted in Catholicism, association with radical practices like psychoanalysis and with the questioning implicit in social science scholarship and journalism, and simple entrenched antisemitism, particularly among the right, all converged in the way assimilated Jews, who in many cases were very marginally self-identified as Jews, were understood and treated during the 1976–1983 right-wing dictatorship.

During the dictatorship Argentina's Jews were caught in metonymy. The discursive connection between Jewishness and difference, and the way Nazism serves as the extreme example of brutal behavior against a nation's perceived others, played out cruelly on the bodies of actual Jews. As we have seen, Jewishness intersects with Argentine state terror discursively and historically in a variety of ways, among them the overrepresentation of Jews as the victims of the dictatorship, some of whom, like Partnoy, Strejilevich, and Timerman, survived to write about their experience. Other Jews, whose family members were detained and disappeared, included those stories in memoirs, novels, films, and other forms of visual art. Many of them invoked their own family's history of loss, and sometimes survival, during the Holocaust, or drew attention to the parallels between Argentine and German state violence. Ironically, the wide deployment of the Holocaust as a universal trope that encourages the reader to accept the gravity of state violence also contributes to the fading of Jewishness when the Holocaust is invoked as signifier, as Jewishness once again folds into modern Argentineity, embedded in its very being.

Jewish embeddedness can take another turn, however, visible at first only to disappear into the larger frame. A stunning example of this phenomenon is Federico Finchelstein's brilliant 2010 study of Fascism in Italy and Argentina. Finchelstein begins the book with a recollection of his classmate, Perla Waserman, a Jewish woman who came to Argentina from Poland "some years before the Holocaust" (1), was imprisoned during the dictatorship, and who became both a member of the Madres de la Plaza de Mayo and a student when her daughter was disappeared, taking her daughter's place in both the university and the resistance. With this verbal portrait, Finchelstein creates an utterly Jewish context for his book.

Finchelstein goes on to discuss the book's "different layers of meaning that could also be described as national and transnational; that is, it opens a critical dialogue with at least seven interlocutors" (10), the fourth of which, he claims, is "the history of antisemitism" (10). Nevertheless, there is barely an overt mention of antisemitism in the book. The index lists just five places in the text where it appears, the longest of which is an autobiographical note on the author's own run-in with an antisemitic reader who likens Finchelstein to Hitler. The index also lists four brief references to Jews. In other words, engagement with Jewishness and antisemitism in the context of both the Italian and Argentine expressions of Fascism is implicit rather than explicit, set up from the outset as the emotional/historical context thanks to Perla Waserman's story. Finchelstein can embed Jewishness into his text precisely because Jewishness has become a (sometimes unspoken) part of the culture. Finchelstein's insistence on the centrality of Jewishness and antisemitism to any understanding of Fascism in Italy and Argentina, only to abandon them in his analysis, is the inverse of Chejfec's offhand acknowledgment of Jewish roots that have little to do with his sense of the essence of his writing even though its Jewish content is palpable. Both are functions of the never simple, often uneasy, embedded Jewishness of Argentina.

CHAPTER EIGHT

# TROUBLING DIFFERENCE

Jewishness, Gender, and Transgressive Sexuality

Like Jewishness, transgressive sexuality has long been available as a sign of troubling difference, ready to be associated with other forms of political and social unorthodoxy. Under conditions of antisemitism and homophobia each may be enlisted to tarnish the other, as we saw in Julián Martel's *The Stock Market* (1891), where the implied homosexuality of the sordid Makster and his associates is enlisted to cast Jewishness itself as a form of social deviance. The insistence on Jewish heteronormativity and robust health in Alberto Gerchunoff's *The Jewish Gauchos of the Pampas* (1910), on the other hand, stands in stark contrast with the caricatured implications of homosexuality and physical degeneracy among the Jews in Martel's novel. Gerchunoff preempts and undercuts the association between Jewish masculinity and effeminacy, defending Jewish manhood, implicitly acquiescing to the denigration of queer sexualities. Antisemitism taking the form of homophobia links Jews to a range of transgressions, from religious to economic to sexual. In an instance of what David Kaminsky calls "interfactionality," Gerchunoff and company embrace dominant norms of sexual behavior as a way of distancing Jewishness from such abjection.[1]

With the invention of the Jewish gaucho, Gerchunoff stakes a claim to the heart of the myth of Argentine masculinity and embraces the heteronormative values that undergird it. Transnational LGBTQIA+ social movements have changed the valence of queerness in recent years, however, just as feminist theory and practice have served to reconfigure ideas about women's sexuality, so that queerness is now available to function as a sign of defiant transgression in the face of repressive power, or even simply as a way to shake up conventional, self-satisfied narratives of nation and society.[2] Historically, though, anxiety about women's sexuality tout court, male homosexuality, and Jewishness intersect in ways that bring us back to the more general anxiety surrounding Jewishness and modernity discussed in chapter 2. Women, queers, and Jews, all markers of difference, are overlapping categories; hegemonic notions of each separate them (the silent "straight" that modifies "women," the silent "male" that modifies "queers" and "Jews," and the phantom class and racial markers that implicitly characterize them all). Yet the residue of otherness links them across what is separate in their spheres.

The link between Jews, femininity, and homosexuals, intended as mutual denigration, comes to Argentina as a legacy of European homophobia, misogyny, and antisemitism.[3] Cultural historians of Europe and the United States point to the turn of the twentieth century, just around the time of the publication of *The Stock Market*, as the moment when both queer identities and the meaning of Jewishness in a secularizing, modern world, emerged as social realities. As Jonathan Freedman reminds us, "Jewish and sexually transgressive identities were molded in each other's image," going on to argue that

> even more so than that of the homosexual, the figure of the Jew arose from a semiotic problem: the inadequacy of any of the emerging nineteenth-century categories to explain the presence and prominence of real, live Jews in such places as Paris, London, New York—the new modern cosmopolis with which that figure, like the homosexual, rapidly became identified. (2001, 523)

As we have already noted, in Argentina the pathologizing of "the Jew" is, paradoxically, both attenuated and intensified by Jews' condition as immigrants: Europeans and therefore desirable on the one hand, scruffy outsiders on the other. The nineteenth century is the time when taxonomies of both race and gender emerge in Europe; it is also the time of national emergence for Latin American nations. Argentina's connection to Jews makes these intersections particularly interesting.

The outsider status crystallized in the predeterminedly womanish figures of the Jew and the male homosexual requires neither actual Jewishness nor actual homosexuality for its potency. For example, the Unitarian hero of one of Argentina's foundational texts, Esteban Echeverría's *The Slaughter Yard* (*El matadero*, c. 1839) is feminized, apparently sodomized, and murdered by the ultra-Catholic, brutish supporters of a purportedly autochthonous land-based party headed by Juan Manuel del Rosas.[4] The thugs who attack him mock his very modernity, what they perceive as his Europeanized foppishness and urbanity. He is not Jewish, but he is rendered less than properly Christian by default (the Rosistas are decidedly, hierarchically, and hypocritically Catholic, and Christianity in this context is necessarily Roman Catholic). He is derided for being less than wholly masculine in his bearing and his clothes; and both insufficiently Catholic and insufficiently masculine, he is tangentially associated with both Jewishness and homosexuality even though there is no overt suggestion that he is actually either Jewish or queer. He stands in contrast with the rough-and-tumble, hypermasculine gauchos and butchers who work in the meat industry that are at the very heart of Argentina's national mythology.

The direct line drawn in the nineteenth century between Jewish men and effeminate queerness has, by the twenty-first, undergone significant revision. It is no coincidence that Edgardo Cozarinsky writes both sexually queer narratives and stories that undermine the stability of Jewish identity, or that Alejandra Pizarnik is never captured entirely by either Jewishness or lesbianism, or that Guillermo Kuitca buries narrative under layers of symbol on the one hand and abstraction on the other. These three queer Jews are avatars of the cosmopolitanism that marks Argentina as a nation and a culture, and that ties a fraught and complex Jewishness inextricably to Argentina's claim to modernity.

Close to a century after Gerchunoff stakes claims to a heteronormative Jewishness in the Argentine countryside, Marcelo Birmajer returns his readers to the days of the Jewish agricultural settlements. His short story "En la noche de bodas" (On their wedding night, 2000) challenges conventional understandings and valuation of appropriate sexuality, turning Gerchunoff on his head. Moreover, it appears in an anthology of homoerotic short fiction, itself an intervention into cultural heteronormativity. "En la noche de bodas" opens with a retelling of the origin story of Moisés Ville, where the Gerchunoff family settled. Birmajer once again recounts the story of the arrival of hopeful Russian Jewish settlers at a remote railroad station where they learn that they have been deceived by scoundrels who took their money but did not give them land they had been promised, leaving them to fend for themselves over a winter that took the lives of many children and the sanity of not a few adults. The narrator's fascination with a young woman's luscious body resonates with Gerchunoff's descriptions of the large-breasted young women whose lush sexuality will be channeled into making multitudes of Jewish Argentine babies. But the reader's sense of familiarity and even complacency is summarily undone by the wild queering of Birmajer's story.

The historical grounding of the narrative creates expectations of conventional realism that are soon dashed, and the safely managed Gerchunoffian sexuality associated with the desire for normativity begins to slip early on. In a scene that resonates queerly with the Gerchunoff vignette in which a young woman milking a cow is the object of masculine desire, Birmajer's narrator likens his future wife to a cow and fantasizes taking her from behind. On their wedding night Birmajer's protagonist learns that his bride, Runia, is unable to have vaginal sex; the explanation she gives is that she is really a man in what seems to be a woman's body, whose gender transformation coincided with migration from the old world to the new. The young woman, Runia, was a lad named Roni in Eastern Europe, a case of transcontinental migration marvelously triggering gender transition. This twenty-first-century story of transgender desire reaches back to a traditional mode of Jewish storytelling, one that embraces the fantastic as a way to understand the divine. Runia's beautiful and voluptuous body has all the markers of conventional, fresh, fertile femininity, but as the narrator tells us it also, oddly, bears the marks of a sexually experienced older woman: "She was twenty, but she bore in her breasts and buttocks the heavy beauty of maturity." [Ella tenía veinte años, pero llevaba en los pechos y en el trasero la pesada belleza de la madurez (2000, 70. All translations from this text are mine.).]

In other words, Runia's body is an image and a paradigm, older than she herself is. It is a kind of avatar, an embodied projection of ideal femininity that masks what might productively be read as the "reality" of Roni's queer masculinity. Roni is desirable to the narrator *because* of his woman's body, but that body does not function in predictable ways. It will not accept vaginal sex, nor can it become pregnant. Nor does Runia/Roni have any desire to bear children: he declares that as a man he finds the idea of having a child inside him rather repulsive. He desires and performs anal, not vaginal, sex. Roni's outward appearance provides the couple with a cover for queer sexual desire. At the moment of penetration he announces his identity: "I am Roni Shipalzsky—said Runia as Efraín entered. From Lodz." [Soy Roni Shipalzsky—dijo Runia mientras Efraín entraba—. De Lodz (76).] Runia claims her masculinity and her full identity at the moment of anal penetration (i.e., at the moment of fulfilling her queer desire as a man), but because it is "Runia" who makes that declaration, the character's gender ambiguity is never entirely resolved.

The new place and the new body are far less real to Roni than is his sense of his own maleness and his own past. The body of a woman is a cover, won, he tells, in a biblical struggle with an angel whose conditions include living only half his life. In the fully realized space of Lodz, Roni was complete, not just Roni Shipalzsky, but "Roni Shipalzsky from Lodz." His presence in the Argentine Jewish agricultural colonies seems contingent, half a life not in terms of time but in terms of space. Moreover, when Runia finally disappears, she is not remembered. Her presence has made no mark.

"En la noche de bodas" is a queer tale whether we take Roni's story at face value—that he really is a man who was divinely transformed into a woman (albeit one without a vagina)—or as a not-so-covert account of gender fluidity and homoerotic (or gender-queer) desire. In the first reading, the fantastic tale has biblical and Hasidic roots that flower into transgressive erotic practice, so that the modern take on queer desire we might expect from a cosmopolitan story written in the twenty-first century collides with both the secretiveness around that desire during the time and place the story is set and the militant heteronormativity that would hold such a transformation utterly impossible in the real world and therefore available only as exuberant fantasy. As Birmajer's story makes abundantly clear, the negative valence attached to sexual transgression and gender fluidity has undergone a major shift during the course of the twentieth century.[5]

Nevertheless, as we saw in the previous chapter, the danger to both sexual and religious outsiders during times of state terror remains very real. Within that context, Leopoldo Brizuela—the editor of the volume in which Birmajer's story appears—expresses and explores, rather than resolves, the conundrum of Jewishness and queerness as otherness from and within Argentineity in his novel *Una misma noche* (The very same night, 2012). Brizuela's protagonist, a writer named Leonardo Bazán, focuses on the Jewishness of his neighbor, who was detained and disappeared during the military dictatorship of the 1970s and 1980s. As the confidential secretary of the aide to David Graiver, the real-life Jewish multimillionaire who apparently helped the urban guerrilla *montoneros* launder and invest their money, the fictional Diana Kuperman was thought to hold information on the militants. The conjunction of Jews, money, and subversion in the mind of the junta, and the protagonist's father's antisemitism and connection to the ESMA, where he received training as a young man, are linked to the protagonist's own memory and sense of familial guilt in his father's complicity with Kuperman's kidnappers.[6] His own feelings of powerlessness as a child merge into his sense of his own otherness as a queer man, an identity he hints at early on in the novel and only much later confirms. A sense of shared otherness with Diana Kuperman appears to be the engine of his obsession with recalling this story. But then, in an extraordinary shift, Bazán declares that his story is not about antisemitism, but about memory and repetition, effectively enacting the incidentalization of Jewishness in the text. Memory and antisemitism may not seem to occupy the same thematic plane, but in this novel they are obliquely related. One does not necessarily obviate the other, although that is what Bazán suggests by the replacement of one by the other:

> I still didn't quite know what I was going to write. But I was sure that in this new version, the crux could no longer be antisemitism. What interested me more and more was the phenomenon of repetition; and the audacity, the risk, the danger of wanting to interrupt it with a law, a sentence, or even a simple novel. (my translation)
>
> [No sabía todavía muy bien qué iba a escribir. Pero estaba seguro de que en esta nueva versión, el eje no podía ser ya el antisemitismo. Lo que me interesaba, cada vez más, era el fenómeno de la repetición; y la osadía, el riesgo, el peligro de querer interrumpirla con una ley, una sentencia o hasta una simple novela. (161)]

Rather than disappearing altogether as the motivation for writing, the antisemitism of the state and that of his father, which casts Jews as suspicious others, recedes in favor of a consideration of the need to remember in order to forestall the repetition of state violence. By disengaging the two and focusing on the latter, Bazán attempts to abandon his identification with Diana Kuperman, her Jewishness mirroring his queerness. Yet the link between the Jew and the queer, though subdued, never goes away in this text; and the question of remembering and repetition attaches to the history of both, even as Bazán means to shift attention to the more immediate questions of the responsibility of Argentine society vis-à-vis the state terror of the 1970s and 1980s and its repercussions for the twenty-first century.

"En la noche de bodas" marks the reassessment of the link between Jewish masculinity and queer sexualities, while the protagonist of *Una misma noche* struggles to submerge both Jewishness and queer desire. Both serve to integrate homoeroticism and Jewishness into Argentineity, an effect of the visual as well as the literary arts. One of Argentina's most successful—and most globalized—contemporary artists is Guillermo Kuitca, whose work we examined in chapter 5. Kuitca's minimal reference to a Jewish past is part of the phenomenon that I earlier characterized as incidental Jewishness, and Kuitca's art is as incidentally queer as it is incidentally Jewish. Rudi Bleys identifies Kuitca as an "Argentinian gay artist" in his study of homoeroticism in Latin American art (145), but mainstream discussions of the artist's work leave out references to his sexuality (or to his Jewish roots, for that matter), either as part of Kuitca's biography or as it is manifested in his art.

Social movements and individual courage have opened the way for the tacit embrace of queer sexuality by at least some segments of Argentine society, as Birmajer's "En la noche de bodas" and the silent acknowledgment of Kuitca's queer presence suggest. Still, José Pablo Feinmann's *La crítica de las armas* (The critique of weapons), published three years after Birmajer's story, rehearses the age-old discursive connections among the disdained categories of being embodied by Jews, queers, and women. Pablo, the narrator in Feinmann's novel, has a fraught relationship with Judaism that is echoed (and thereby reinforced) by his fascination with and horror of homoerotic desire. Moreover, he is obsessed with his mother, whose power he fears and whose insights he ridicules. He mocks her relentlessly, as if to ward off her power. Pablo's mother has recognized something of her son in a film that she has seen pathologizing homosexuality and traumatizes him by assuming he is homosexual and intervening to cure him of it.[7] Pablo himself simultaneously describes and denies his attraction to his friend Hugo Hernández, whose surname is reassuringly *castizo*—that is, unproblematically Iberian, ostensibly with unsullied bloodlines. Pablo admires Hugo's body, wishing his were like it. Most specifically, he compares his own rounded, somewhat feminine buttocks to Hugo's discreet, slim behind. Pablo's insistence on not being sexually attracted to Hugo is of the "doth protest too much" variety. Hugo, Pablo claims, holds no sexual appeal for him; rather his friend arouses desires in him that are more profound than sex. Yet even as Pablo asserts his own heterosexuality by arguing that his attraction to Hugo is not sexual, he implies that because sexual relations for him necessarily involve women they are inconsequential.[8] In other words, what attracts him to Hugo is an eroticism that goes much deeper than mere physicality. No wonder his mother thinks he's gay.

Queer desire haunts Pablo, and he acknowledges that desire even as he buries it. Pablo often returns to this fixation on the buttocks and on anal sex, literally protecting his ass by reiterating just how closed and inaccessible he must prove it to be. Moreover, he does so in a series of wry—and outlandishly hyperbolic—similes that terminate with a devastating comparison to his mother's inability to love him adequately:

> I've got to be impregnable, the most hetero of heteros. My ass has to be as tightly closed as the horizon of history, more impenetrable than the Amazon, more impossible to attain than social justice, more unreachable than the Kingdom of Heaven, more inaccessible and remote than your heart. (my translation)
>
> [debo ser inexpugnable, el más hétero de todos los héteros, debo tener el culo más cerrado que el horizonte de la historia, más impenetrable que el Amazonas, más imposible que la justicia social, más inalcanzable que el Reino de los Cielos, más inaccesible y remoto que tu corazón. (168)]

Pablo reveals his own dreadful conduct as a parent in the brief recollection of his own son's coming out, returning once again to his fixation on the buttocks and anal sex. When his son comes out to him, Pablo replies flippantly, "okay, kid, it's your ass, not mine."

Pablo's disdain for women is constant in *La crítica de las armas*, of which his dismissive attitude toward his mother is only one instance. He considers her a fool, yet she often has important insights. She is terrified by the film *The War of the Worlds*, convinced that Martians will soon invade the Earth. Just as seeing the film *The Third Sex* convinces her that Pablo is gay, she believes that the world is literally under siege, allowing Pablo to mock her. The Martian invasion is a metaphor for the state terror that is at the core of the novel, but Pablo does not acknowledge that she perceives a figurative truth worth attending to.[9]

Feinmann's Pablo is not the only character in contemporary Argentine fiction and film who exhibits anxiety around masculinity and Jewishness. In both Daniel Burman's *Waiting for the Messiah* and Gustavo Kusminsky's novel *Médanos: Premio de narrativa hispanoamericana* (Sand dunes: Prize winner in Latin American narrative), for example, the male character's Jewishness is associated with his normalized heterosexuality. In both texts the Jewish male is confronted with sexually challenging women, and in both his Jewishness becomes part of the sexual encounter. In the Burman film, Ariel is attracted to his coworker Laura in large part because as a queer woman she is sexually exotic, a change from what he perceives as the stultifying normativity that embraces not only heterosexuality but also ethnic exclusivity and the constraints of marriage, monogamy, and traditional Jewish manhood. For her part, Laura's perception of Ariel as Jewish is a crucial part of her desire to seduce him. She identifies what for him is a bizarre analogy between his religion and her sexuality. Laura associates Jewishness with being gay because for her they are both outsider positions. This is something Ariel does not understand, since the inside he is trying to escape is precisely that of Jewishness, and her transgressive sexuality is of a piece with the unencumbered life he desires. Ariel's transition through postadolescent exploration into what he hopes will be an adulthood of horizons broader than those afforded by the boundary lines of Barrio Once, and participation in Argentine society outside what he calls the bubble of his Jewish upbringing, is measured in part by his relationship with Laura. The bubble, so carefully constructed to keep Jewish Argentina safe and to ensure its continuation, safeguards against not only outside threats, over which it has limited control, but also from the seduction of assimilation.

Kusminsky's opportunistic and cynical writer-protagonist, Marcos, is unlike Burman's Ariel, who is endearing, if egocentric to the point of heartlessness. Yet Marcos also has a sexual encounter that becomes a referendum on Jewishness. He is unable to perform sexually with Fina, a beautiful woman from an oligarchic family, after she demands that he beat her with his belt. As a result, she insults his masculinity with an antisemitic tirade. Until this moment, Marcos's Jewishness is an unspoken presence in their encounter; his failure to satisfy her triggers what is latent in their cocaine-inflected lovemaking (20–22). Two hundred years of Argentine political and social history, including the consolidating of national territory, the complexity of class-tinged gender politics, and the emergence of a precarious intelligentsia, are contained in their encounter.

Kusminsky's Marcos is hardly a sexual innocent and certainly not a nice guy. In the novel's first scene he rapes a woman with whom he had spent the night, ignoring her refusal to have sex with him, and leaving her bleeding. Yet Fina's deeply held antisemitism, the product of several generations of refinement (hence her name), following on Marcos's aversion to her demand for him to inflict pain on her, locates him in the space of the noble victim. By refusing to whip her, he is implicitly denying her the expiation of her historical guilt; he will not inflict sexually pleasurable punishment on a woman whose body exposes and hides the scars of masochistic beatings. Like the oligarchy itself, whose crimes are known but visible only in the most private circumstances, the scars of whipping on Fina's buttocks can be seen only on her terms. On the land her family killed to possess, soybeans now grow, apparently benignly. The oligarchs have even stripped the land of the emblem of Argentineity, the cattle culture established in the wake of attempted genocide. Similarly bare of meaning is the art gallery that Fina owns, empty like her apartment, Marcos suggests, and as vacant as her soul, the soul of Argentina's elite. Marcos's body will not acquiesce to Fina's desire to purge that historical guilt.

In Burman, on the other hand, sexual transgression is appealing: it is a sign of the modern. Although Laura proclaims her transgression and makes use of it for playing at outsiderness, Ariel knows that only those well inside and secure can play at otherness safely. Neither for Ariel nor for Laura's lover Ani is outsider status simply a matter of play. In a painful confrontation between the two women, Laura refuses the label "lesbian," and when she does identify herself sexually, she says that she is "gay," a much trendier term, and one that gives Burman the opportunity to play on words: "*Dijo gay o goy?*" (Did she say gay or goy?) Ariel wonders, confusing sexual with ethnic identity from within a Jewish perspective. Ani claims not the chic term "gay," but the more deeply transgressive "lesbian." Laura intends her declaration that she is gay to signify that she, like, Ariel, is a marginalized outsider; but for Ariel, "gay" and "goy" lie on the same side of the insider-outsider divide, both fully located within the dominant culture. For Ariel, whose energy is entirely directed at escaping the marginalization of outsider status, Laura's charm is precisely the difference between them. As different as their fictions are, both Burman and Kusminsky place the onus on the women in their texts. Laura is too self-centered to understand Ariel's Jewishness and what it means; Fina not only bears the ancestral guilt of the ruthless and antisemitic oligarchy, she is an empty-headed dilettante as well.

Contemporary queer theory has focused on those transgressive sexualities that realign the gendered objects of sexual desire, but sexual transgression surely includes Fina's masochist demands, to say nothing of the very act of women's escape from the limited bounds of marital sex. Whereas all participants in same-sex relations are perceived as transgressors within the context of modern European and North American sexual practice, only women have traditionally been considered transgressors in nonmarital heterosexual practice. Most notably, female prostitutes have, historically, been reviled as fallen and debased; their male clients are simply engaging in accepted social practice. Jewish prostitution, then, is another site of intersection between transgressive sexuality and Jewishness.

In "Medics, Crooks, and Tango Queens" (*Médicos, maleantes y maricones*), Jorge Salessi brilliantly examines the links between the anxiety around outlaw sexuality, including its heterosexual varieties, and the perceived threat of immigration. He argues that the workforce brought into Argentina to help modernize the nation, making it a player in the international economy centered in Europe,

> was now a foreign force living within national borders and capable of striking against and paralyzing the meat and grain exporting economy that kept enriching the landowning class. An Argentine sexual science seeking to define strict border controls around the definitions of sex and gender, class and nationality, was an urgent response to this threat. (143)

It is a little startling that the connection between transgressive sexuality and immigration as threats to the modernizing nation should be so starkly stated. The resonances usually seem more subtle, one threat echoing the other, but Salessi goes on to document how the links made by turn-of-the-century social hygienists whose crusades to build a nation marry the two anxieties. The emerging social configurations in the nation's capital, he notes, could be regulated, at least in part, by managing sexuality and creating a taxonomy for it:

> Implemented to control the new social formations of Buenos Aires, this sexual science gave rise to a taxonomy of categories of sexual deviance, such as "pederasty," "the third sex," "sapphism," "sexual inversion," "uranism," and "homosexuality." (143)

Jews are hardly alone as representatives of the dangerous immigrant classes: Italian anarchism, syndicalism, and prostitution (both male and female) are important points of distress. Italians, after all, constituted the majority of immigrants at this time. Also unnerving was the rise of women's greater participation in professions, education, and the public sphere in general, and the rising fear of what was labeled "uranism," (mostly) male same-sex desire. Salessi cites George L. Mosse to drive home his point:

> The plot not only involves "sapphic" women from "all over Europe" and Italian "pederasts," but also Jewish men, represented as "feminine" and "sexually inverted," who threatened the security

> of the state. Mosse explains that the myth of a homosexual conspiracy parallels the myth of an international Jewish conspiracy. At the end of the century "[both] Jews and homosexuals were perceived as a 'state within the state'" [Mosse, 138]. As we have already seen, the foreign women who worked in the brothels, in addition to being represented as lesbians, were characterized as Jewish. (155)

In this emerging sexual science, all transgressive sexuality—that is, all sexual behavior and desire not contained by heteronorms—is linked. Prostitution, same-sex desire, pedophilia, transgender, and women's defiance of traditional gender roles are all medicalized and taxonomized into submission. Significantly but not unpredictably, the condemnation of prostitution is one-sided. Sex workers, but not their clients, are transgressors; unlike women who are perceived to be under the socially sanctioned sexual protection of one man (a father or brothers to protect her virginity; a husband to monopolize and contain her sexual activity), prostitutes are social outlaws who threaten social stability.[10] Men who use the services of prostitutes, however, behave well within patriarchal heteronorms; their forays into brothels, many of which serve as virtual men's clubs where men of like social standing come together, are not perceived as a threat to society, at least when those men do not imperil the social, political, and economic status quo. In the early twentieth century, men of social standing were expected to frequent brothels, but "brothel anarchists" (anarquistas prostibularios) were condemned by police and public health officials alike.[11]

Beatriz Sarlo juxtaposes the twin anxieties caused by (implicitly straight) women's sexuality and male homosexuality in a footnote—a queer aside—that implies a connection between the two, and between them and the peripheric modernity of the title of her book, without making that connection overt. The footnote merits citing:

> The programs of modernity coexist, even among the elites, with the persistence of old judgmental attitudes about women and sexuality. An anonymous letter that [Vanguardist poet Oliverio] Girondo, anyway, considered worthy of keeping, can be found in the archive of the bibliophile Washington Pereyra and can be read, partially, in the journal *Xul*, no. 6, quoted by Néstor Perlongher. The eroticism of Girondo's poetry enters into dialogue with a piece of brothel pornography in which the female sexual object

occupies center stage in the text. In the same archive I found a letter to Girondo by the sculptor Riganelli (June 24, 1924), where one of the circumstances of the homosexual question can be seen: "After you left I went out to confirm certain suspicions with respect to thepersonwe'dbeenspeakingaboutandtheytoldme-he'sa*hermaphrodite*. Imagine my delight that this person could come to my home, that people might take me for him! I beg you to come to my house to advise me what I should do, I'm so furious I can barely see." (my translation)

[Los programas de la modernidad conviven, aun en las élites, con la persistencia de viejos juicios sobre la sexualidad y la mujer. Una carta anónima que, de todos modos, Girondo consideró digna de conservarse, se encuentra en el archivo del bibliófilo Washington Pereyra y puede leerse, parcialmente, en la revista *Xul*, no 6, citada por Néstor Perlongher. El erotismo de la poesía de Girondo entra en diálogo con una pornografía prostibularia donde la mujer objeto sexual ocupa el primer plano del discurso. En el mismo archivo encontré una carta del escultor Riganelli a Girondo (junio 24 de 1924), donde se muestra uno de los estados de la cuestión homosexual: "Después que usted se fue he salido para confirmar ciertas sospechas respecto al individuodelquehe-mosestadohablandoymehandichoqueesun*hermafrodita*. ¡Imagínese la gracia que me hace de que este individuo frecuente mi casa! para que me tomen por el mismo individuo; ruego a usted se llegue hasta mi casa para aconsejarme lo que debo hacer, estoy que no veo de rabia." (1988, ch. 1, note 20)]

Sarlo, like Girondo, considers both the anonymous letter and the signed one "worthy of keeping," even though she somehow cannot integrate them into the body of her text. And they *are* worthy of keeping, inasmuch as they juxtapose male fascination with women's transgressive (hetero)sexuality with an exaggerated fear of homosexuality represented in the breathless enjambment of Riganelli's characterization of the queer man who frequents his home, the high sarcasm failing to mask his apparent terror in being "turned into" his acquaintance, his blind fury, and his sense of helplessness before what he perceives to be an existential threat.

Néstor Perlongher, incidentally Jewish and famously queer, quotes from that same anonymous letter in a footnote of his own, in which he says that Girondo's reader, who signs himself "un prorongo, vulgo priapo" ["an undistinguished, ordinary lecher" (Perlongher 1984, citing Girondo, citing the reader)], is stimulated in his own lechery by one of Girondo's poems. Anonymous and marginal, this correspondence nevertheless resists being relegated to utter silence. Sarlo and Perlongher alike struggle to find a way to wedge it into their work, even though the discourse discourages it. My attempt here may be as awkward as theirs.

Girondo attracts Perlongher's interest not because they share an object of desire (the written record suggests an uncomplicated heterosexuality on Girondo's part), but because they are both determined to free sexuality from bourgeois piety. Perlongher conscripts Girondo's erotic writing for his program of liberating sexuality more generally, celebrating what he calls the "obscene" (25) poems of "Las chicas de Flores" (The girls of Flores) in *20 poemas para ser leídos en el tranvía* (20 poems to be read on the trolley), which had been domesticated by literary critics and historians into a less threatening "sensuality." Girondo's overtly sexual poems are decidedly heterosexual in nature, but they are part of the liberation of sexuality that serves Perlongher's larger project.

Inversely, the apparent heteronormativity of César Tiempo's *Versos de una . . .* (Poems of a . . .) has more than a trace of queerness about it. As Ben Sifuentes-Jáuregui observes, César Tiempo performs a kind of transvestism when he not only invents, but writes as, a Jewish Russian prostitute. Yet even as Tiempo takes on a female persona in the writing of this book as Clara Beter, he suppresses of the very sign of abject femininity in the sly title that withholds the damning word "whore."

Tiempo plays a drag version of hide-and-seek in dealing with both Jewishness and abject femininity. First he translates his name, Israel Zeitlin, to a Spanish equivalent, César Tiempo, a move that, like drag, both covers over and makes evident the transition from the truth of the body to the truth of the disguise. The Jewishness of his original name appears to be utterly overdetermined. The translation, which on the surface may seem literal, involves a play of languages. Zeitlin is a matronymic surname, following Slavic rules, and found among Jews from places like Russia, Poland, and Lithuania. (The writer himself was born in Ukraine.) The translation of "Zeitlin" to "Tiempo" rests on a play on words that wrests *zeit* ("time" in German) from *Zeitl* (a woman's given name). Moreover, the meaning of the writer's given name, Israel, is hardly straightforward. Zeitlin/Tiempo modifies one of its generally accepted meanings, "God rules," but with a shift from the sacred to the secular. God and Caesar, polar opposites in Christian lore, are collapsed by the

Jewish writer. In addition, although César is a perfectly legible and reasonably common given name in Spanish, "Tiempo" is not a traditional Spanish surname. It sounds Spanish but rings artificial, much as drag signals its own artificiality. Similarly, it is clear that Tiempo did not adopt his pseudonym to hide his Jewishness for fear of antisemitic attacks. On the contrary, much of his work dealt with Jewish themes, not least of which was his condemnation of antisemitism. This hide-and-seek interplay is reflected in César Tiempo's claim to have published *Versos de una . . .* as a joke, even as he is solemnly meticulous about the details of Clara Beter's life in Ukraine. Moreover, the volume was taken seriously; readers were taken in by the ruse.

Throughout *Versos de una . . .* , drag's actualization of the self, even as the self appears to be manifestly "other," is the dominant mode. The combination of sexuality, sentimentality, melodrama, and gender impersonation framed as an intentional joke tie Cesar Tiempo's *Versos de una . . .* to a camp sensibility that Susan Sontag would contemplate decades later and in another country. Moreover, in "Notes on Camp" Sontag may have been the first to link Jewishness to homosexuality as avatars of modernity and to do so in a thoroughly positive way. In this pivotal 1964 essay, in which Sontag explains "the peculiar relation between Camp taste and homosexuality," she makes the analogy between Jews and gays, averring that

> the analogy is not frivolously chosen. Jews and homosexuals are the two outstanding creative minorities in contemporary western culture. Creative, that is, in the truest sense: they are creators of sensibilities. The two pioneering forces of modern sensibility are Jewish moral seriousness and homosexual estheticism and irony. (529)

Sontag argues that both Jews and gays want to legitimate themselves in the larger society, and that they offer moral and political credentials (Jews) and esthetic credentials (gays) as a way to do so. The argument holds for Jews in Argentina as much as for the US Jews Sontag had in mind:

> Jewish liberalism is a gesture of self-legitimization. So Camp taste which definitely has something propagandistic about it. Of course, the propaganda is in just the opposite direction. The Jews pinned their hopes for integrating into modern society on promoting the moral sense. Homosexuals have pinned their integration into society on promoting the esthetic sense. (529)

Sontag engages in a provocative coupling and de-linking: she presents the comparison between Jewishness and homosexuality, remarking that it may seem startling at first, but she insists that it is not frivolously invoked. The Jew and the homosexual are both outsiders with a shared desire to integrate into society, but each approaches integration in a different, even contradictory, way: Jews with moral seriousness, homosexuals with a refusal of seriousness and embrace of the esthetic. The specifically queer esthetic that both celebrates and undercuts the larger culture finds its parallel in the Jewish desire to reform as well as gain entry to society; both contain an implicit critique of the status quo. Yet both the Jewish subject and the homosexual subject embrace this imperfect culture, each in their own way.

By linking Jewishness and queerness via sensibility, Sontag diverts the reader's attention from what looms largest and most threatening for Gentiles and straight people. Neither Jews' non-Christian religious way of being nor homosexuals' transgressive sexuality could possibly underpin their respective bids for inclusion. Instead, Jews and homosexuals each offer a sensibility that is constitutive of modernity and that might be their entry card into what they intend to be a more inclusive culture. Though written from a US-European perspective, Sontag's remarks resonate with the intersections of queerness and Jewishness in Argentina's claim on modernity. Even more, perhaps, because Argentina is itself on the threshold, peering in from the edge of the outside. One way to frame the relationship between queer and Jew in modernity, in fact, is via the Argentine paradigm, in which—as I have argued—Jews oscillate between occupying the figurative space of the not-modern other and that of the modern European. In Argentina Jews are also European and as such carry the modern with them, in contrast to Europe, where, Naomi Seidman argues, Jewish claims to enter European modernity are "notoriously unreciprocated" (50).

Sontag's taxonomy, which distills a kind of essence of queerness and Jewishness for the sake of argument, seems to leave no space for the messy conjunction of queer Jewish people. Her campy queer subject is implicitly male, as are her Jews. Ironically, in formulating this theory of modernity, Sontag submerges her own subject position as a secular Jewish lesbian, irrevocably connected to, but at the margins of, both Jewishness and gay male camp.[12] Sontag, who wrote the introduction to the English version of Edgardo Cozarinsky's first book, *Urban Voodoo* (*Vudú urbano*), maintains an authorial distance from both Jewishness and queerness in "Notes on Camp," while Cozarinsky explores both in his fiction and films but rarely brings them into close contact.[13] His 2005 film *Night Watch* (*Noche de ronda*), made on his return to Buenos Aires after living in Paris for many years, for example, explores the city through the occasionally supernatural adventures of a gay male prostitute on All Soul's Night, a decidedly non-Jewish reference point.

Years after Sontag published "Notes on Camp," Naomi Seidman, in "Queer Ashkenaz," argues against the conventional, negative view of Jewish queerness by contrasting it with the implicitly homophobic and antisemitic modern European culture to which it aspires. Instead, she offers an analysis from within Jewishness that, like Sontag's, gives a positive valence to the queer-Jew pairing. Instead of being negatively perceived, Jewish queers as unmanly men and sexually predatory (or at least simply sexual) women, Jews are provocatively queer as men who insist on an internally determined mode of masculinity that prizes passionate connection between men. Seidman's argument owes much to Daniel Boyarin's analysis of Jewish masculinity, which, while not about queer sexuality per se, persuasively argues that what the dominant culture labels feminine is, rather, ideal Jewish masculinity that goes back to the Babylonian Talmud (1997).

The figure absent from all these constructs is the Jewish lesbian. Jewish lesbians are, following Terry Castle's analysis, phantasmagoric creatures, not because they do not exist, but rather because they occupy a small and historically reviled space in the heteronormative cultural imaginary. Castle's "apparitional lesbian," however, refuses to stay repressed; the culture invokes her at any hint of gender transgression. Taibele Efron (1912–1977), a case in point, defied gender norms, took one new name and then another, and became a key player in the rise of radio and television in Argentina. A quarter of a century after César Tiempo fashioned his eruditely playful nom de plume and established himself as a central figure in his own cultural moment, Efron performed a similar sleight of name, one that traces the distance between her origins, her identity, and her aspirations. Her Yiddish name, Taibele, means "little dove"; the Spanish "Paloma" is a simple translation. Her subsequent name change to "Blackie" is less straightforward. While working at a North American cultural institute in Argentina, Efron came across a recording of Negro spirituals and taught herself to sing them. Her biographer, Hinde Pomeraniec, recounts that the stage name "Blackie" was chosen for her by her radio listeners in 1934 after she won a contest that effectively introduced Black music from the United States to an Argentine audience. She soon shifted from spirituals to jazz, which was becoming popular in Buenos Aires. Although for Spanish speakers, the foreign word "Blackie" does not carry the racial charge that it does for English speakers, Efron's own father called his daughter on her appropriation of a culture she did not know. His solution was to send her to the United States to learn about it. In 1937 Efron went to New York, lived with her brother, a student at Columbia University, hung around Harlem, and studied first at Columbia (in what was then called the Institute for Primitive Music) and then at the historically Black Tuskegee Institute.

In the documentary film *Blackie: una vida en blanco y negro* (Blackie: A life in black and white), Efron, who confounded racial as well as gender norms, attributes her success to doing things that other women did not do. No doubt as a result of her transgression of gender roles and disregard of traditional gender behavior by becoming a jazz musician and putting together her own combo, and as a pioneer television producer whose marriage ended in divorce, Efron was presumed to be a lesbian. Myriam Escliar, who wrote what she calls a "novel/biography" of Efron, rejects stories of her subject's lesbianism, and Efron herself reacts with indignation at the assumption, saying that people thought she was a lesbian simply because she behaved in ways thought unsuitable for a woman. Efron herself was very private, and Escliar was unable to get access to her family for information. Her primary informant was Efron's companion, a woman she names only as Leocadia, who offers one singular detail about their relationship.[14] Efron had insomnia and could sleep only in Leocadia's arms. Sleeping with Leocadia can easily be understood through class differences. Efron is not only Leocadia's employer; she also uses her as a mother substitute. Read through that lens, Leocadia's are maternal arms. Read through queer desire, however, the lesbian appears. Nevertheless, Efron herself vehemently denies the suggestion that she was a lesbian:

> And it was very hard. They said all kinds of things, for example that I was a *lesbian*, since nobody ever heard anything about any love affairs I might have had. They treated me like an eccentric (my translation)
>
> [Y fue durísimo. Se decía de todo, por ejemplo, que era *lesbiana*, ya que no se me conocían aventuras amorosas. Se me trató como a una excéntrica (Efron, qtd. in Horvath, 70)]

Efron clearly expresses resentment about being thought a lesbian. Although we cannot know definitively about her sexuality, we do know for certain that she was transgressive in many other ways, as a singer and as a Jewish daughter who married a non-Jew, in her work as a producer, and in her entry into Black jazz culture. As such she reads as socially, if not necessarily sexually, queer. Efron's decision to travel to the United States to experience the jazz world in itself was hardly normative. Her later work as an influential producer, director, and interviewer on Argentine television was also unusual for a woman; and as she points out, after her separation from her husband, people did not see her involved romantically with men. Nor was she a maternal figure. "They treated me like an eccentric," a term of queerness following so quickly on the heels of her observation that people thought she was a lesbian. Actual same-sex desire is only one part of the queerness ascribed to Efron: her refusal to enact typical femininity—whether Argentine or Jewish—is of a piece with lesbianism in the popular imagination.

Women's sexual transgression is, at its source, an escape from patriarchal control, and as such resonates with queerness: daughters choosing their own sexual partners, wives refusing domestic servitude and abuse, women as prostitutes, particularly as prostitutes who resist being victimized and insist on their own subjectivity. Sexual transgressions, including queer sexuality, have borne a negative valence in the antisemitic west, associating Jewishness with degeneracy and therefore with homosexuality. Acknowledgment of sexual transgression in the context of Jewishness contributes to the anxiety about breaking down boundaries in the modern age: Jews enter and confuse the mainstream, all within a framework of heteromasculine normativity. Once women's perspectives are taken into account, the meaning of escape from a stultifying marriage or the conditions under which women engage in the sex trade is radically altered. The recuperation of sexual transgression with the rethinking of sex workers and runaway wives within the Jewish community is of a piece with progressive thinking generally and complicates the intersections of Jewishness, modernity, Argentineity, gender, and sexuality. In the realm of heterosexual transgression, Angélica Gorodischer's "Camera Obscura" (La cámara oscura) captures the moment of change during which sympathy shifts from the abandoned husband and family to the dishonored and disrespected runaway wife, and Nora Glickman's retelling of the Raquel Liberman story does the same. The very meaning of commercialized sex has changed: the prostitute (an active noun, suggesting the woman held responsible and disdained for her behavior) is more recently understood as the prostituted (i.e., trafficked, victimized) woman. Florencia Mujica and Daniel Najenson's documentary The Impure (*Impuros*) makes a case both for remembering the women trafficked by the Zwi Migdal and for holding those who exploited them accountable. The powerful presence in the film of Sonia Sánchez, herself a survivor of sex trafficking, relentlessly impresses upon the viewer the suffering and degradation of these prostituted women, insisting that they not be forgotten.[15]

Yet as much as these sexually transgressive behaviors, together with their revalencing at the hands of (mostly) women storytellers, revise heteronormativity, they do not fundamentally challenge it. Disobedient daughters marry perhaps inappropriate men, runaway wives abandon their husbands for other men and establish steady relationships. Prostitutes become heroes of triumph-over-adversity stories with Raquel Liberman as the prototype, are saintly and kind, as Tiempo's Clara Beter, or are objects of pity, completely undone, as is Sara in Feierstein's *Mestizo*.[16] One exception might be María Inés Krimer's prostitute in *La inauguración* (The inauguration), but she is dead, having tried to escape her traffickers. Her replacement, a petty thief who has killed an abusive stepfather and is not averse to having sexual relations with her captor, is the center of the novel in all her moral ambiguity, nobody's idea of a mother or grandmother whose actions can be reclaimed for the family's honor.

Lesbians, meanwhile, tend not to be recuperated within the family saga; they remain transgressive and defiant of the sexual norms that would contain them and make them manageable within the boundaries of heterosexuality. Insofar as the national narrative of modernity maps onto the patriarchal, heteronormative family, stories of lesbians do not compute. Reina Roffé's 1976 novel *Monte de Venus* (Mount of Venus) represents an extreme version of the suppression of lesbianism. Shortly after the novel was published, the right-wing junta that served as Argentina's government condemned the book as obscene and removed it from bookstores; the publisher got rid of copies in its warehouse and scrubbed references to the book and its author from its catalog (1985, 913). The novel, with its sexually transgressive challenge to society and its political challenge to the state, was effectively disappeared. It was not reissued until 2013, just about four decades after it vanished from sight. The novel has two main characters, Julia Grande and Barú, known only by that one name. Julia, poor and from a Catholic family, is a classic picaresque character, scrabbling to survive. Most often the victor in the small skirmishes of her life, she is betrayed by one of her women lovers, a teacher and writer, who blackmails Julia into giving up her child to her. Roffé does not overtly link Jewishness to women's sexual transgression in the novel. In fact, Jewishness is virtually absent in the text, though it is possible that Barú's name is a short form of Baruch or Barucha. Over the course of the novel Barú becomes increasingly involved in the resistance, a political counterpoint to Julia's sexual challenge to the dominant culture.

It is perhaps pertinent that Barú's narrative is solely focused on her life at school; the reader learns nothing of her family or its past, which, as we have seen, is the primary site of Jewish rootedness in so many narratives.[17] As it happens, the Jewish story Roffé would recall later in *El cielo dividido* (The divided sky) is the immigration story of Moroccan Sephardim, which diverges from the conventional story of Jews in Argentina. Moroccan Jews also tell the story of their migration and recall the familiar smells of a grandmother's cooking, but they confound the geopolitical epithet "ruso."

Whereas the feminizing of the Jewish male in the Western imaginary forges a discursive link between queer sexuality and Jewishness along the axis of masculinity, Jewishness and lesbianism have no easy purchase as linked concepts in heteronormative culture. At most, they function as a failed chiasmus, as in *Waiting for the Messiah*, in which Laura perceives a connection between her marginalization as a gay woman and Ariel's marginalization as a Jew. He, of course, sees no such parallel; for Ariel, Laura's expansive sexuality marks her as fully part of the larger modern world he aches to enter. As in Roffé's novel, the lesbian in the Jewish text is not Jewish, and it is only with difficulty that the Argentine cultural imaginary can make room for lesbian Jews.

Susana Blaustein Muñoz's 1980 autobiographical documentary *Susana* suggests that Argentina, and more specifically the provincial city of Mendoza, has no place for flesh-and-blood lesbians either. The film depicts the young filmmaker struggling to come out to her family under the constraints of culturally and socially imposed heteronormativity, in which Jewishness plays a quiet but significant part. Susana ultimately leaves Argentina, first to live in Israel and then in the United States, where, presumably, she can live her sexuality more freely. Blaustein left for Israel before the coup, but in 1977 she found herself in Stockholm, part of a flourishing lesbian community, at the same time that Sweden opened its borders wide to political refugees from Latin America's Southern Cone. Her current film project documents her return to Sweden and to the Finnish lover Kristina, with whom Blaustein had long been out of touch. Now married to Kristina, Susana explores their history and their relationship. In the fund-raising promotional clip for the film, still unmade at the time of this writing, Jewishness, linked to provincial Argentineity and family, seems to have receded into the deep background, as the women's once raucous and transgressive outlaw sexuality has mellowed into state-sanctioned marriage in another country.

Alejandra Pizarnik's Jewishness also reaches backward, into her roots, rather than occupying a central place in her poetic concerns. Undoubtedly the most renowned Argentine Jewish lesbian writer of the twentieth century, Pizarnik resists easy categorization. Jewishness seeps into Pizarnik's writing surreptitiously; only the subtlest of readers seem capable of excavating it in any convincing way.[18] Her forays into lesbianism in the writing published during her life tend toward the horrific, highly charged eroticized sadism worthy of the Marquis himself. In *The Bloody Countess* (*La condesa sangrienta*) the pleasure of the submissive partner is not anywhere apparent. Pizarnik draws her reader into the dark side of sexuality, where sex, pain, power, and death—the sexual torture and murder of an unwilling peasant by an aristocrat—emerge as beautiful and thrilling. Evil in *The Bloody Countess* is an effect of class privilege, evoking complicity with the pleasure of inflicting pain, dominance for the sake of one-sided pleasure, impunity, and entitlement, from the unapologetic point of view of the torturer. There is nothing in this text that suggests a critique of this structure of radical inequality. There is nothing of political queerness or of Jewish ethics here. Pizarnik the poet seduces her readers into complicity with evil, for how else can we characterize the torture and murder of young women for the sake of one's own sexual/textual pleasure?[19]

With the exception of *The Bloody Countess*, which flamboyantly displaces transgressive sexuality onto another time, another place, and an actual historical figure, Pizarnik deliberately suppressed her sexually charged writing, never publishing it during her lifetime.[20] Years after Pizarnik's death, Fiona Mackintosh gained access to Pizarnik's unpublished manuscripts, allowing her to explore Pizarnik's self-censorship, especially of the "many prose pieces with lesbian sexual encounters as their focus, none of which were published by Pizarnik (nor by her literary executors)" (519). Mackintosh generously cites passages that allow her reader to see a sometimes-double suppression, in which Pizarnik crosses out overt references to lesbian sexuality and then keeps even the revised texts from publication. In some cases the redacted lines are visible; in others the erasures are absolute. Although Mackintosh writes primarily about Pizarnik's self-censorship with reference to lesbian sexuality, she also devotes a few paragraphs to the places where Pizarnik makes Jewishness legible by caricaturing Yiddish-inflected speech, only to leave it out of her published work.

When Ana Beciu published her posthumous edition of Pizarnik's *Poesía completa* (Complete poetic works), she included some previously unpublished work, but by no means all of it. Although the volume includes some prose, the "many prose pieces of lesbian encounters" are nowhere to be seen, and the one, raw, erotically charged autobiographical passage is buried in a long prose poem. It did not take long for readers to single out the five lines in which Pizarnik celebrates the pleasure of well-performed cunnilingus, likening the lover's pubic hair to "a disheveled rabbi."[21] The adjective in Spanish is *desaseado*, which carries with it the suggestion of a lack of attention to personal hygiene. The juxtaposition of the lesbian body and rabbinic funkiness crosses so many lines of propriety that it is hard to know where to begin. The passage offers a brilliant example of poetic compression in which any single one of the taboo-breaking poetic moves the poet makes would have been remarkable in itself. It would have been enough for Pizarnik to name the act of cunnilingus; she names it multiple times, reveling in the techniques of the tongue and turning colloquial terms describing female genitalia and oral sex into poetic language.

> I speak of cunt and I speak of death,
>     all is cunt, and I have licked cunts in numerous countries and only felt pride in my virtuosity—the mahatma gandhi of tonguing, the Ein-
>     stein of cunnilingus, the Reich of lapping it up, the Reid of breaking trail through pubic hair like disheveled rabbis—oh the pleasure of filth![22] (my translation)
>
> [hablo de la concha y hablo de la muerte,
>     todo es concha, y yo he lamido conchas en varios países y sólo sentí orgullo por mi virtuosismo—la mahtma gandhi del lengüeteo, la Ein-
>     stein de la mineta, la Reich del lengüetazo, la Reid de abrirse camino entre pelos como de rabinos desaseados—¡oh el goce de la roña! (412)]

It would have been enough to elevate the word "cunt" in a line that equates its power with the power of death and that resonates with epic poetry ("I sing of arms and the man"), and then to insist on both the metaphysical aspect of cunt ("todo es concha") and its fundamental carnality, bringing the reader back to the alarming word itself each time. It would have been enough to celebrate a sexual expertise developed though years of practice. It would have been enough to evoke the unkempt rabbi, breaking the code of reverence before such a figure. It would have been enough to evoke the wild and messy pubic hair of the lover. But to double down on the transgression and reduce the rabbi to a metaphor for the tangle of a woman's pubic hair is simply breathtaking. Here, in this buried passage in a withheld poem, Pizarnik intertwines the explosive elements of joyously overt lesbian pleasure and somewhat rancid, but also sacred Jewish masculinity; buries the bomb in a rambling, unpublished text; and leaves its detonation to her posthumous reader. Also unusual in this poem is a palpable sense that Pizarnik is having fun; the speaker clearly revels in comparing her cunnilingual brilliance to that of some of the great revolutionary thinkers of the twentieth century, gaily claiming her place among these powerful men, her tongue now firmly planted in her cheek.[23]

Women's transgressive sexuality takes a different road to recuperation when it can claim heteronormativity and lobby for simple sexual equality: the argument that women have the same right to sexual freedom as men is less likely to encounter resistance when it is made within the safe boundaries of heterosexuality. Perhaps the most exuberant example of this recuperation of women's (hetero)sexuality is Diana Raznovich's *Mater erótica* (Erotic *mater*, 1992), dedicated to her mother and consisting of two narratives, both of which take place in what was East Berlin shortly after the Wall came down. In the first, a forty-two-year-old woman has a rambunctious affair with her friend's adolescent son; in the second an older man who has been a double agent has sex with a sixteen-year-old girl. Consensual sadomasochism, degradation role-playing, bondage, and anal as well as genital sex all come into play in these sex-positive tales, whose descriptions more than border on the pornographic. Social markers of race, ethnicity, religion, class, and age are eclipsed by the fact of desire, even as the seismic geopolitical shifts taking place in the Germany of the 1990s ground the texts politically outside of Argentina. Jewishness is absent from these tales, in sharp contrast to its place in Raznovich's 1995 play *Rear Entry* (*De atrás para adelante*), a work in which heterosexual desire is displaced by transgender identity and the desire for affirmation. The family depicted in the play is overtly, not incidentally, Argentine and Jewish, and Dolly (née Javier) is centrally, not incidentally, transgender. The Jewish patriarch must be tricked into embracing his transgressive, and highly successful, adult child in order to maintain his own precarious hold on middle-class status. The play is an almost classic farce, containing elements of both mistaken identity and bathroom humor: Simon Goldberg created his financial empire manufacturing toilets, and Dolly saves the threatened business by marketing vibrantly colored toilet paper. Simon must be wrenched into recognizing and accepting his transgender child; for the rest of the family Dolly's transition is a matter of fact. The play presents Dolly, formerly Javier, as a happily married mother and a brilliant businesswoman. Simon, mired in antiquated notions of gender and plagued by the homophobia that has estranged him from his child, is the odd man out in a family that works to reintegrate Dolly and, in the process, save the family business. Jewishness is, on the one hand, normalized in *Rear Entry*, and on the other is gently mocked for its link to bathroom obsessions and, by extension, to problems of defecation—here not the blocked bowels that plague the Pechoff family in Szichman's novels, but the fact that the bathroom biz is going down the toilet. When Simon finally acknowledges and accepts Dolly as his child, transgender becomes normalized, another way of being in the Jewish family, and the very key to maintaining the family's survival and its place in a precarious socioeconomic system.

Although its tone and register are radically different from Raznovich's *Rear Entry*, Julia Solomonoff's 2009 feature film *The Last Summer of La Boyita (El último verano de la Boyita)* is also a study in struggle to normalize alterity. In Solomonoff's movie, as in Raznovich's play, Jewishness is an already-normalized difference that nevertheless retains something of intractable otherness, while transgender (in the play) and intersexuality (in the film) are troubling issues to be resolved. The eleven-year-old protagonist of *The Last Summer of La Boyita*, Jorgelina, is a Jewish girl who precipitates the discovery of the intersexuality of a young adolescent named Mario. The film follows Jorgelina's desire to understand how to integrate that difference into a world in which distinctions between childhood and adolescence, no less than those between the urban middle class and the rural working poor, are also a challenge to navigate.[24] Jorgelina's natural curiosity about her own body (she examines it, she wanders off with a gynecology textbook to examine the illustrations, and she asks her sister about her experience of puberty) makes her the ideal focal point of the film. Jorgelina accepts everything before her as natural, has no preconceived notions of what is normal, and so asks questions about everything.

Mario's intersexuality confounds the simple binary of conventional sex and gender. When Jorgelina asks her doctor father about male menstruation, having seen signs of it in Mario, all she wants is a logical explanation of the facts she has observed. But her friend's intersexuality also opens up distinctions based on class and education. Elba, Mario's mother, has ignored indications of her child's physical anomaly, explaining that she did not follow up with a doctor's advice to seek treatment for him because Mario is so normal and healthy. Mario's rustic, rural father, on the other hand, polices the gender binary rigorously, first reprimanding Mario and Jorgelina for their playful cross-gender masquerade and later beating Mario for exhibiting traits of womanhood. Jorgelina's father, who is charming, urban, wise, and compassionate, tries to convince Elba that she needs to have Mario treated medically. Mario's mother is portrayed as a caring but uneducated and misguided woman. Her sense of her child as a fundamentally healthy human being gets no purchase in the film, except, perhaps, by Jorgelina. Elba is distraught not because Mario is sexually anomalous but because she realizes that her husband will not accept this news easily. Her sense of her child as a fundamentally healthy human being is, however, overwhelmed by the medical expertise of Jorgelina's father, and the viewer is implicitly asked to agree with him. The filmmaker portrays Mario's father as an ignorant brute and Jorgelina's as an enlightened, caring, educated professional. Both men, however, coincide in their enforcement of binary gender conventions.

As Solomonoff's film suggests, the resignification of sexual ambiguity and gender queerness is an irregular process. Buenos Aires is home to a vibrant LGBTQIA+ culture, and the development of Judíos Argentinos Gays began in 2004. The organization became an affiliate of DAIA in 2015, thus entering the mainstream of Jewish Argentine culture.[25] Even so, Maximiliano Pelosi's 2010 documentary *Otro entre otros* (An other among others) tells a story not unlike Blaustein Muñoz's *Susana*, three decades earlier, detailing the pressure of heteronormativity within family and community. Still, the once-powerful mooring cable that bound homophobia, misogyny, and antisemitism into a powerful tool for cultural annihilation has slowly been giving way to narratives that recuperate queer folk and transgressive women. Sexual and gender transgression can now intertwine with Jewishness as modes of liberation, and the association between Jewishness and queerness, writ large, reverberates with the creative productive energy of writers like Edgardo Cozarinsky, for whom Jewish identity cannot be quite fixed even as clandestine queer desire is rendered visible, performers like Paloma Efron, whose transgression of gender roles could be understood by many only in sexual terms, and artists like Guillermo Kuitca, whose canvases only sometimes bear even the most subtle Jewish and queer traces.

# BY WAY OF CONCLUSION

In 2003 Tamara Kamenszain published a collection of poetry called *El ghetto*. The title suggests a segregated world where Jews are kept apart from society as a whole and brings to mind the centuries-old European restrictions on Jewish bodies and Jewish movement. Nevertheless, a key poem in the collection assumes a very different relationship between Jews and the space of the nation. "El árbol de la vida" (Tree of life) places Jewish life and death at the very heart of Argentineity. The poem opens with a cry of mourning, "Mi duelo" (My grief), uttered from a Jewish cemetery on the outskirts of Buenos Aires. (All translations from the poem are my own):

> My grief, what I am seeing
> is Greater Buenos Aires from a Jewish cemetery.
>
> [Mi duelo, lo que estoy viendo
> es el Gran Buenos Aires desde un cementerio judío. (43)]

In mourning, the speaker's vision radiates out from the cemetery, and from that site of Jewish death she lays claim to Greater Buenos Aires, itself a kind of sacred Argentine ground. The cemetery is emblematic of the Jewish past, but also, importantly and necessarily, it is from there that the living Jewish woman, the daughter who has traversed the city and its outskirts to get to the site of her father's grave, declares her presence. The speaker's route to the geographical heart of the poem takes her from Quilmes and Ezpeleta, near the coast of greater Buenos Aires, to the inland cemetery. She passes through a vibrant social landscape that includes a florist's shop, an evangelical church promising an end to suffering, and the iconic aroma of sausages cooking on an outdoor grill:

In the doorway the florist crosses herself
before a parade of relatives and neighbors
improvised skullcaps, women of easy tears
gather in the line of mourners
it is not for my sorrow, they keep me at a distance, I am
    seeing them
I do not join this timid crowd
I am left, headed the other way, with my solitary loss
through Quilmes and Ezpeleta to La Tablada floating
beneath the smoke of sizzling chorizos,
of muddy unpaved streets
dead roads and, at the end, an evangelical signboard.
"End your suffering" the slogan on the sign announces
as stone upon stone I bury
the badly translated photocopy of the Kaddish
deep in my handbag.

[En la puerta la florista se persigna
ante un cortejo de parientes y vecinos
solideos improvisados, mujeres de llanto fácil
se congregan en la fila de los deudos
no es por mi duelo, me segregan, los estoy viendo
no me sumo a esa muchedumbre abatatada
me resta a contramano mi pérdida solitaria
por Quilmes y Ezpeleta hasta La Tablada flotando
bajo el humo de chorizos arrebatados,
de calles barrosas sin apisonar
vías muertas y, al final, una tarima evangelista.
"Pare de sufrir" anuncia la humorada del cartel
cuando piedra sobre piedra entierro
mal traducida la fotocopia de kaddish
en el fondo de mi cartera. (43)]

The mourners who trace that path cut a visibly Jewish line through Christian space: the woman who crosses herself, the scent of pork sausages, the church with its uplifting sign. The remarkable thing about these neighborhoods and the sensory experience of passing through them is precisely how unexceptional they are. Like the cemetery, which at first evokes a kind of Jewish universality, the route the speaker takes is both generically quotidian and locally recognizable. She eventually names the cemetery; it is La Tablada, a Jewish place in the middle of otherwise Gentile terrain, familiar, specific, evocative, and personally meaningful to Kamenszain's readers. That terrain, moreover, is benign: the florist offers a prayer to her god for the Jewish dead, and the evangelical church makes its promise to all passersby.

Once she has traversed the muddy streets of Greater Buenos Aires and reached the gravesite, the speaker confronts her mourning and claims the flowering of a living future that encompasses both Jewish and non-Jewish elements of the cityscape she has taken in during the course of her journey. Grief and the grim landscape are transformed, as the poem ends with a flowering into the future.

> My grief, what I am seeing
> will be now and forever this greenery that I dedicate to you.
> Today all my roots bloom in the treetops.
>
> [Mi duelo, lo que estoy viendo
> será de aquí en más este verdor que te dedico.
> Hoy florecen en las copas de los árboles todas mis raíces. (44)]

The roots of the speaker's past are the source and nourishment of the trees in her field of vision: it is those roots that flower in the treetops she sees before her. Staking a claim to Argentina, the speaker announces that "all her roots" are rendered visible in the new budding of the trees that symbolize the nation's vibrant life.

In this poem, as in most of the books, films, and works of visual art I have discussed in the previous chapters, it is the Jewish artist, writer, musician, thinker, or filmmaker whose work cuts Jewish furrows into Argentine culture. The metaphor of planting wheat and reaping doctors gives way to another, in which the generations of Jews in Argentina have planted seeds of Jewish meaning in Argentine culture. The Jewish claim to Argentineity has been made largely by Jews themselves, and they have crafted a rich presence in the larger Argentine landscape.[1]

That Jewish creative workers have been successful in their labors is due in no small part to the fact that the larger culture was already receptive to Jewishness as a site of meaning, thanks to the already existing, but complex, connection between Jewishness and cosmopolitan modernity. The paradox that Jewishness poses—that it is simultaneously emblematic of modernity and of the lingering traces of the premodern—both sets the stage for and echoes the paradox that Jewishness poses for Argentina: that it is woven into but not entirely at one with Argentineity. Inscribing Jewishness into the objects they make, Jewish artists, writers, and filmmakers, as well as shopkeepers, psychoanalysts, teachers, and political actors, make Jewish Argentineity a legible, coherent phenomenon for the culture as a whole. Although the collective narrative that gives meaning to Jewishness can never be fully under their control, Jewish Argentines, with their presence and their labor, stake a claim to the nation and create an Argentina in which Jewishness is an intrinsic element.

# NOTES

## PREFACE

1. The reader should feel free to read this term either to refer to the light Jesus and his teaching brought to the world or to the turn toward reason eighteen centuries later. Or both.

2. In the context of Latin America, see, for example, my own work on gender, sexuality, and national identity in *After Exile*, Sommer's *Foundational Fictions*, Achugar's study of the production of nation via the canonization of a narrow range of texts that exclude those authored by women and marginalized others, and Masiello's *Between Civilization and Barbarism*.

3. Doris Sommer has eloquently demonstrated that the love story in nineteenth-century Latin America functioned as a metaphor for nation building. Conflict between lovers in those texts is largely a function of differences between groups (political, racial, social), not within them.

## CHAPTER 1

1. See the indispensable history of Argentine Jewry by Haim Avni, *Argentina and the Jews: A History of Jewish Immigration*.

2. There is, of course, important scholarship on Afro-Argentineity and indigeneity, but dominant Argentine culture has long presented itself as essentially European. This is the point made by Gordillo and Hirsch (2003) and Cottrol (2007).

3. Erin Graff Zivin makes a similar claim in her excellent study of the figure of the Jew and the idea of Jewishness in Latin America, *The Wandering Signifier*.

4. Postmodernity, particularly the postmodernity *avant la lettre* that Juan José Brunner proposes and Senkman mentions, is not in the interest of the peripheral nation-state, which prizes the solidity, presence, and dignity of modern (national) subjectivity, confirmed by other like nation-states (Brunner 1987, ctd. in Senkman

126). Senkman convincingly argues that modernity's grand narratives and real consequences have disadvantaged developing nations, but that peripheral postmodernity does not offer a satisfying solution.

5. For an analysis of national identity among Argentine (and other Southern Cone) exiles and expatriates, see Kaminsky, *After Exile: Writing the Latin American Diaspora*.

6. There is, currently, a debate over the spelling of the word "antisemitism" and its variants. "Anti-Semitism," with a hyphen and a capital *s*, remains the preferred spelling in many style guides, but I am in agreement with those, such as Deborah Lipstadt, who point out that "anti-Semitism" implies that there is something called "Semitism" that one can be against, or that "Semite" is a meaningful ethnic (or religious or racial) classification. "Antisemitism" is a practice of othering, oppression, and hatred directed toward Jewish people. As such it is its own entity.

7. The reference to the character's claim to nobility is likely not a swipe at the German Jewish philanthropist Maurice von Hirsch, who in fact inherited his title from his father. Von Hirsch established the Jewish Colonization Association in 1891, the same year Martel's novel was published.

8. The pseudonymous Martel is not unique in his antisemitic patriotism. The more mainstream, deeply Catholic and right-wing Manuel Gálvez, whose lifelong anti-immigration stand was nourished by antisemitism, wrote a novel, *El mal metafísico* (The metaphysical malady, 1900), that represents Jews in troublingly stereotyped ways.

9. Gerchunoff was born in what is now Ukraine in 1883. His family came to Argentina, settling first in Moisés Ville in 1889 and, after his father's death at the hands of a fugitive gaucho, in another of the Jewish colonies. In 1895 Gerchunoff moved definitively to Buenos Aires, where he worked as a college professor, writer, and journalist. He published *Los gauchos judíos* in 1910, in homage of the centenary of the May Revolution, which laid the groundwork for Argentine independence.

10. Both the urban speculators of *The Stock Market* and the Jewish colonists in Entre Ríos and elsewhere keep the indigenous other at bay. Nevertheless, there is a haunting portrait in the Moisés Ville museum of Filomeno Zárate, an indigenous man of the Abipones nation, who walked into the Jewish settlement one day. He never told anyone his history, but he made himself a presence in the colony, living among the Jewish settlers for many years. Brief reference is made to him in Eva Guelbert de Rosenthal's *Memoria oral de Moisés Ville*.

11. This, in contrast to the writer-protagonist in Gustavo Kusminsky's novel *Médanos: Premio de narrativa hispanoamericana* (Sand dunes: Prize winner in Latin American narrative), who wins literary awards via corruption and celebrates them via sexual violence.

12. Raquel Liberman's story of being prostituted by the Jewish crime syndicate Zwi Migdal has been retold numerous times and will be discussed in a subsequent chapter.

13. The swindling of Jews has enjoyed a long tradition in Hispanic culture. If, as is likely, they had read the Spanish epic poem *The Poem of the Cid* (*El poema del mío Cid*) in school, the Argentine agents would have remembered that one of the episodes in the poem celebrating the national hero's honor, loyalty, bravery, and general superiority concerns the Cid's tricking two Jewish moneylenders and running off with the loan they'd made him. The money stolen from Raquel and Vidas enabled the Cid to raise a small army and, ultimately, to ingratiate himself with his king.

14. The struggle to maintain Moisés Ville as a Jewish space in the face of decline in the latter part of the twentieth century and new people coming in in the early part of the twenty-first seems to have fallen to a small group of women who encourage Jewish tourism, maintain the museum, house visitors, and conduct tours. Connecting with Jewish tourism is a way of maintaining the town's Jewish character and history, so that Jewishness in Argentina has become a globalized project.

## CHAPTER 2

1. This formulation is still current. Recently, the Buenos Aires government promoted urban development projects with the phrase "hacer Buenos Aires."

2. There is a resonance here with Bhabha's "mimic men," but with an important difference. Bhabha's mimic men are native Indians who identify with the colonizer. In Argentina, it is the descendants of the colonizers who themselves are not a dominant force in the global order, who claim Europeanness.

3. Pratt 27–28. Pratt's thoughtful analysis of modernity in Latin America as necessarily imbricated with a series of others (geographical, historical) tends to set Argentina aside.

4. Universal male suffrage was enacted as law in 1912. Women got the vote in 1947.

5. I am grateful to Alicia Partnoy (personal communication) for reminding me of this.

6. A third axis of Argentine otherness compresses race, gender, class, and geography into a single term that rests on Asian difference. "Chinita," which literally means "little Chinese female," refers to poor, rural, mestiza women and functions as a term of both affection and denigration.

7. Borges's fascination with Jewish mysticism has been well studied, most notably by Jaime Alazraki (1972), Saúl Sosnowski (1976), and Edna Aizenberg (1984).

8. To be sure, this mother is also an outsider of sorts, an immigrant from Brazil who came to Argentina as a child whose hazy ancestry renders her claims to high-end ancestry not so easily refuted.

9. It is not just Jews who leave spatiality for temporality. For Kovadloff, Europe as a whole is organized spatially, in contrast to South American nations "founded on the predominant inscription of man in time" (Kovadloff 79).

10. In contrast, Sarlo is explicit in the importance of changing meanings and contested practices of gender, particularly around the proper behavior of women and new technologies that make women's greater freedom—from the end of corsets to electric streetlights, from the phonograph to private cars.

11. Alicia Partnoy notes that the end of the word is puzzling—"ira" is not an adjectival ending in in Spanish. "But," she says, "it makes us think of rage, ire" (Partnoy, personal correspondence).

12. Partnoy (personal communication) wonders if "the omission of indigenous and black people [in Gelman's portmanteau of Argentine ethnicity might] be because they, unlike the others, are not to be blamed" for complicity in Che Guevara's death.

13. It is, perhaps, worth quoting Sznaider at length:

> Cosmopolitanism combines appreciation of difference and diversity with efforts to conceive of new democratic forms of political rule beyond the nation-state. . . . In this view, cosmopolitanism differs fundamentally from all views of vertical differentiation that seek to place social difference in a hierarchical relation of superiority and subordination, whereas universalism is the dissolution of all difference and represents the countervailing principle to hierarchical subordination. Universalism obliges us to respect others as equals in principle, yet for that very reason it neglects what makes others different. On the contrary, the particularity of others is sacrificed to an assumed universal equality that denies its own origins and interests. Universalism thereby becomes two-faced, involving both respect and hegemony. Cosmopolitanism differs in its recognition of difference as a maxim of thought, social life, and practice, both internally and externally. It neither orders differences hierarchically nor dissolves them, but accepts them as such—indeed invests them with positive value. It is sensitive to historic cultural particularities, respecting the specific dignity and burden of a group, a people, a culture, a religion. Cosmopolitanism affirms what is excluded both by hierarchical difference and by universal equality—namely perceiving others as different and at the same time equal. (5–6)

See, among others, Elizabeth Minnich and Catherine MacKinnon for the feminist critique of universalism in the legal realm. Seyla Benhabib also critiques what she calls "moral universalism," but she goes on to argue for a "dialogic universalism" that allows for difference. See also Mitchell Cohen on "rooted cosmopolitanism" and Kwame Anthony Appiah on cosmopolitan patriotism.

14. In fact, Tamar Garb maintains that antisemitism (in contrast to anti-Jewishness, which is religious in nature) is a product of the scientific racism of the nineteenth century (22). Sznaider invokes Marx to articulate the paradox of

the simultaneous identification of the Jews with the premodern and the modern, with the Enlightenment as the defining moment and phenomenon of modernity:

> Marx put the Jews center stage in the European drama of modernity. Jews became the symbol of all modern paradoxes. As figures of particularity, they undermined the universal claim of the Enlightenment, still living in fantasy worlds of close-knit communities. At the same time, Jews were also the symbol of community's opposite: transnationalism, homelessness, abstraction, multiple loyalties, and the money economy. (21)

15. The juxtapositon of "Israelite" and "Argentine" in the AMIA's very name highlights both the separateness of the terms and their inexorable link. In contrast to the modern "Argentina," the term "Israelite" now seems redolent with antiquity (perhaps even more in English than in Spanish), but it was not uncommon terminology at the time the AMIA was established. In addition, even though the "mutuality" inscribed in the title no doubt originally referred to the bond linking the members of the Jewish Argentine community, the national response to the bombing justifies a post-bombing reading that connects local Jews to the Argentine nation as a whole.

16. Pratt, op. cit. p. 35, synthesizes the work of a range of thinkers on the distinction between modernization and modernity. She quotes Norbert Lechner (1990) on "instrumental" versus "normative" rationalism and Rodrigo Montoya (1992), who contrasts modernization as a capitalist, Westernizing project to modernity's autonomy and self-determination, among others.

17. It is, for example, the theme of Cristina Peri Rossi's "Las estatuas o la condición del extranjero," in which the speaker is as invisible to the natives as are the statues in the town square. For a full discussion of the invisibility of the exile, see Kaminsky, *After Exile*.

18. See David Sharp, "Possession of the Ball," for a further discussion of the soccer episode.

19. See Donna Guy, *Sex and Danger in Buenos Aires*, for a comprehensive, thoughtful overview of the history and cultural meaning of prostitution in Argentina. Guy neither highlights nor diminishes Jewish participation in the trafficking of women.

# CHAPTER 3

1. "un argentino es un español que se cree norteamericano y en realidad no es nada más que un italiano pobre; por eso sufre como un judío." (Pron citing Drucaroff citing Pron, 2009).

2. I am grateful to Carla Manzoni for bringing *Vientos de agua* to my attention.

3. See *After Exile* (1999), where I explore claims to national identity by political exiles, and *Argentina: Stories for a Nation* (2008), where I examine Argentines' crafting of a national identity in relation both to their own dreams and to their spectral appearances in the dreams of others.

4. Sandra Harding argues that, inasmuch as all knowledge is produced from a standpoint, it cannot be value-neutral. Instead, the researcher's own awareness of her or his positionality is a precondition of what she calls "strong objectivity."

5. Goldberg's title, "Literatura judía latinoamericana: Modelos para armar" (Latin American Jewish writing: A model kit), slyly references the Gentile Argentine novelist Julio Cortázar, who has probably never been categorized in quite that way before.

6. Juan José Saer reminds us that the Montoneros' genealogy includes the ultra-Catholic, right-wing, and antisemitic Movimiento Nacionalista Tacuara (MNT). "The ideology of [left-wing groups, particularly the famous Montoneros] was extremely shady: many came from right-wing nationalist origins, like the group Tacuara, which was nationalist, ultra-Catholic, antisemitic and pro-Nazi" (ctd. in Scorer, 185).

7. *La crítica de las armas* is Feinmann's second novel about this protagonist. The first, *La astucia de la razón*, concerns Pablo's relationship with Western philosophy. Like Feinmann himself, the character is a politically engaged philosopher.

8. Daniel Hendler plays the first three Ariels. The fourth is played by Alan Sabbagh, who looks nothing like Hendler. The assimilating Jew, played by Hendler, is slim, smooth-shaven, and handsome. Sabbagh, in contrast, has a soft-looking body and an unfashionable beard, and although he gets the girl, a beautiful and sexy Orthodox woman, he is decidely no matinee idol.

9. "Once" (pronounced own-say), the name of the neighborhood, translates as the number eleven.

# CHAPTER 4

1. "Zakhor" translates roughly to the admonition "Remember," with the implied stipulation that remembrance carries with it the expectation of action.

2. Szichman first published *Los judíos del Mar Dulce* in 1971. He has since revised the novel. My discussion refers to the original version, which Szichman says is marred by a desire for vengeance, a linguistic and cultural schizophrenia resulting from his then-recent move from Buenos Aires to Venezuela. "En la novela estaba presente mi profunda exasperación, un gran desenfado, una enorme necesidad de exhibirme como un enfant terrible. Pero faltaba algo. Un principio organizador. Una especie de andamiaje que sustentara el edificio narrativo" (Szichman, 2013). (My profound exasperation was present in the novel—a great sense of abandon, an enormous need to show the world I was an *enfant terrible*. But it was missing something. An

organizing principle. A kind of scaffolding that would support the narrative structure [my translation].) I am drawn to the very rawness of the original version.

3. Szichman's own hand is highly visible as well, insofar as he has taken the original novel and rewritten it, making the confection of the text visible to the persistent reader.

4. Having grown up in Spain, Neuman now refers to himself as "Hispano-Argentine."

5. *Una vez Argentina* represents another set of Argentine Jewish texts, those of continuing diaspora. Sergio Waisman's *Leaving* is another, written in English about Jewish Argentines who emigrated to the United States. Writers Pablo Urbanyi (Canada), Nora Strejilevich, Alicia Borinsky, and Alicia Partnoy (United States) are also among Argentine Jewish émigrés whose work can be fruitfully read in the light of multiple migrations.

6. See, for example, the opening scene of Fabian Hofman's *I Miss You* (*Te extraño*).

7. See Senkman (2000) for a discussion of Jewish memory in *El árbol de la gitana*.

8. Such haunting is explicit in the text: Her mother is visited by a ghostly figure she calls "la Dama Blanca"; the Italian grandmother sees herself looking at herself in a case of self-haunting; and although the laconic and bitter Jewish grandmother never speaks of her ghosts, the protagonist is certain that she too is haunted.

9. That story is a parable of a young man who learns that the only way to move a large boulder is to break it into small stones, like the heart: "—¿Quién mueve de su sitio un corazón entero? El corazón, para avanzar, ha de estar en pedazos" (293). [Who moves a whole heart from its place? The heart, to move forward, has to be in pieces.] Which is where the book ends.

10. In the narrative Christopher Columbus meets up with her ancestor, Micer Nicolo Oderigo, Genovese ambassador. Oderigo tells Columbus about his conversation with Samuel Dujovne, teacher of the Chazars. Thus does the mix of religions, nationalities, and family begin in the space of the imagination, to be made material in Argentina, several hundred years later. Oderigo's descendant, a Genovese sea captain named Giuseppe Oderigo, winds up going to Argentina, invited by Rivadavia, to set up trade with Paraguay, where he is held more or less captive, not permitted to leave. Columbus is fascinated by Oderigo's story of traveling to the land of the Chazars, since Columbus had read about them in a book by Yehuda Ha-levy (26–27), suggesting that Columbus himself was Jewish or converso.

11. Dujovne and Feierstein implicitly agree with feminist philosopher María Lugones, an Argentine living in the US, for whom claims to purity are suspect at best.

12. When the paramilitary come for him during the dirty war, he has already been dead for three years, but his widow burns the books he published (202).

13. Alicia tells us that she does not learn to make gefilte fish from her Jewish grandmother and that her Italian grandmother's only recipe is for a decidedly

non-Italian white sauce. Her mother barely manages to show her how to make her cauliflower pudding, another white, bland food (23). The women of the family most emphatically do not bear the responsibility for preserving ethnic identity with elaborate food preparation.

14. For a thorough discussion of this gender distinction, see Kaminsky, *After Exile*.

15. The overt link between death of an early generation and the birth of the new, as well as of how this is connected to diaspora, occurs in the paternal line as well, when, on the night of Alicia's father's birth, the family receives a letter saying that the newborn's grandfather has died in a pogrom (203).

## CHAPTER 5

1. Similarly, as I suggested in chapter 4, Mario Muchnik's *Mundo judío: Crónica personal* also makes Jews legible to a Gentile readership.

2. See Kaminsky 2011 for a full discussion of the scene in *Waiting for the Messiah*.

3. See Mirelman for a detailed discussion of the events and the historical, social, and economic context. The estimate of more than one thousand injured is taken from the City of Buenos Aires's official website, http://www.buenosaires.gob.ar/areas/ciudad/historico/calendario/destacado.php?menu_id=23203&ide=275. Other sources claim seven hundred dead and about four thousand wounded.

4. Other memory-texts of the Tragic Week include the play *Ala de criados* (Servants' wing) by Mauricio Kartun (2009). Mario Szichman, in *At 8:25 Evita Became Immortal*, plays the Tragic Week for dark comedy. The day after the Pechof family arrives in Buenos Aires the events of the week begin, making the family patriarch believe that he had been tricked, and that the family had never left Poland.

5. See Mollie Lewis Nouwen for a discussion of this text.

6. In an integrationist move, Saslavsky also casts a Jewish actress, Berta Singerman, in the role of an Italo-Argentine diva.

7. For an excellent discussion of the intersection of culture and politics around the AMIA bombing, see Edna Aizenberg's *Books and Bombs in Buenos Aires*.

8. Of the twenty-nine people who died in the embassy bombing, four were Israelis and twenty-two were Argentines. Two hundred and forty-two were injured.

9. Personal conversation with Dobry.

10. See Fried (2005) for a discussion of the punctum as the guarantor of nontheatricality of the photograph.

11. Although the numbers vary slightly, the *Jewish Encyclopedia* conservatively counts forty-seven Jews killed, ninety-two severely injured, and five hundred slightly wounded in the pogrom, and approximately seven hundred Jewish-owned homes and six hundred businesses were plundered and destroyed. The riots were instigated by charges of the ritual murder of a Christian child (i.e., the antisemitic medieval

blood libel charge that, zombie-like, refuses to die). http://www.jewishencyclopedia.com/articles/9350-kishinef-kishinev. Accessed 15 Apr. 2013.

12. Personal conversation, 6 Mar. 2013.

13. I am indebted to Noni Benegas, personal conversation, for this reference.

14. "Jewishness is embodied there with her characteristic charge of ambivalence, and consists in extensive reflections marked by an emphasis, somewhere between offhand and moving, for example, on a visit to the synagogue of Segovia." ["Lo judío se plasma allí con su carga característica de ambivalencia, y consiste en extensas reflexiones marcadas por un énfasis entre casual y patético, por ejemplo, en una visita a la sinagoga de Segovia"] (Nora Catelli [2012], n.p.).

15. See Mizraje for a lucid discussion of this work.

16. The translator Helen Lane has a short piece on Satz; Polo Garcia's was the only scholarly article I could find dedicated to his work, although Senkman and others mention him.

17. See Kuperminc's artist's book, *Borges y la Cábala: Senderos del verbo* (*Borges and the Kabbalah: Paths to the word*), created together with Saúl Sosnowski.

18. Guillermo Kuitca. Walker Art Center, Opening day artist's talk, 26 June 2010.

19. In his discussion of Kuitca, Bob Duggan writes, "Alluding to his family's Russian and Jewish roots stretching back to Odessa, Kuitca claims that '[s]omehow, my family was traveling in that stroller. That was the ship that was bringing my family from Odessa.' Just when you think you have Kuitca's puzzle solved, he adds another item to the map legend and makes you begin all over again" (Duggan n.p.).

20. This line of thinking was triggered by an exhibit of the work of Venezuelan visual artist Carlos Cruz Diez shown in a retrospective at MALBA in Buenos Aires in 2011–2012. Working with thin and narrow strips of different material (wood, metal, resin), differently colored along each narrow side and again along the edge, Cruz Diez experiments with color and movement, creating patterns that appear and change as the viewer moves from one viewing angle to another.

## CHAPTER 6

1. See Sitman (2008) for a discussion of *Sur*'s commitment to anti-Fascism during the Second World War. Among the Jewish contributors to *Sur* mentioned by Sitman are Waldo Frank, who encouraged Ocampo to undertake the creation of *Sur* in the first place, philosopher Benjamin Fondane, essayist Máximo José Kahn, and writer Giuliana Tedeschi.

2. In a 2010 interview Cozarinsky states, "I had been brought up completely outside religion, completely outside tradition. It wasn't a question on the part of my parents of denying, there was no denial. It's just that they were not religious and they didn't feel attached to any Jewish tradition" (*Itineraries*, n.p.).

3. See Nudler, *Tango Judío*, and Judkovski, *Buenos Aires, fervor . . . y tango*.

4. Given his published writing we may think of Costantini himself as "incidentally Jewish," though "published" is the key word here. As we noted in chapter 2, Costantini left an unfinished manuscript based on the life of Raquel Liberman.

5. Alan Astro (5) observes that virtually no Yiddish has entered Argentine vocabulary, which may account for the footnotes. On the other hand, the novel was published in Spain, with a minuscule Jewish community that in turn is largely Sephardic, so the translations may be for the sake of the Spanish reader. See also Szichman, who uses Yiddish amply in his expanded trilogy but includes a glossary rather than footnotes to solve the translation problem.

6. After discovering that her friend Mario is menstruating, Jorgelina, caught between her promise not to reveal his secret and her concern for her friend, has told her father, which leads to Mario's being beaten by his father.

7. Although the writer-director says this is a Mexican film—made with a Mexican crew and Mexican funding, with, she pointedly remarks, no help from Argentina—the movie is set in Argentina, is cast with Argentine actors, tells a specifically Argentine story, and is written and directed by an Argentine child-exile, now grown and living in Mexico. The film, then, raises its own questions of national identity.

8. The child in Alicia Steimberg's *Musicians and Watchmakers* (*Músicos y relojeros*), a text in which Jewishness is not at all incidental, goes to church and builds an altar to the Virgin, presaging the scenes in these two films in which the little-girl protagonists are drawn to the figure of the Virgin Mary. Steimberg's child protagonist is drawn to Catholicism for its aesthetics and spirituality, as well as by her own desire to belong.

9. The film is familiar in its implicit contrast between city and the threatening, chaotic natural world. World literature offers a frame of reference here, with Conrad's *Heart of Darkness*, Rivera's *La vorágine*, Carpentier's *Los pasos perdidos*, and James Dickey's *Deliverance*, but it is the geographically and historically more immediate Horacio Quiroga's *Los desterrados* that emerges as its touchstone. Both brothers have the old Losada edition of the Quiroga short-story collection in their homes.

10. Although the surname Rosenthal is recognizably Jewish in Argentina—it was the name of the head of the Anti-Defamation League's Latin American branch who was outspoken about antisemitism during the dictatorship—it is also a Scandinavian name, which may be a sly reference to Viggo Mortensen's background. Misperceptions of Jewishness give another twist to the questions I am raising here. Angelica Gorodischer is married to a Jewish man whose name she took, and is often thought to be Jewish, not least, I imagine, because at least one of her best-known stories is about a Jewish family history.

11. Director Diego Lerman made the novel into a movie called *The Invisible Eye* (*La mirada invisible*).

12. A number of elements indicate that the film has shifted levels of reality, including the metamorphosis of a pretty woman who catches Leonardo's attention in the film's first scene into a somewhat sadistic dentist with whom he has an affair,

and the marginally surrealistic figures—clowns and musicians—who skew a shopping mall scene and herald the complete breakdown of the norms of film realism as shoppers become a dancing chorus behind an oblivious Leonardo, making manifest the carnivalesque, grotesque excess of globalized capitalism. Within Leonardo's movie, this scene, and several others that read as production numbers, overtly break the illusion of the otherwise realist film and hint that we are watching a film within a film. These scenes also signal that smaller details, like the bright red cover of his son-in-law's manuscript and the arbitrary appearances of the neuroscientist Spivak, are symbolic.

## CHAPTER 7

1. Kovadloff goes even farther, provocatively suggesting that the individual essentialized as "the Jew" is not visible as a national subject and therefore is, from the beginning, discursively disappeared.

2. The dossier is unsettlingly confused. It records as Alicia's Communist books that in fact her mother authored when Alicia was still a little girl. Conflating parent and child, it ahistoricizes Jews, and, by making them interchangeable, diminishes them.

3. "También me preguntó si era judía pero se respondió a sí mismo: 'No importa; yo no tengo problema'" (19).

4. For a harrowing account of the DAIA's complicity with the dictatorial regime, see Feitlowitz 1998, particularly chapter 3, "Life Here Is Normal" (89–109).

5. In stark contrast, Marshall Meyer, a US rabbi living in Argentina, used his public position as a religious leader (he was founder of the Latin American Rabbinical Seminary in Buenos Aires and leader of the Beth El Congregation in the same city) to openly criticize the military regime and to work for the release of the disappeared.

6. *Testimonios* are firsthand accounts of state violence.

7. See, for example, the CONADEP report *Nunca más* (1984).

8. Israel, of course, is the exception; it is both a Jewish nation and a modern one. When, humiliated as a Jew, Samuel leaves Argentina, he goes to Israel, feeling ashamed of his own cowardice in the face of torture.

9. Her book has appeared on the syllabi of many women's studies courses, especially those concerned with global feminisms or human rights.

10. Examples include dissertations by Noemí Acedo Alonso (2015) and Daniela Goldfine (2015), Patricia DeRocher's study of transnational *testimonio* (2018), and M. Edurne Portela's study of trauma in Argentine women writers (2009).

11. The same source puts the number of Jewish immigrants who came to Argentina between 1918 and 1933, laying the foundaton for future Eastern European Jewish immigration, at seventy-nine thousand. It also notes that Argentina

tightened its immigration laws in 1938. See United States Holocaust Memorial Museum, "Holocaust Encyclopedia," http://www.ushmm.org/wlc/en/article.php?-ModuleId=10007824, accessed 12 Nov. 2014).

12. See Goldfine (2015) for a discussion of the injunction to pass down history from generation to generation.

13. The Recoleta Cultural Center is well known and easily accessible, within easy walking distance to downtown Buenos Aires. Its exhibits are free and open to the public, and they are usually very well attended.

14. Reina Roffé's short story "La noche en blanco" (Sleepless night) also draws a maternal map linking the Holocaust to the Argentine dictatorship. In it, the mother of a small child leaves the little girl with her neighbor, a Holocaust survivor, knowing that she is about to be taken away by the paramilitary. See Robinson (2017) for a full discussion of this text, and for an example of the unease outside Argentina of equating the disappearances of the Argentine dictatorship with the Holocaust.

15. For a full discussion of sites of memory, see Nora.

16. These will be two different stories not only (and much less) because their subjects are different, but because they stand in different relationship to the language that surrounds them: although they both live in Argentina, the father does not, he claims, have the dexterity to write in Spanish. He will write in Yiddish, the son in Spanish.

17. For a thorough analysis of the failure of memory under conditions of trauma in Fingueret's novel, see Kaminsky (2014).

18. "I do not consider myself a Jewish writer, although I have Jewish roots. Only sometimes Jewish issues or topics appear in my work. I would say that my main source of inspiration are phrases that I read or listen to. From them I create situations. And from the situations, stories are made, either novels or shorter narrations" (Mastakar 2017, n.p.).

19. Kovadloff (op. cit. 86) also uses the term "genocide" to characterize the state terror of this period.

20. In the same way, a single homoerotic kiss between two adolescent boys in the film marks the presence of queer desire, making it visible, but just as quickly abandons it.

# CHAPTER 8

1. Interfactionality, according to Kaminsky, is a mechanism of intersectional oppression whereby members of different oppressed classes are pitted against another by offers of contingent privilege based on mutually distinctive characteristics they share with those in power.

2. The transnational social movement, with a focus on gay men and lesbians, began in the late 1960s. It was fueled by activism around the AIDS epidemic

in the 1980s and has been buttressed by the development of queer theory on the one hand and the mainstreaming of LGBTQIA+ issues nationally and globally. The acronym stands for Lesbian, Gay, Bisexual, Transgender (alternatively, Transsexual or Two-Spirit), Queer (alternatively, Questioning), Intersex, Asexual (alternatively, Ally), with the plus sign indicating that this list is incomplete and in process.

3. See, for example, "the German-Jewish literary critic, Mayer," who, in 1975, "[linked] the fate of the Jews with those of homosexuals and women, cited by Natan Sznaider" (Sznaider 152, note 51, citing Mayer 1975).

4. "Unitarian" here refers to the liberal political party that favored a strong central government, in contrast to the conservative Federalists, led by Juan Manuel de Rosas, who was twice governor of the province (not just the city) of Buenos Aires (1829–1832 and 1835–1852), assuming dictatorial powers and establishing a system of state terror. By the late 1840s Rosas had consolidated his power over the country as a whole.

5. The story opens itself to readings through both male homoeroticism and trans desire, both of which I suggest here.

6. The ESMA (Escuela Superior de Mecánica de la Armada) was the naval academy in Buenos Aires that became notorious for being used as a clandestine prison and torture center during the 1976–1983 dictatorship. It is now a museum dedicated to historical memory and human rights.

7. The film is *The Third Sex*. IMDB lists two films of that title, a lost documentary from 1934 and a 1957 feature film from Germany directed by Veit Harlan, a filmmaker accused, and eventually exonerated, of collaboration with the Nazis.

8. This homophobic protestation of virile male Jewish heterosexuality is also present in Neuman's *Una vez Argentina*. When in early adolescence the protagonist gets into a fight with a bigger, tougher schoolmate and opens his lip, he assures his place among the virile. The incident includes teasing about sodomizing each other, but the two quickly recuperate their claim to heterosexuality by declaring that their incipient sex play isn't queer because they themselves are straight (32).

9. Feinmann certainly understands the mother's too-literal interpretation of the film. He is a screenwriter as well as a novelist, and he not infrequently encodes his own truths in screenplays that may seem frivolous on the surface.

10. Male prostitutes are less frequently represented, but when they are (as in Cozarinsky), they tend to be poor and otherwise marginalized.

11. See Salessi for a discussion of law enforcement and public health officials whose political transgressions are linked to the illicit sexuality of the brothels but unregulated by class structure.

12. In fact, Victoria Ocampo praised Sontag for being a strong woman intellectual who nevertheless was charmingly feminine in the most heteronormative of ways.

13. Cozarinsky first wrote *Urban Voodoo* in English, later translating it into Spanish. Sontag published her response to the book, "The Exile's Cosmopolis," in 1985, the year it appeared in Spanish.

14. Leocadia, who appears in the documentary, appears to be Jewish as well, and she also worked in television.

15. The documentary was released as *Impuros* in 2018, with directorial credit given to both Mujica and Najenson. The version released in the US, *The Impure*, carries a 2017 release date, with directorial credit given only to Najenson. I am grateful to Daniela Goldfine for bringing the film to my attention.

16. Sara represents both the immigrant and the traumatized. Others speak of her time as a prostitute, but she does not; instead Sara lives in terror and "speaks" in a way that can barely be understood, almost as if she speaks from the Kristevan chora. Her speech is pregrammatical, the syntax is gone, cause and effect, subject-verb-object structure never come together.

17. The novel includes one overtly Jewish reference, to a stereotypically disheveled Jewish math teacher named Goldman at the school the women attend. The students refer to him as "the Jew," calling attention to his presence by effectively othering him.

18. Florinda Goldberg's study is exemplary, as is Evelyn Fishburn's.

19. David William Foster (1991) argues that *La Condesa sangrienta* reinforces the homophobic trope of the evil lesbian, but Sylvia Molloy dismisses Foster's reading, suggesting that by transgressing the limits of sexual legitimacy, the figure of the Countess "makes lesbian sense" as a "figure of disruption" (Molloy 1997, 255).

20. Catherine Grant (1996) persuasively argues that Pizarnik was constrained first by her own desire to become accepted as a serious poet under conditions that severely limited women and later by others intent on protecting her reputation. Grant also reminds us that little by little Pizarnik's raucously humorous and transgressive texts have been making their way into the light of day.

21. See Bollig (2013) and Fishburn (2007). It is in fact reasonable to argue that this section of the poem actually begins earlier, with the invocation of the mother, into whose body the speaker wants to return. The description of the mother, "un animal carnívero que ama la vegetación lujuriosa" (a carnivorous animal that loves lustful vegetation), suggests women's homoerotic desire, with its reference to eating flesh and the love of lecherous vegetation.

22. "Roña," which I have translated as "filth," is actually a very rich word that also carries connotations of itchiness, mange, and the children's game, tag.

23. Fishburn's important essay on humor and wordplay in Pizarnik's work (2007) notes that these elements rarely appear in the work published during Pizarnik's lifetime.

24. The "Boyita" of the film is an Argentinian-made amphibious camper-trailer popular in the 1970s. Jorgelina and her father drive to the countryside with the Boyita hitched to the back of their car. On one level the Boyita represents childhood, but it also suggests ambiguity—it functions on land and in the water. Moreover, it can be read as a bilingual pun—the masculine noun ("boy") attached

to the feminine diminutive suffix ("-ita"), and as such available as a reference to Mario's intersexuality.

25. See JAG, "Home page" (blog), http://jagargentina.blogspot.com/, accessed 3 Sept. 2020, and Fundación Judaica, "JAG (Judíos Argentinos Gays) se incorpora como entidad adherida a la DAIA," http://www.judaica.org.ar/jag/jag-judios-argentinos-gays-se-incorpora-como-entidad-adherida-a-la-daia/, accessed 3 Sept. 2020.

# CONCLUSION

1. The great exception is Jorge Luis Borges, whose fascination with and exploration of Jewishness, discussed briefly in chapter 5, is well studied and itself the source of inspiration for other artists and writers.

# BIBLIOGRAPHY

Acedo Alonso, Noemí. "Po/ética de la escucha: Un estudio de la representación del dolor físico infligido y el sufrimiento en la escritura testimonial de Nora Strejilevich." Universitat Autònoma de Barcelona, Departament de Filologia Espanyola, 2015.
Achugar, Hugo. "El Parnaso es la nación o reflexiones a propósito de la violencia de la lectura y el simulacro." *Las otras letras: Literatura uruguaya del Siglo XIX*, edited by Leonardo Rossiello, Grafitti, 1994, 27–46.
Agamben, Giorgio. *Remnants of Auschwitz: The Witness and the Archive*. Translated by Daniel Heller-Roazen, Zone Books, 2008. 1st edition, 1999.
Aizenberg, Edna. *Books and Bombs in Buenos Aires*. UP of New England, 2002.
———. *The Aleph Weaver: Biblical, Kabbalistic, and Judaic Elements in Borges*. Scripta Humanistica, 1984.
Alazraki, Jaime. "Borges and the Kabbala." *TriQuarterly*, vol. 25, 1972.
Anonymous. "Tango que me hiciste goy." *Página 12*, n.d.
Anzaldúa, Gloria. *Borderlands/La Frontera: The New Mestiza*. Aunt Lute, 1987.
Appiah, Kwame Anthony. *Cosmopolitanism: Ethics in a World of Strangers (Issues of Our Time)*. Norton, 2006.
Arnés, Laura A. "La lesbiana y la tradición literaria argentina: *Monte de Venus* como texto inaugural." *Lectora*, vol. 17, 2011, pp. 41–52.
Astro, Alan. "The Durability of Yiddish in Argentina." Seventh Woodrow Borah International Colloquium: Writing Across the Americas: Policies, Politics, Poetics. Tel Aviv University, 6 May 2012.
Avni, Haim. *Argentina and the Jews: A History of Jewish Immigration*. Translated from the Hebrew by Gila Brand, U of Alabama P, 1991.
Baron, Salo Wittmayer. "Ghetto and Emancipation: Shall We Revise the Traditional View?" *Menorah Journal*, June 1928.
Bayer, Osvaldo, and Juan Gelman. *Exilio*. Legasa, 1984.
Benhabib, Seyla. *Situating the Self: Gender, Community, and Postmodernism in Contemporary Ethics*. Routledge, 1992.
Benjamin, Walter. *Collected Letters*, vol. 2, 1972.

Bhabha, Homi. "Of Mimicry and Man: The Ambivalence of Colonial Discourse." *October*, vol. 28, Spring 1984, pp. 125–33.
Birmajer, Marcelo. "En la noche de bodas." *Historia de un deseo: El erotismo homosexual en veintiocho relatos argentinos contemporáneos*, edited by Leopoldo Brizuela, Planeta, 2000, pp. 70–79.
———. *La despedida*. La Otra Orilla, 2010.
———. *Tres mosqueteros*. Debate, 2001.
———. *Ser judío en el siglo XXI*. Milá, 2002.
Bleys, Rudi C. *Images of Ambiente: Homotextuality and Latino/a American Art 1810–Today*. Continuum, 2000.
Bollig, Ben. "How Many Ways to Leave Your Country? On Exile and Not-Belonging in the Work of Alejandra Pizarnik." *The Modern Language Review*, vol. 104, no. 2, April 2009, pp. 421–37.
Borges, Jorge Luis. "Emma Zunz." *El aleph*. Emecé, 1971, pp. 61–68.
———. "El indigno." *El informe de Brodie*. Emecé, 1970, pp. 25–36.
———. "Gunnar Thorgilsson." *Historia de la noche*. Emecé, 1977, p. 59.
———. "El muerto." *El aleph*. Emecé, 1971, pp. 29–36.
———. "La muerte y la brújula." *El aleph*. Emecé, 1971, pp. 133–48.
Boyarin, Daniel. *Unheroic Conduct: The Rise of Heterosexuality and the Invention of the Jewish Man*. U of California P, 1997.
Boyarin, Daniel, Daniel Itzkovitz, and Ann Pellegrini, editors. *Queer Theory and the Jewish Question*, Columbia UP, 2003.
Braylan, Marisa, Daniel Feierstein, Miguel Galante, and Adrián Jmelnizky. *Informe sobre la situación de los detenidos-desaparecidos judíos durante el genocidio perpetrado en Argentina 1976–1983*. Centro de Estudios Sociales DAIA, 2007.
———. *Report on the situation of the Jewish detainees-disappeared during the genocide perpetrated in Argentina*. Social Research Center of DAIA, 2000, digitized 2009.
Brizuela, Leopoldo. *Una misma noche*. Alfaguara, 2012.
Brodsky, Adriana, and R. Rein, editors. *The New Jewish Argentina*. Brill, 2013.
Brodsky, Marcelo. *Buena memoria: Un ensayo fotográfico*. Distributed Art Publishers, 2007.
Buber, Martin. *I and Thou*. Scribners, 1937.
CONADEP. *Nunca más* (Report of the National Commission on the Disappearance of Persons), 1984.
Castle, Terry. *The Apparitional Lesbian: Female Homosexuality and Modern Culture*. Columbia UP, 1993.
Catelli, Nora. "Los *Diarios* de Alejandra Pizarnik: Estrategias de lectura." *Congreso Internacional Alejandra Pizarnik (1936–1972): Balances y perspectivas*. 28 y 29 de noviembre de 2012, Université Paris de Sorbonne, Paris IV.
Chejfec. Sergio. *Lenta biografía*. Buenos Puntosur, 1990.
———. *My Two Worlds*. Translated by Margaret B. Carson, Open Letter, 2011.
———. *Mis dos mundos*. Candaya, 2008.
Cohen, Mitchell. "Rooted Cosmopolitanism." *Dissent*, 1992, pp. 478–83.

Colombres, Adolfo. "Modernidad dominante y modernidad propia." *América como civilización emergente*. Amargord, 2008, pp. 95–113.

Costantini, Humberto. *Rapsodia de Raquel Liberman*. Unpublished manuscript.

———. *De dioses, hombrecitos y policías*. Casa de las Américas, 1979.

Cottrol, Robert J. "Beyond Invisibility: Afro-Argentines in their Nation's Culture and Memory." *Latin American Research Review*, vol. 42, no. 1, February 2007, pp. 139–56.

Cozarinsky, Edgardo. *La tercera mañana*. Tusquets, 2010.

———. *El rufián moldavo*. Seix Barral, 2004.

———. *The Moldavian Pimp*. Random House, 2007.

———. *Lejos de dónde*. Tusquets, 2014.

———. *La novia de Odessa*. Emecé, 2001.

———. *The Bride from Odessa*. Translated by Nick Caistor, Farrar, Straus and Giroux, 2001.

DAIA. *Special Report on Jewish Detained and Disappeared (1976–1983)*. 1984.

DeRocher, Patricia. *Transnational Testimonios: The Politics of Collective Knowledge Production*. U of Washington P, 2018.

Deutsch, Sandra McGee. *Crossing Borders, Claiming a Nation: A History of Argentine Jewish Women, 1880–1955*. Duke UP, 2010.

———. "The Argentine Right and the Jews, 1919–1933." *Journal of Latin American Studies*, vol. 18, no. 1, May 1986, pp. 113–34.

Díaz, Esther. *Buenos Aires: Una mirada filosófica*. Biblos, 2000.

Dobry, Edgardo. "Pizarnik y Gelman ante la ley inaccesible." *Cuadernos Líricos*, vol. 17, 2017, https://journals.openedition.org/lirico/3914. Accessed 29 Jan. 2019.

Dobry, Edgardo, Geneviève Fabry, and Valentina Litvan, editors. *La rebelión de los hijos: El judaísmo en la literatura latinoamericana contemporánea entre tradición y asimilación*. Special issue of *Cuadernos Líricos* 19, 2018, https://journals.openedition.org/lirico/. Accessed 28 Jan. 2019.

Drucaroff, Elsa. *El infierno prometido. Una prostituta del Zwi Migdal*. Sudamericana, 2006.

Duggan, Bob. "Map Quest: Guillermo Kuitca's 'Everything.'" https://bigthink.com/Picture-This/map-quest-guillermo-kuitcas-everything, 16 Aug. 2010. Accessed 18 Aug. 2020.

Dujovne Ortiz, Alicia. *El árbol de la gitana*. Aguilar, 1997.

———. *Las perlas rojas*. Alfaguara, 2005.

Edurne Portela, M. *Displaced Memories: The Poetics of Trauma in Argentine Women's Writing*. Bucknell UP, 2009.

Efron, Gustavo, and Darío Brenman. "El atentado y las representaciones sociales a través de los medios." *Indice* (BA), vol. 36, no. 23, 2005, pp. 231–53.

Escliar, Myriam. *Blackie, con todo respeto: Biografía novelada*. Milá, 2007.

Fainstein, Graciela. *Detrás de los ojos*. Icaria, 2006.

Feierstein, Ricardo. *Contraexilio y mestizaje: Ser judío en la Argentina*. Milá, 1996.

———. *Mestizo*. Mila, 1994.

———. *Mestizo: A Novel*. Translated by Stephen A. Sadow, U of New Mexico P, 2000.
———. *La logia del umbral*. Busqueda De Ayllu, 2001.
———. *La historia de los judíos argentinos*. Planeta, 1993.
Feinmann, José Pablo. *La astucia de la razón*. Grupo Editorial Norma, 2001.
———. *La crítica de las armas*. Grupo Editorial Norma, 2003.
———. *La sombra de Heidegger*. Seix Barral, 2005.
———. *Heidegger's Shadow*. Translated by Joshua Price and María Constanza Guzmán, Texas Tech UP, 2016.
Feitlowitz, Marguerite. *A Lexicon of Terror: Argentina and the Legacies of Torture*. Oxford UP, 1998.
Filippo, Virgilio. *Los judíos*. Tor, 1939.
Finchelstein, Federico. "The Anti-Freudian Politics of Argentine Fascism: Antisemitism, Catholicism, and the Internal Enemy, 1932–1945." *Hispanic American Historical Review*, vol. 87, no. 1, 2007, pp. 77–110.
———. *The Ideological Origins of the Dirty War: Fascism, Populism, and Dictatorship in Twentieth Century Argentina*. Oxford UP, 2014.
———. *Transatlantic Fascism: Ideology, Violence, and the Sacred in Argentina and Italy, 1919–1945*. Duke UP, 2010.
Fingueret, Manuela. *Hija del silencio*. Planeta, 1999.
———. *Daughter of Silence*. Translated by Darrell B. Lockhart, Texas Tech UP, 2012.
Fishburn, Evelyn. "Different Aspects of Humor and Wordplay in the Work of Alejandra Pizarnik." *Árbol de Alejandra: Pizarnik Reassessed*, edited by Fiona Joy Mackintosh and Karl Posso, Támesis, 2007, pp. 36–59.
———. "Reflections on the Jewish Imaginary in the Fictions of Borges." *Variaciones Borges*, vol. 5, 1998, pp. 145–56.
Foster, David William. *Gay and Lesbian Themes in Latin American Writing*. U of Texas P, 1991.
Foucault, Michel. *History of Sexuality*. Translated by Robert Hurley, Random House, 1978.
Frank, Waldo. *Memoirs of Waldo Frank*, edited by Alan Trachtenberg, U of Massachusetts Press, 1973.
Freedman, Jonathan. *Klezmer America: Jewishness, Ethnicity, Modernity*. Columbia UP, 2009.
———. "Coming Out of the Jewish Closet with Marcel Proust." *GLQ: A Journal of Lesbian and Gay Studies*, vol. 7, no. 4, 2001, pp. 521–51.
Freund, Gisele. *The World in My Camera*. Translated by June Guicharnod, Dial Press, 1974.
Fried, Michael. "Barthes's Punctum." *Critical Inquiry*, Spring 2005, pp. 539–74.
Futoransky, Luisa. *El Formosa*. El Centro Editores, 2009.
Gálvez, Manuel. *El mal metafísico*. Tor, 1900.
Garb, Tamar. "Introduction: Modernity, Identity, Textuality." *The Jew in the Text*, edited by Linda Nochlin and Tamar Garb, Thames and Hudson, 1995.

Gelman, Juan. "Pensamientos." *Cólera buey*. La Tertulia, 1968.
———. *Mundar*. Era, 2008.
Gerchunoff, Alberto. *Los gauchos judíos*. Talleres Gráficos Joaquín Sesé, 1910.
———. *The Jewish Gauchos of the Pampas*. Translated by Prudencio de Pereda, U of New Mexico P, reprinted in 1998.
Giorgi, Gabriel. "Sueños de exterminio: Perlongher." *Ciberletras*, vol. 9, 2003, http://www.lehman.cuny.edu/ciberletras/v09/giorgig.html. Accessed 29 Sept. 2008.
———. *Sueños de exterminio. Homosexualidad y representación en la literatura argentina*. Beatriz Viterbo Editora, 2004.
Girondo, Oliverio. *20 poemas para ser leídos en el tranvía*. La Facultad, 1922.
Glickman, Nora. *The Jewish White Slave Trade and the Untold Story of Raquel Liberman*. Garland, 2000.
———. *Una tal Raquel. Teatro: Cuatro obras de Nora Glickman*. Nueva Generación, 2000, pp. 19–60.
Glusberg, Samuel. *La levita gris: Cuentos judíos de ambiente porteño*. Editorial Babel, 1924.
Goldberg, Florinda F. "Judíos del Sur: El modelo judío en la narrativa de la catástrofe argentina." *Estudios Interdisciplinarios de América Latina y el Caribe*, vol. 12, no. 2, 2000–2001, pp. 139–52, http://eial.tau.ac.il/index.php/eial/article/view/983/1018. Accessed 11 Mar. 2020.
———. "Literatura judía latinoamericana: Modelos para armar." *Revista Iberoamericana*, vol. 66, no. 191, April–June 2000, pp. 309–32.
———. *Alejandra Pizarnik: "Este espacio que somos."* Hispamérica, 1994.
Goldfine, Daniela. *Stories of Memory/Memory in Stories: Issues of Memory and Identity in Contemporary Jewish Argentine Cultural Production*. 2015. University of Minnesota, Ph.D. dissertation.
González de Trumper, Lilí, and Ester Gabriel de Falcov, editors. *Aromas y sabores de las bobes de Moisés Ville*. Editorial Milá, 2006.
Gordillo, Gastón, and Silvia Hirsch. "Indigenous Struggles and Contested Identities in Argentina: Histories of Invisibilization and Reemergence." *The Journal of Latin American Anthropology*, vol. 8, no. 3, 2003, pp. 4–30.
Gorodischer, Angélica. "Camera Obscura." Translated by Diana Vélez, *Scents of Wood and Silence: Short Stories by Latin American Women Writers*, special issue of *Latin American Literary Review*, vol. 19, no. 37, 1991, pp. 96–105.
Grant, Catherine. "A private revolution? Alejandra Pizarnik's *La bucanera de pernambuco o Hilda la polígrafa*." *Journal of Latin American Cultural Studies*, vol. 5, no. 1, 1996, pp. 65–82.
Guelbert de Rosenthal, Eva, editor. *Memoria oral de Moisés Ville*. Museo Histórico Comunal de Moisés Ville, 2008.
Güiraldes, Ricardo. *Don Segundo Sombra*. Buenos Aires, 1926.
Guy, Donna. *Sex and Danger in Buenos Aires: Prostitution, Family, and Nation in Argentina*. U of Nebraska Press, 1991.

Harding, Sandra. *Whose Science? Whose Knowledge? Thinking from Women's Lives.* Cornell UP, 1991.

Hernández, José. *El gaucho Martín Fierro.* Buenos Aires, 1872.

———. *La vuelta de Martín Fierro.* Buenos Aires, 1879.

Horvath, Ricardo. *Memorias y recuerdos de Blackie.* Todo es Historia, 1979.

Hussar, James A. "*Los gauchos judíos* de Alberto Gerchunoff en su centenario." *Hispanófila*, vol. 163, 2011, pp. 39–52.

*Itineraries of a Hummingbird.* "Edgardo Cozarinsky," published in *Antique Children*, no. 2, 2010, repr. https://www.itinerariesofahummingbird.com/edgardo-cozarinsky1.html. Accessed 7 Nov. 2019.

Jacobson, Shari. "Modernity, Conservative Religious Movements, and the Female Subject: Newly Ultraorthodox Sephardi Women in Buenos Aires." *American Anthropologist*, vol. 108, no. 2, pp. 336–46.

Jenckes, Kate. *Witnessing Beyond the Human: Addressing the Alterity of the Other in Post-Coup Chile and Argentina.* SUNY Press, 2017.

Judíos Argentinos Gays. Blogspot. http://jagargentina.blogspot.com/. Accessed 3 Sept. 2020.

Judkovski, José. *Buenos Aires, fervor . . . y tango. Una historia con judíos.* Fundación IWO, 2003.

Kamenszain, Tamara. *El ghetto.* Sudamericana, 2003.

———. "Toda escritura es femenina y judía." *Pluralismo e identidad. Lo judío en la literatura latinoamericana.* Milá, 1996, pp. 129–32.

Kaminsky, Amy. *After Exile: Writing the Latin American Diaspora.* U of Minnesota Press, 1999.

———. *Argentina: Stories for a Nation.* U of Minnesota Press, 2008.

———. "¿Dijo gay o goy? Identidades étnicas y prácticas sexuales en *Esperando al Mesías* de Daniel Burman." *Revista Iberoamericana*, vol. 77, no. 236–37, July–Dec. 2011, pp. 993–1004.

———. "Memory, Postmemory, Prosthetic Memory: Reflections on the Holocaust and the Dirty War in Argentine Narrative." *Hispanic Issues on Line*, vol. 12, Spring 2014, pp. 104–17, http://hispanicissues.umn.edu/assets/doc/06_KAMINSKY.pdf. Accessed 12 Sept. 2019.

Kaminsky, David. "Intersectionality and Interfactionality," *Pop-o-litics. A blog about media literacy and politics.* January 26, 2020. https://pop-o-litics.com/2020/01/26/intersectionality-and-interfactionality/.

Kartun, Mauricio. *Ala de criados.* Atuel, 2009.

Katrak, Ketu. *Politics of the Female Body: Postcolonial Women Writers of the Third World.* Rutgers UP, 2006.

Kaufmann, Paola. *El lago.* Planeta, 2005.

———. *The Lake.* Translated by Miranda France, Alma Books, 2007.

Kociancich, Vlady. *Los bajos de temor.* Tusquets, 1992.

Kohan, Martín. *Ciencias morales.* Editorial Anagrama Bs As, 2007.

———. *Dos veces junio*. Sudamericana, 2002.
Kovadloff, Santiago. "Un lugar en el tiempo: La Argentina como vivencia de los judíos." *Hispamérica*, vol. 42, Dec. 1985, pp. 79–89.
Kreimer, Juan Carlos. *Todos lo sabíamos*. de la Flor, 2008.
Krimer, María Inés. *La inauguración*. El Ateneo, 2011.
———. *Sangre kosher*. BPR, 2010.
———. "Shabat." *Página 12*. 27 Jan. 2018. https://www.pagina12.com.ar/91883-shabat. Accessed 31 Aug. 2020.
Kristeva, Julia. "Women's Time," *Signs*, vol. 7, no. 1, 1981, pp. 31–35.
Kuperminc, Mirta, and Saúl Sosnowski. *Borges y la Cábala: Senderos del verbo/Borges and the Kabbalah: Paths to the Word*. Artist's book, limited edition. Buenos Aires, Argentina, 2006.
Kusminsky, Gustavo. *Médanos: Premio de narrativa hispanoamericana*. Mansalva, 2010.
Lane, Helen R. "Mario Satz: Cosmic Choreographer." *Review: Literature and Arts of the Americas*, vol. 13, no. 24, pp. 15–19.
Lejeune, Phillipe. *Le Pacte autobiographique*. de Seuil, 1975.
Lerman, Gabriel. "Album de familia." *Pagina 12*, 8 Feb. 2009.
Lewis, Anthony. Review of Jacobo Timerman, *Prisoner without a Name, Cell without a Number*. *The New York Times*, 10 May 1981, p. 7.
Lipstadt, Deborah E. *Antisemitism: Here and Now*. Schocken, 2019.
Lockhart, Darrell. *Jewish Writers of Latin America—A Dictionary*. Garland, 1997.
Lockhart, Melissa. "The Censored Argentine Text: Griselda Gamabro's *Ganarse la muerte* and Reina Roffé's *Monte de Venus*." *Interventions: Feminist Dialogues on Third World Women's Literature and Film*. Bishnupriya Ghosh and Brinda Bose, eds. Taylor & Francis, 1997.
Lojo, María Rosa. *Sábato: En busca del original perdido*. Corregidor, 1997.
López Mejía, Adelaida. "La visión satírica de Humberto Costantini: De dioses, hombrecitos y policías." *Chasqui: Revista de Literatura Latinoamericana*, vol. 20, no. 2, 1991, pp. 86–97.
Ludmer, Josefina. *The Corpus Delicti: A Manual of Argentine Fictions*. Translated by Glen Close, U of Pittsburgh P, 2004 (translation of *El cuerpo del delito*. Eterna Cadencia, 1999).
Lugones, María. "Purity, Impurity, and Separation." *Signs*, vol. 19, no. 2, Winter 1994, 458–79.
Lukin, Liliana. "Sobre el tránsito de los cuerpos (Cuerpos en viaje, o de cómo las lecturas transforman mi cuerpo, mientras va leyendo los cuerpos narrados en la escritura)." *Noaj: Revista Literaria*, no. 18–19 (Jerusalem, Aug. 2011), pp. 30–32.
Mackinnon, Catherine. *Toward a Feminist Theory of the State*. Harvard UP, 1989.
Mackintosh, Fiona. "Self-Censorship and New Voices in Pizarnik's Unpublished Manuscripts." *Bulletin of Spanish Studies*, vol. 87, no. 4, 2010, pp. 509–35.
Mactas, Raquel. *Los judíos de Las Acacias*. Self-published, 1936.

Martel, Julián. *La bolsa*. Buenos Aires, 1891.

———. *The Stock Market*. Translated by Tomás Romero, 1948. New Mexico State University, MA thesis.

Masiello, Francine. *Between Civilization and Barbarism: Women, Nation, and Literary Culture in Modern Argentina*. U of Nebraska P, 1992.

Mastakar, Manasi. "Sergio Chejfec: I do not consider myself a Jewish writer." *The Free Press Journal*, 26 Nov. 2017, https://www.freepressjournal.in/weekend/sergio-chejfec-i-do-not-consider-myself-a-jewish-writer/1176716. Accessed 3 Dec. 2018.

Mayer, Hans. *Aussenseiter*. Suhrkamp, 1975.

Medina, Enrique. *Las muecas del miedo*. Galerna, 1981.

Minnich, Elizabeth. *Transforming Knowledge*. Temple UP, 2004.

Mirelman, Victor A. "The *Semana Trágica* of 1919 and the Jews in Argentina." *Jewish Social Studies*, vol. 37, no. 1, Winter 1975, pp. 61–73, http://www.jstor.org/stable/4466861. Accessed 16 Jan. 2017.

Mizraje, María Gabriela. "Un talmudista entre evangélicos: A propósito de Samuel Glusberg, 'La levita gris y otros textos.'" *Chasqui: Revista de Literatura Latinoamericana*, vol. 39, no. 2, Nov. 2010, 114–32.

Molloy, Sylvia. "From Sappho to Baffo: Diverting the Sexual in Alejandra Pizarnik." *Sex and Sexuality in Latin America*, edited by Daniel Balderston and Donna J. Guy, New York UP, 1997, pp. 250–58.

Mosse, George. *Nationalism and Sexuality: Middle Class Morality and Sexual Norms in Modern Europe*. U of Wisconsin P, 1988.

Muchnik, Mario. *Mundo judío: Crónica personal*. Lumen, 1984.

Narayan, Uma. *Dislocating Cultures: Identities, Traditions, and Third World Feminisms*. Routledge, 2013.

Neuman, Andrés. *Una vez Argentina*. Alfaguara, 2014.

Nora, Pierre. *Les Lieux de mémoire* (Gallimard). Abridged translation, *Realms of Memory*, Columbia UP, 1996–1998.

Nouwen, Mollie Lewis. *Oy, My Buenos Aires: Jewish Immigrants and the Creation of Argentine National Identity*. U of New Mexico P, 2013.

Nudler, Julio. *Tango Judío: Del ghetto a la milonga*. Sudamericana, 1998.

Ocampo, Victoria. "Susan Sontag y una encuesta." *Testimonios. Décima serie, 1975–1977*. Sur, 1977, pp. 30–38.

Orgambide, Pedro. *Aventuras de Edmund Ziller en tierras del Nuevo Mundo*. Grijalbo, 1977.

Ostrom, Katherine. "*Literatura Policial*: Gender, Genre, and Appropriation in Argentine and Brazilian Hard-Boiled Crime Fiction." 2011. University of Minnesota, Ph.D. dissertation.

Partnoy, Alicia. *The Little School*. Cleis Press, 1986.

———. *La escuelita*. La Bohemia, 2008.

———. "Poetry as a Strategy of Resistance in the Holocaust and the Southern Cone Genocides." *The Jewish Diaspora in Latin America and the Caribbean: Fragments of Memory*, edited by Kristin Ruggiero, Sussex Academic Press, 2005, pp. 234–46.
Peri Rossi, Cristina. "Las estatuas o la condición del extranjero." *El museo de los esfuerzos inútiles*. Seix Barral, 1983, pp. 131–32.
Perlongher, Néstor. "El sexo de las chicas." *Xul*, no. 6, 1984.
Piglia, Ricardo. *La ciudad ausente*. Buenos Aires, 1992.
Piña, Cristina. *La palabra como destino: Un acercamiento a la poesía de Alejandra Pizarnik*. Botella al Mar, 1981.
Pizarnik, Alejandra. *La condesa sangrienta*. Aquarius, 1971.
———. *Poesía completa*, edited by Ana Beciu, 2nd ed., Lumen, 2001.
Plager, Silvia. *Como papas para varenikes*. Vergara, 2004.
———. *Mi cocina judía*. Sudamericana, 2014.
Polo García, Victorino. "La novela argentina contemporánea: Aproximación a la narrativa de Mario Satz." *Anales de Literatura Hispanoamericana*, vol. 21, 1992, pp. 457–66.
Pomeraniec, Hinde. *Blackie: La mujer que hacía hablar al país*. Capital Intelectual, 2010.
Posse, Abel. *La Reina del Plata*. Emecé, 1988.
Pratt, Mary Louise. "Modernity and Periphery: Toward a Global and Relational Analysis." *Beyond Dichotomies*, edited by Elizabeth Mudimbe-Boyi, SUNY Press, 2002, pp. 21–48.
Prell, Riv Ellen. *Fighting to Become Americans: Assimilation and the Trouble Between Jewish Women and Jewish Men*. Beacon, 2000.
Pron, Patricio. "Un intercambio epistolar con Elsa Drucaroff." *PatricioPron Blogspot*, 2009. http://patriciopron.blogspot.com/2009/06/un-intercambio-epistolar-con-elsa.html.
Rajca, Andrew C. "Remnants of the Disappeared: Subjectivity and the Politics of Postdictatorial Cultural Memory in Sergio Chejfec's *Los planetas*." *Dissidences*, vol. 5, no. 9, article 8, 2013.
Rama, Angel. *La ciudad letrada*. Comision Uruguaya pro Fundacion Internacional, 1966.
Ran, Amalia. *Made of Shores: Judeo-Argentinean Fiction Revisited*. Lehigh UP, 2011.
———. "Nuestra *Shoá*: Dictaduras, Holocausto y represión en tres novelas judeorioplatenses." *Letras Hispanas*, vol. 6, no. 1, 2009, pp. 17–28.
Raznovich, Diana. "Rear Entry." *Defiant Acts: Four Plays by Diana Raznovich/Actos desafiantes*, edited by Diana Taylor and Victoria Mártinez, Bucknell UP, 2002.
———. *Mater erótica*. Ediciones Robinbook, 1992.
Reati, Fernando. *Nombrar lo innombrable. Violencia política y literatura argentina 1975–1985*. Legasa, 1992.

Rein, Raanan. *Argentine Jews or Jewish Argentines?* Brill, 2010.

———. *Fútbol, Jews, and the Making of Argentina.* Translated by Martha Grenzeback, Stanford UP, 2014.

Rivera, Andrés. *El profundo Sur.* Emecé, 2006. Repr. Madrid: Veintisiete Letras, 2007.

———. *Kadish.* Seix Barral, 2011.

Robinson, Cheri. "The Violence Within and the Violence Without: 'La noche en blanco' by Reina Roffé." *Mester*, vol. 45, no. 1, 2017, https://escholarship.org/uc/item/7th3b1fx. Accessed 1 Aug. 2018.

Roffé, Reina. "La noche en blanco." *Aves exóticas: Cinco cuentos con mujeres raras.* Leviatán, 2004, pp. 25–38.

———. *El cielo dividido.* Sudamericana, 1996.

———. *Monte de Venus.* Corregidor, 1976. Repr. Astier Libros, 2013.

———. "Omnipresencia de la censura en la escritora argentina." *Revista Iberoamericana*, vol. 51, no. 1, 1985, pp. 909–15.

Rosenberg, Sara. *Un hilo rojo.* Espasa, 1998.

Rozenmacher, Germán. "Tristezas de la pieza de hotel." *Cuentos completos.* Centro Editor de América Latina, 1971, pp. 9–18.

———. "*Blues* en la noche." *Cuentos completos.* Centro Editor de América Latina, 1971.

Rubin, Gayle. "The Traffic in Women: Notes on the 'Political Economy' of Sex." *Toward an Anthropology of Women*, edited by Rayna R. Reiter, Monthly Review Press, 1975, pp. 157–210.

Sábato, Ernesto. *Abaddón el exterminador.* Buenos Aires, 1975.

Saer, Juan José. *El río sin orillas: Tratado imaginario.* Seix Barral, 2006.

Salessi, Jorge. "Medics, Crooks, and Tango Queens: The National Appropriation of a Gay Tango." Translated by Celeste Fraser Delgado. *Everynight Life: Culture and Dance in Latin/o America*, edited by Celeste Delgado and José Muñoz, Duke UP, 1997, pp. 141–74.

———. *Médicos maleantes y maricas: Higiene, criminología y homosexualidad en la construcción de la nación Argentina (Buenos Aires: 1871–1914).* Beatriz Viterbo Editora, Biblioteca Estudios Culturales, 1995.

Sarlo, Beatriz. *Una modernidad periférica: Buenos Aires 1920 a 1930.* Nueva Vison, 1988.

Sarmiento, Domingo Faustino. *Facundo, o Civilización i barbarie en las pampas argentinas.* 1868.

Satz, Mario. "Borges, El Aleph y La Kábala." *Oro en la piedra: Homenaje a Borges, Murcia, 1987*, edited by Victorino Polo García, Editora Regional de Murcia, 1988, pp. 337–44.

Scorer, James. *City in Common: Culture and Community in Buenos Aires.* SUNY Press, 2016.

Sebreli, Juan José, editor. *La cuestión judía en la Argentina.* Tiempo Contemporáneo, 1968.

Seidman, Naomi. "Reading 'Queer' Ashkenaz: This Time from East to West." *TDR: The Drama Review*, vol. 55, no. 3, Fall 2011, pp. 50–56.
Senkman, Leonardo. "Discurso histórico y ficción en Adán Buenosayres." *Hispamérica*, vol. 22, no. 61, April 1992, pp. 3–21.
———. *El antisemitismo en Argentina*. Centro Editor de América Latina, 1989.
———. "Klal Yisrael at the Frontiers: The Transnational Jewish Experience in Argentina." *Identities in an Era of Globalization and Multiculturalism: Latin America in the Jewish World*, edited by Judit Bokser Liwerant, Eliezer Ben-Rafael, Yosef Gorny, and Raanan Rein, Brill, 2008, pp. 125–50.
———. *La identidad judía en la literatura argentina*. Pardés, 1983.
———. "La nación imaginaria de los escritores judíos latinoamerianos." *Revista Iberoamericana*, vol. 46, no. 191, April–June 2000, pp. 279–98, http://revista-iberoamericana.pitt.edu/ojs/index.php/Iberoamericana/article/viewFile/5769/5915.
———. "La rebelión de hijos emancipados: Judeidad y diáspora en escritores exiliados judíos latinoamericanos." *Cuadernos LIRICO* [online], no. 19, 2018, doi: 10.4000/lirico.6140. Accessed 29 Jan. 2019.
Sharp, David. "Possession of the Ball: Recovering Identity in Ricardo Feierstein's *Mestizo*." *Global Graffiti*, vol. 1, 2010, https://globalgraffmag.wordpress.com/2010/07/02/possession-of-the-ball-recovering-identity-in-ricardo-feierstein's-mestizo/. Accessed 7 Feb. 2019.
Shua, Ana María. *The Book of Memories*. U of New Mexico P, 1998.
———. *El libro de los recuerdos*. Sudamericana, 1994.
Sifuentes-Jáuregui, Ben. *Transvestism, Masculinity, and Latin American Literature: Genders Share Flesh*. Palgrave, 2002.
Sitman, Rosalie. "Protest from Afar: The Jewish and Republican Presence in Victoria Ocampo's *Revista Sur* in the 1930s and 1940s." *Rethinking Jewish Latin Americans*, edited by Jeffrey Lesser and Raanan Rein, U of New Mexico P, 2008, pp. 132–60.
Sommer, Doris. *Foundational Fictions: The National Romances of Latin America*. U of California P, 1991.
Sontag, Susan. "Notes on Camp." *Partisan Review*, vol. 31, no. 4, 1964, pp. 515–30.
Sosnowski, Saúl. *Borges y la Cabala: La búsqueda del verbo*. Hispamérica, 1976.
———. *La orilla inminente. Escritores judíos argentinos*. Legasa, 1987.
Spivak, Gayatri. *The Postcolonial Critic: Interviews, Strategies, Dialogues*. Routledge, 1990.
Steimberg, Alicia. *Músicos y relojeros*. Centro Editor de América Latina, 1971.
Strejilevich, Nora. *Una sola muerte numerosa*. North-South Center Press, 1997.
———. *A Single, Numberless Death*. U of Virginia P, 2002.
Suárez, Patricia. *Las polacas*. Colección Ibiku, 2012.
Szichman, Mario. *At 8:25 Evita Became Immortal*. Translated by Roberto Picciotto, Ediciones del Norte, 1983.

———. *A las 20:25, la señora entró en la inmortalidad.* Ediciones del Norte, 1981.
———. *Los judíos del mar dulce.* Editorial Galerna, 1971.
———. "Los judíos del mar dulce: de la iracundia a la sátira." Aug. 2013, http://marioszichman.blogspot.com/2013/08/los-judios-del-mar-dulce-de-la.htmlblog.
Sznaider, Natan. *Jewish Memory and the Cosmopolitan Order.* Polity Press, 2011.
Tal, Tzvi. "Terror, etnicidad y la imagen del judío en el cine argentino contemporáneo." *Nuevo Mundo. Mundos Nuevos,* 2010, http://nuevomundo.revues.org/. Accessed 2 Nov. 2015.
Tavosnanska, Gregorio. *Ydel, el judío pampa.* Corregidor, 1999.
Tiempo, César. *Versos de una. . . .* Amgehino, 1998 (1926).
Tierney Tello, Mary Beth. "From Silence to Subjectivity: Reading and Writing in Reina Roffe's 'La Rompiente.'" *Latin American Literary Review,* vol. 21, no. 42, 1993, pp. 34–56.
Timerman, Jacobo. *Prisoner without a Name, Cell without a Number.* Vintage, 1981.
Toker, Eliahu, editor. *Buenos Aires esquina sábado: Antología de César Tiempo.* Ediciones Archivo General de la Nación, 1997.
———. *Trayectoria de una idea: 50 años de periodismo judeo-argentino.* Fund. M. Anilevich, 1999.
Trachtenberg, Alan. *Classic Essays on Photography.* Leete's Island Books, 1980.
Tsing, Anna. *Friction: An Ethnography of Global Connection.* Princeton UP, 2011.
Valenzuela, Luisa. *El Mañana.* Seix Barral, 2010.
Viñas, David. *En la semana trágica.* J. Alvarez, 1966.
Wald, Pinie. *Koschmar. Pesadilla: Novela crónica de la semana trágica* (Nightmare: A chronicle-novel of the tragic week, translated by Simja Sneh). Editorial Milá, 1988; repr. 1998, Editorial Amgehino.
Waldegaray, Marta Inés. "Andrés Rivera, escritor social." *Cuadernos Lírico,* vol. 8, 2013, pp. 221–34.
Yerushalmi, Yosef Hayim. *Zakhor: Jewish History and Jewish Memory.* U of Washington P, 1996.
Zivin, Erin Graff. *The Wandering Signifier: Rhetoric of Jewishness in the Latin American Imaginary.* Duke UP, 2008.
Zuker, Cristina. *El tren de la victoria: Una saga familiar.* Sudamericana, 2003.

# FILMOGRAPHY

Bielinsky, Fabián, dir. *Nueve reinas* (*Nine Queens*), 2000.
Blaustein, David, dir. *Botín de guerra* (*Spoils of War*), 2000.
———. *Hacer patria* (*Forging a Nation*), 2007.
Blaustein Muñoz, Susana, dir. *Susana,* 1980.
Burman, Daniel, dir. *Derecho de familia* (*Family Law*), 2006.
———. *El abrazo partido* (*Lost Embrace*), 2004.

———. *El nido vacío* (*The Empty Nest*), 2008.
———. *El rey del Once* (*The Tenth Man*), 2016.
———. *Esperando al Mesías* (*Waiting for the Messiah*), 2000.
Campanella, Juan José, dir. *Vientos de agua* (TV miniseries), 2006.
Cozarinsky, Edgardo, dir. *Ronda nocturna* (*Night Watch*), 2005.
Dietsch, Sebastián, and Ionantan Klajman, dirs. *Mar del Plata*, 2012.
Hofman, Fabián, dir. *Te extraño* (*I Miss You*), 2010.
Kamin, Bebe, dir. *Los chicos de la guerra* (*The Children of the War*), 1984.
Katz, Ana, dir. *Una novia errante* (*A Stray Girlfriend*), 2007.
Lerman, Diego, dir. *La mirada invisible* (*The Invisible Eye*), 2010.
Lichtmann, Gabriel, dir. *Cómo ganar enemigo* (*How to Win Enemies*), 2014.
Markovitch, Paula, dir. *El premio* (*The Prize*), 2011.
Menis, María Victoria, dir. *La cámara oscura* (*Camera Obscura*), 2008.
Pelosi, Maximiliano, dir. *Otro entre otros*, 2010.
Piterbarg, Ana, dir. *Todos tenemos un plan* (*Everybody Has a Plan*), 2012.
Ponce, Alberto, dir. *Blackie: Una vida en blanco y negro*, 2012.
Saslavsky, Luis, dir. *Ceniza al viento* (*Ashes to the Wind*), 1942.
Solomonoff, Julia, dir. *Hermanas* (*Sisters*), 2005.
———. *El último verano de la Boyita* (*The Last Summer of La Boyita*), 2009.
Szwarcbart, Herman, dir. *Un pogrom en Buenos Aires*, 2007.
Torres Ríos, Leopoldo, dir. *Pelota de trapo* (*Ragged Football*), 1948.
Yellen, Linda, dir. *Jacobo Timerman: Prisoner without a Name, Cell without a Number*, 1983.

# INDEX

*Absent City, The* (*La ciudad ausente*) (Piglia), 20
Acedo Alonso, Noemí, 211n10
Achugar, Hugo, 201n2
Agamben, Giorgio, 159
agricultural colonies: Jewish, xii, 1, 11, 12, 15–18, 30, 54, 95, 124, 131, 202n7, 202n10; in film, 104–105; 131; in literature, 14–15, 33, 54, 58, 61–62, 64, 67, 69, 70, 75, 81, 138, 173–75. *See also* Moisés Ville
Aizenberg, Edna, 110, 203n7, 208n7
Alazraki, Jaime, 110, 203n7
alterity. *See* otherness
AMIA (Asociación Mutual Israelita Argentina), 98, 205n15; bombing 32, 76, 92, 99–100, 112, 148, 153, 208n7
antisemitism, 19, 28, 31–32, 38–40, 50, 100, 110, 124, 142, 160, 170, 175–76, 204–205n14, 206n6; casual, 54–55, 62, 125; and dictatorship, 134–35, 142–50, 160, 169, 175; European, 17, 175, 187, 208–209n11; 160, 164, 169, 210n10; in fiction, 4–8, 10–11, 12, 54–55, 56, 61, 72, 95–97, 110, 111, 125, 143, 145–46, 164, 175–76, 179–80, 202n8; in film, 134–35; and homophobia, 6–7, 12, 171, 172, 179, 187, 189, 196; spelling of, 202n6; traditional vs. ideological, 143–44
anxiety, 37, 61, 96; and assimilation xiv, 11, 131; and gender/sexuality, 26, 45, 172, 178, 181, 189; Jewish, 32, 33, 55, 56, 57, 94, 100, 101, 130, 137–38; and modernity, 4–5, 8, 22, 33, 37, 38–39, 45, 172, 178, 189
Anzaldúa, Gloria, 147
Appiah, Kwame Anthony, 204n13
*árbol de la gitana, El* (The Gypsy woman's tree) (Dujovne Ortiz), 31, 73, 77, 79–87, 106, 207n7, 207n10
Argentineity, 27–28, 37, 50, 52, 118, 119–20, 173, 180. *See also* Argentineity and Jewishness. *See also under* Catholicism; identity; immigration; Jewishness; whiteness
Argentineity and Jewishness, 1–4, 16–20, 22–31, 50–52, 91–92, 141–43, 160, 169, 199–200; and AMIA bombing, 32, 99–100; in fiction, 11–12, 14–15, 20, 31, 33–37, 54–58, 60, 63, 64–65, 67–68, 72, 75–78, 79, 83, 128–29, 138–39, 164–65, 175, 177–78; in film, 33–34, 37–38, 59, 92–95, 135–38; in Gentile writers, 20, 31–32, 110;

Argentineity and Jewishness *(continued)*
  in poetry, 26–29, 197–99; and
  tango, 100–103; in visual art, 88,
  119–20. *See also under* Jewishness
*Arqueology of the Journey* (*Arqueología
  de un trayecto*) (Kuperminc), 88–89
*Ashes to the Wind* (*Cenizas al viento*)
  (Saslavsky), 98–99, 208n6
Asociación Mutual Israelita Argentina.
  *See* AMIA
assimilation, xiv, 32, 33, 44, 48, 49,
  54, 102, 133, 137, 138, 150; and
  Catholicism, 131–33; in fiction,
  11–12, 32, 56–57, 60, 67–68,
  74, 75–76; in film, 37, 59, 92,
  94–95, 131–33, 138, 179; and
  food, 30; and gender, 11–12, 137,
  138; and intermarriage, 13, 77;
  and modernity, 33, 37, 125, 131;
  unsuccessful, 56–57; mentioned 1,
  12, 16, 129, 150. *See also* incidental
  Jewishness
Astro, Alan, 210n5
*astucia de la razón, La* (The cunning of
  reason) (Feinmann), 206n7
*At 8:25 Evita Became Immortal* (*A
  las 20:30 la señora entró en la
  inmortalidad*) (Szichman), 45, 60,
  71, 208n4
Avni, Haim, 201n1 (ch 1)

Baron, Salo Wittmayer, 109
Bayer, Osvaldo, 163–64
Beciu, Ana, 192
Benhabib, Seyla, 204n13
Benjamin, Walter, 91, 123
Bielinsky, Fabián, 105, 125; *Nine
  Queens*, 104
Birmajer, Marcelo, 130, 17; *La
  despedida*, 129–30; "En la noche
  de bodas," 173–75, 176–77; *Tres
  mosqueteros*, xv, 1

Blackie. *See* Efron, Paloma
*Blackie: Una vida en blanco y negro*
  (Blackie: A life in black and white)
  (Ponce), 188
blackness, 14, 23, 29, 110, 187–88,
  204n12. *See also* race
Blaustein Muñoz, Susana, 191; *Susana*,
  191, 196
Blaustein, David: *Hacer patria*, 18–19;
  *Spoils of War*, 167
Bleys, Rudi, 177
*Bloody Countess, The* (*La condesa
  sangrienta*) (Pizarnik), 192, 214n19
"*Blues* en la noche" (Blues in the
  night) (Rozenmacher), 57–58
Bollig, Ben, 109–10, 214n21
*Book of Memories, The* (*El libro de los
  recuerdos*) (Shua), 74
Borges, Jorge Luis, 110, 112, 163,
  203n7, 209n17, 215n1; "Death
  and the Compass," 110; "The Dead
  Man," 110; "Emma Zunz," 45,
  110; "Gunnar Thorgilsson," 115;
  and Jewish identity, 24, 110; "The
  Unworthy Friend," 110
*Borges and the Kabbalah* (*Borges
  y la Cábala*) (Kuperminc and
  Sosnowski), 209n17
Boyarin, Daniel, xiv, 127, 187
Brenman, Darío, 99–100
"Bride from Odessa, The" ("La novia
  de Odessa") (Cozarinsky), 60–62,
  64, 68, 78–79
Brizuela, Leopoldo, 175; *Una misma
  noche*, 175–77
Brodsky, Marcelo 165; *Buena memoria*,
  167; *NEXO 7*, 165–67
Brunner, Juan José, 201n4
Buber, Martin, 4
"Budapest" (Cozarinsky), 39–40
*Buena memoria* (Good Memory)
  (Brodsky), 167

# INDEX

Burman, Daniel, 92, 105; Ariel films, 59–60, 77, 92–95, 135; *The Empty Nest*, 13, 102–104, 135–38, 139–40; *Family Law*, 59–60, 92–95; *Lost Embrace*, 13–14, 59, 60, 93; *The Tenth Man*, 59, 60, 92–95; *Waiting for the Messiah*, 33–34, 58, 59, 92–94, 137, 178–80, 191, 208n2

"Camera Obscura" ("La cámara oscura") (Gorodischer), 18, 68, 70–71, 78–79, 90, 189
Camorra, La, tango quintet, 100–102
Campanella, Juan José, *Vientos del agua*, 18, 47, 89
Castle, Terry, 187
Catelli, Nora, 109
Catholicism, 131–33, 149, 169, 206n6, 210n8; and Argentineity, xiii, 23, 24, 26, 72, 106, 133, 142, 147, 172–73, 202n8. *See also* intermarriage
Chejfec, Sergio, 159, 170; *Lenta biografía*, 153, 154–59; *My Two Worlds*, 34; *The Planets*, 159–60
*Children of the War, The* (*Los chicos de la guerra*) (Kamin), 134–35
"cielo dividido, El" (The divided sky) (Roffé), 191
civilization vs. barbarism, 8, 22–23, 25, 133
Cohen, Mitchell, 204n13
Colombres, Adolfo, 3
colonialism, 3, 11, 12, 28–29, 30, 47, 203n2
*Como papas para varenikes* (Like potatoes for *varenikes*) (Plager), 83
cosmopolitanism, 204n13; and Jewishness, 12, 24–33, 99, 173, 199; and modernity 2, 29–30, 32, 33; and nationalism 28–29

Costantini, Humberto, 42, 210n1; *De dioses, hombrecitos y policías*, 126
Cottrol, Robert, 201n2
Cozarinsky, Edgardo, 54, 124, 173, 186–87, 196, 209n1, 213n10; "The Bride from Odessa," 60–62, 64, 68, 78–79; "Budapest," 39–40; "Émigré Hotel," 62–64, 106; *Lejos de dónde*, xiv, 54–55; *The Moldavian Pimp*, xv; *Night Watch*, 186–87; "Real Estate," 70, 138–40; *La tercera mañana*, 105–106; *Urban Voodoo*, 186, 213n13
*Crítica de las armas* (Critique of weapons) (Feinmann), 24–25, 55–56, 77, 177–78, 206n7, 213n9

DAIA (Delegation of Argentine Jewish Organizations): and the dictatorship, 144–46, 161–62, 211n4; and Judíos Argentinos Gays, 196. See also *Report on the Situation of Jewish Detained and Disappeared*; *Special Report on Jewish Detained and Disappeared*
*Daughter of Silence* (*Hija del silencio*) (Fingueret), 73, 153–54, 158–59, 212n17
"Dead Man, The" ("El muerto") (Borges), 110
"Death and the Compass" ("La muerte y la brújula") (Borges), 110
Delegation of Argentine Jewish Organizations. *See* DAIA
DeRocher, Patricia, 211n10
*despedida, La* (The farewell) (Birmajer), 129–30
*Detrás de los ojos* (Behind the eyes) (Fainstein), 167
Deutsch, Sandra McGee, 143–44

diaspora, 1, 13, 49, 79, 88–89, 108, 114, 125, 137, 147, 148, 150, 151, 162, 207n5, 208n15. *See also* displacement; exile

Díaz, Esther, 40

dictatorship (1976–1983), 2, 49–50, 85, 98, 142–50, 159–70, 175–76, 190, 213n6; in fiction, 24, 35–37, 43, 44, 56, 73, 75–76, 81, 143, 145–46, 147–49, 153–54, 158, 159–60, 175–76, 212n14; in film, 132, 134–35, 167–68; and gender violence, 43–44; and Jewishness, 72–73, 143–48, 167–69, 175, 211n1; in testimonio, 145, 148–49, 169; in visual art, 112–13, 114, 117, 165–67. *See also under* antisemitism; DAIA; Holocaust; incidental Jewishness; Jewish legibility

Dietsch, Sebastián: *Mar del Plata*, 126–27

difference. *See* otherness

*dioses, hombrecitos y policías, De* (On gods, little men, and police) (Costantini), 126

displacement, 73, 88–89, 108, 112, 119, 150. *See also* diaspora; exile

Dobry, Edgardo, 100

*Don Segundo Sombra* (Güiraldes), 28

*Dos veces junio* (Two times June) (Kohan), 37

Dreishpoon, Douglas, 117–18, 120

Drucaroff, Elsa, 47; *El infierno prometido*, 42–43

Duggan, Bob, 209n19

Dujovne Ortiz, Alicia, 106, 207n11; *El árbol de la gitana*, 31, 73, 77, 79–87, 106, 207n7, 207n10; *Las perlas rojas*, 79, 143

Echeverría, Esteban, *The Slaughter Yard*, 172–73

Edurne Portela, M., 211n10

Efron, Gustavo, 99–100

Efron, Paloma (Taibele), 187–89, 196. *See also Blackie: Una vida en blanco y negro*

embedded Jewishness, 2, 91, 101, 141–42, 147, 170; in anti-dictatorship narratives, 143; and antisemitic nationalism, 142–45, 147–49, 159–60, 164–65, 168, 169; explained 141–42; in contrast to incidental Jewishness, 141; in Kuitca, 114–15, 116, 118–19

"Émigré Hotel" ("Hotel de emigrantes") (Cozarinsky), 62–64, 106

"Emma Zunz" (Borges) 45, 110

*Empty Nest* (*El nido vacío*) (Burman), 13, 102–104, 135–38, 139–40

*En la semana trágica* (During the Tragic Week) (Viñas), 95–96

Escliar, Myriam, 188

essentialism: provisional vs. strategic, 53

*Everybody Has a Plan* (*Todos tenemos un plan*) (Piterbarg), 133–34

exile, 34, 49–50, 75, 79–82, 84–86, 87, 146, 154, 162, 167, 169, 205n17, 207n5; and gender, 24, 84–86, 208n14; and identity, 202n5, 205n17, 206n3. *See also* diaspora; displacement

*Facundo* (Sarmiento), 22–23

Fainstein, Graciela: *Detrás de los ojos*, 167

*Family Law* (*Derecho de familia*) (Burman), 59–60, 92–95

father/child relationships, 13–14, 15, 24–25, 34–37, 59–60, 70, 83, 93–94, 95, 108, 154–58, 178, 195–96, 197, 208n15, 210n6. *See also* patriarchy

Feierstein, Ricardo, xv, 82, 87, 88, 124, 207n11; *La logia del umbral,* 37, 55, 87, 147–48; *Mestizo,* 34–37, 50, 55, 69, 71–73, 86, 87, 124, 190, 205n18

Feinmann, José Pablo, 206n7; *La astucia de la razón,* 206n7; *La crítica de las armas,* 24–25, 55–56, 77, 177–78, 206n7, 213n9; *Heidegger's Shadow,* xiv

Feitlowitz, Marguerite, 162, 164, 211n4

femininity, 7, 8, 10, 11, 26, 53, 99, 102, 174, 184; as attributed to men, xiv, 3, 5–6, 26, 39, 53, 171–73, 177, 181–82, 187, 191; transgressive, 12, 71, 180, 184, 188–94, 196

feminist analysis, 3, 12, 29, 45, 51, 53, 168, 171–72, 201n2, 204n13, 207n11, 208n14, 207n11; and Jewish studies xi, xiv, 3

Filippo, Virgilio, 142

Finchelstein, Federico, 142, 170

Fingueret, Manuela, 153; *Daughter of Silence,* 73, 153–54, 158–59, 212n17

Fishburn, Evelyn, 108–109, 110, 214n18, 214n21, 214n23

food: and identity, 30–31, 61, 83–84, 207–208n13; and memory, 54, 68, 191

*Formosa, El* (The Formosa) (Futoransky), 73, 74, 77, 89

Foucault, Michel, xiii

Frank, Waldo, 24, 209n1

Freedman, Jonathan, 172

Freund, Gisele, 123–24

Fried, Michael, 208n10

Futoransky, Luisa, *El Formosa,* 73, 74, 77, 89

Gálvez, Manuel, 202n8

Garb, Tamar, 204n14

*Gaucho Martín Fierro, The* (*El gaucho Martín Fierro*) (Hernández), 17, 28

gauchos, 12, 17, 31, 173; Jewish, xv, 12, 30, 54, 67–68, 124, 171. See also *Gaucho Martín Fierro*; *Jewish Gauchos of the Pampas*; *Ydel, el judío pampa*

Gelman, Juan, 26; *Mundar,* 106–108; "Pensamientos," 26–29, 204n12

gender, 2, 84, 103, 201n2, 203n6, 204n10, 68; in Birmajer, 13, 173–75; in Burman, 13–14, 58, 136–37, 178–79, 180; in Chejfec, 156–57; in Dujovne Ortiz, 86; in Echeverria, 172–73; in Feierstein, 36–37, 86; in Gerchunoff, 11–12, 13; in Gorodischer, 70, 71; and Jewishness, xiii–xv, 11–12, 15, 25, 26, 31, 37, 44, 64, 71, 102–103, 156–57, 171–72; in Kusminsky, 178, 179–80; in Martel, 4–11, 12; in prostitution stories, 41–45, 70–71, 189–90; and sexuality, xiii–xv, 2–4, 48–49, 51, 124–25, 174–75, 180–82, 187–89, 191, 196; in Tavnosanska, 14–15; in Tiempo, 40–41; violence, 43–44, 125, 179, 202n11. See also femininity; masculinity; transgender

Gerchunoff, Alberto, xv, 4, 28, 32, 49, 54, 67, 100, 128–29, 150, 173–74, 202n9; *The Jewish Gauchos of the Pampas,* 4, 11–13, 28, 91–92, 95, 171

*Ghosts at the Lodz Ghetto* (*Fantasmas en el ghetto de Lodz*) (Kuperminc), 151

Girondo, Oliverio, 182–84

Glickman, Nora, 41–42, 109; *Una tal Raquel,* xv, 42, 68, 70–71, 78, 79, 109, 189

Glusberg, Samuel, 24, 111

Goldberg, Florinda, 52, 108, 160, 162–65, 206n5, 214n18
Goldfine, Daniela, 211n10, 212n12
Gordillo, Gastón, 201n2
Gorodischer, Angélica, 210n10; "Camera Obscura," 18, 68, 70–71, 78–79, 90, 189
grandmother figures, 42, 61–62, 63–64, 70–71, 77, 78–79, 81, 84, 131, 168, 207n8, 207n13
Grant, Catherine, 214n20
Guevara, Che, 26–28
Güiraldes, Ricardo, *Don Segundo Sombra*, 28
"Gunnar Thorgilsson" (Borges), 115
Guy, Donna, 205n19

*Hacer patria* (Forging a Nation) (Blaustein), 18–19
Harding, Sandra, 206n4
*Heidegger's Shadow* (*La sombra de Heidegger*) (Feinmann), xiv
Hernández, José, *El gaucho Martín Fierro*, 17, 28
Hernández, Rafael, 17
heteronormativity, 12–13, 59, 171, 173–74, 175, 178–79, 182, 184, 189–90, 191, 194, 196. See also homophobia
*hilo rojo, Un* (A red thread) (Rosenberg), xv, 144
Hirsch, Baron Maurice von, 11, 17, 18, 54, 124, 202n7
Hirsch, Marianne, 151
Hirsch, Baron Maurice von, 17, 18, 54, 124, 202n7
Hirsch, Silvia, 201n2
*Hispamérica*, xv, 126
Hofman, Fabián, *I Miss You*, 167, 168, 207n6, 212n20
Holocaust, 53, 95, 98, 99, 109, 123–24, 150–59, 160; and 1976–83 dictatorship, 142–43, 144–47, 149–50, 153–54, 158, 159–67, 168–69, 212n14; Argentina as refuge from, xiv, 18, 98–99, 150; in Brodsky, 166–67; in Kuitca, 151; in Kupferminc, 112, 114, 151–53; narratives, 62–64, 153–59; as universal signifier, 160–65, 169, 212n19
homoeroticism. *See* lesbianism; queerness, transgressive sexuality
homophobia, 12, 96, 171–73, 177–78, 181–83, 187, 188, 195, 196, 213n8; and interfactionality, 171. *See also* heteronormativity
*How to Win Enemies* (*Cómo ganar enemigos*) (Lichtmann), 126
hybridity, 3, 26–28, 37, 72, 80–83, 86, 87, 110, 207n11

*I Miss You* (*Te extraño*) (Hofman), 167, 168, 207n6, 212n20
identity, xi, xii, 53, 56, 118, 140, 180, 201n2, 202n5, 206n3; Argentine (national) xii, xiii, 2, 21, 22, 27, 28–29, 35, 47–50, 72, 73, 79, 210n7, Argentine with reference to Jews; 2, 16, 38, 48–49, 99–100, 149; –based scholarship, 51; instability of, 51–52, 64, 79, 83, 173, 174, 196, 210n10; Jewish, xiii, 2, 30, 33, 48–49, 50–55, 58, 59, 60–63, 72, 74, 75, 77, 79, 82, 85, 94, 110, 123, 126, 135, 138–39, 141, 159–60, 168–69; Jewish-Argentine, 25–26, 30–31, 34–36, 56, 59, 61, 73, 78, 99, 102–103, 128–29, 130–31, 135–37, 158, 165; Jewish Argentine and gender, 37, 58; as performance, 60–61, 77, 79, 102–103, 104, 105, 113
immigration, 21–23, 30, 74, 88–90; ambivalence toward, 16–17, 23, 25; Jewish in Argentina, xii, xiv,

1, 2, 3, 4, 15–19, 22–25, 27, 29, 31–32, 47–48, 89–90, 126, 150, 172, 211n11; and modernity, 2, 12, 29–30, 31–32, 33, 53, 59; in narrative, 56–58, 61–64, 67–68, 75, 77–78, 79, 90, 191; and transgressive sexuality, 174, 181–82. *See also* migration

*inauguración, La* (The Inauguration) (Krimer), 44–45, 190

incidental Jewishness, 50, 51, 105, 123–40, 141; and Costantini, 210n4; and Cozarinsky, 124; and dictatorship, 160, 167–68, 176; in film, 102–103, 126–27, 131–38, 139–40, 167–68; and Freund, 123–24; in narrative, 76–77, 124–26, 127–31, 134, 138–40, 159–60, 176; and normalization of Jewishness, 125, 126, 128–29, 136, 160; and Partnoy, 149, 168–69; and Perlongher, 183; and tango, 100–102, 125; in visual art, 167, 118, 120, 177. *See also* Jewish legibility

indigeneity, 2, 3, 12, 16, 21, 22, 23, 28, 29, 87, 110, 167, 201n2, 202n10, 204n12

*infierno prometido, El* (The promised Hell) (Drucaroff), 42–43

interfactionality, 171, 212n1

intermarriage: assimilation and 13, 77; in film, 59, 94–95; in narrative, 24–25, 55–56, 75, 77–78, 79, 81–82, 106

intersex, 195–96, 214–15n24

Israel, xii, 3, 63, 82, 191, 211n8; embassy bombing, 32, 99, 148, 208n8; in *The Empty Nest*, 102, 104, 136–38; and Jewish identity, 48; and masculinity xiii, 13–14, 59, 136

Italians in Argentina; 17, 19–20, 27–28, 29, 30, 38, 47–48, 132, 134, 181, 207n8, 207–208n13

Jacobson, Shari, xiv

JCA (Jewish Colonization Association). *See* agricultural colonies.

Jenckes, Kate, 159–60

Jewish cultural landscape, 50–51

*Jewish Gauchos of the Pampas, The* (*Los gauchos judíos*) (Gerchunoff), 4, 11–13, 28, 91–92, 95, 171

Jewish legibility, 18, 34, 91–121, 125, 148, 200, 208n1; during the 1976–83 dictatorship, 148–50; in film, 92–95, 99, 102–103, 104–105, 110; and incidentality, 125, 127, 128; and the "Jewish Pact," 106–109; in narrative, 34, 75, 91–92, 95–98, 100, 105–106, 110, 125, 159; in poetry, 100, 106–10, 192; in tango, 100–102, 125; and pseudonyms 110–11; and visibility, 91, 92, 98, 99, 100, 104–106, 110–15, 120–21; in visual art, 112–20. *See also* incidental Jewishness; visibility

Jewish studies, xi–xii

Jewishness: as constitutive of Argentineity, xii, xv, 1–3, 19–20, 26–28, 32, 47–49, 72, 76–77, 120; contested meanings of, 2, 4–8, 11, 12–13, 32, 53; and criminality, 32, 38–40; meaning of, xiii–xv, 25, 32, 47, 48, 51–53, 77, 100, 147, 150, 199–200; as metaphor, xiii, 1–2, 10, 47, 48, 164–65, 204–205n14; as a mode of Argentineity, 13, 20, 25–26, 28, 126, 128–31, 138; and the premodern, xiii, 25, 31–32, 53, 199–200, 204–205n14; and sexuality, xiv, 6–7, 12, 171–73, 177, 181–82, 185–86. *See also* Argentineity and Jewishness; embedded Jewishness; incidental Jewishness, modernity and Jewishness. *See*

Jewishness *(continued)*
  *also under* Argentineity; anxiety; cosmopolitanism; identity; otherness
*judíos de Las Acacias, Los* (The Jews of Las Acacias) (Mactas), 33
*judíos del Mar Dulce, Los* (The Jews of the sweetwater sea) (Szichman), 68–69, 206–207nn2–3
Judkovski, José, 101, 125

*Kadish* (Kaddish) (Rivera), 145–46
Kamenszain, Tamara, 197; "Mi duelo," 197–99
Kaminsky, David, 171
Katz, Ana, *A Stray Girlfriend*, 51–52
Kartun, Mauricio, 208n4
kashrut, 30, 131. *See also* food
Kaufmann, Paola, *The Lake*, xiv
Klajman, Ionatan, *Mar del Plata*, 126–27
Kociancich, Vlady, 125
Kohan, Martín: *Dos veces junio*, 37; *School for Patriots*, 134
*Koschmar* (Nightmare) (Wald), 98
Kovadloff, Santiago, 25–26, 33, 42, 142–43, 203n9, 211n1, 212n19
Kreimer, Juan Carlos, *Todos lo sabíamos*, 127–29, 130
Krimer, María Inés, 44, 45; *La inauguración*, 44–45, 190; *Sangre kosher*, 43, 44; "Shabat," 44
Kristeva, Julia, 25, 214n16
Kuitca, Guillermo, 114–21, 151, 173, 177, 196, 209n19; *El Mar Dulce*, 115–17, 118; *1–30,000*, 114, 117–18, 120; *Tablada Suite*, 114–15, 118
Kuperminc, Mirta, 87–89, 112–14, 119, 151–53; *Arqueology of the Journey*, 88–89; *To Be a Witness*, 112–13; *Borges and the Kabbalah*, 209n17; *Ghosts at the Lodz Ghetto*, 151; *On the Way*, 87–88; *The Skin of Memory*, 153; *That Place*, 152; *La vida espuma*, 153
Kusminsky, Gustavo, *Médanos: Premio de narrativa hispanoamericana*, 178, 179–80, 202n11

*Lake, The* (*El lago*) (Kaufmann), xiv
Lane, Helen R., 209n16
*Last Summer of La Boyita* (*El último verano de la Boyita*) (Solomonoff), 131–33, 195–96
Latin American Jewish Studies Association (LAJSA), xi
legibility, Jewish. *See* Jewish legibility
Lejeune, Phillipe, 106
*Lejos de dónde* (Far from where) (Cozarinsky), xiv, 54–55
*Lenta biografía* (*Slow biography*) (Chejfec), 153, 154–59
Lerman, Diego, 210n11
Lerman, Gabriel, 127–28
lesbianism, 189, 190; and Jewish Argentineity, 181–82, 189, 191; obscured, 51, 186, 187, 192, 214n20; in Pizarnik, 108, 173, 191–94, 214n19; 214n21; presumptive, 187–89; in Roffé, 190–91; in scholarship, xi, 51; in social movements, 212–13n2; in *Susana*, 191; in *Waiting for the Messiah*, 34, 180, 191
Liberman, Raquel, 41–42, 70–71, 109, 189, 190, 202n12, 210n4. *See also* Glickman; *Una tal Raquel*
Lipstadt, Deborah, 202n6
*Little School, The* (*La escuelita*) (Partnoy), xv, 145, 148–49, 168
Lockhart, Darrell, 52
*logia del umbral, La* (The lodge of the threshold) (Feierstein), 37, 55, 87, 147–48

*Lost Embrace* (*El abrazo partido*) (Burman), 13–14, 59, 60, 92, 93
Lowenthal, Wilhelm, 17, 18
Ludmer, Josefina, 38–39
Lugones, María, 207n11
Lukin, Liliana, 161

Mackinnon, Catherine, 204n13
Mackintosh, Fiona, 192
Mactas, Raquel, 32; *Los judíos de Las Acacias*, 33
*Mañana, El* (Valenzuela), xiii
*Mar del Plata* (Dietsch and Klajman), 126–27
*mar dulce, El* (The sweetwater sea) (Kuitca), 115–17, 118
Markovitch, Paula, *The Prize*, 132–33, 135, 167
Martel, Julián, 202n8; *The Stock Market*, 4–11, 12, 171–72, 202n7
masculinity, 17, 37, 86, 87, 136, 171, 174–75, 176; and heteronormativity, 12–15, 177–80, 191; Jewish, xv, 11, 13–15, 127, 130, 171, 176, 178, 179, 187, 194; and modernity, 4, 25
Masiello, Francine, 201n2
*Mater erótica* (Erotic mater) (Raznovich), 194
Mayer, Hans, 213n3
*Médanos: Premio de narrativa hispanoamericana* (Sand dunes: Prize winner in Latin American narrative) (Kusminsky), 178, 179–80, 202n11
Medina, Enrique, *Las muecas del miedo*, 164
memory, xv, 48, 206n1, 207n7; contested, 74–75; and history, 51, 64, 67–69, 72–77, 79–83, 105, 208n4; in Holocaust narratives, 150, 151–59; and identity, 48, 50, 54, 67–69, 76; loss and recovery, 37, 71–72; and photography, 69–72, 166–67; and state terror, 34–35, 161, 166–67, 175–76, 212n17, 213n6
mestizaje. *See* hybridity
*Mestizo* (Feierstein), 34–37, 50, 55, 69, 71–73, 86, 87, 124, 190, 205n18
Meyer, Marshall, 211n5
*Mi cocina judía* (My Jewish kitchen) (Plager), 83–84
"Mi duelo" (My grief) (Kamenszain), 197–99
migration, 1, 50, 53, 87–90, 207n5; and displacement, 73, 79–81, 82, 150; internal, 12, 33, 75; and transformation, 63, 174. *See also* immigration
Minnich, Elizabeth, 204n13
Mirelman, Victor, 208n3
misogyny, 12, 31, 172, 177, 178–80, 196
Mizraje, María Gabriela, 209n15
modernity in Argentina: and Jewishness, xii–xiii, xiv–xv, 1–3, 4, 29–30, 31–34, 38–39, 42–43, 49, 52, 53, 55, 59, 72, 98, 100, 111, 24, 125, 129, 130–31, 132–33, 137, 143, 145, 147, 160, 169, 172, 173, 185–87, 189, 199, 204–205n14; and modernization, 33, 203n2, 205n16; and sexuality 173, 175, 180–87, 189–91. *See also under* anxiety
Moisés Ville, 11, 15–16, 17–18, 30, 67, 89–90, 104, 173, 202n9, 202n10, 203n14
*Moldavian Pimp, The* (*El rufián moldavo*) (Cozarinsky), xv
Molloy, Sylvia, 214n19
*Monte de Venus* (Mount of Venus) (Roffé), 190–91
Mosse, George, 181–82

mother-daughter relationships, 168–69; in fiction, 42, 43, 78–80, 82, 83–85, 86, 153–54, 158, 211n2; in film, 59, 131–33; in poetry, 214n21; in visual art, 114, 152. *See also* mothers

mother-son relationships: in fiction, 24–25, 56–57, 139, 177–78, 203n8; in film, 58, 59, 92–93, 195–96; in poetry, 107. *See also* mothers

mothers, xiv, 7, 45, 71, 77–80, 103, 112, 156, 167–68; absent, 60, 156; runaway, 68, 70, 139, 189, 190, 194

Muchnik, Mario, 67, 208n1

*muecas del miedo, Las* (Fear grimaces) (Medina), 164

*Mundar* (Worlding) (Gelman), 106–108

*Musicians and Watchmakers* (*Músicos y relojeros*) (Steimberg), 68, 73–74, 78, 210n8

*My Two Worlds* (*Mis dos mundos*) (Chejfec), 34

mysticism: Jewish, 51, 110, 112, 114, 147

Nazism. *See* Holocaust

Neuman, Andrés, 78, 79, 106, 207n4; *Una vez Argentina*, 37, 73–74, 75–77, 106, 130, 213n8

*NEXO 7: LOS CAMPOS* (NEXUS 7: THE CAMPS) (Brodsky), 165–67

*Nice Jewish Girls*, xi

*Night Watch* (*Noche de ronda*) (Cozarinsky), 186–87

*Nine Queens* (*Nueve reinas*) (Bielinsky), 104

"noche de bodas, En la" (On their wedding night) (Birmajer), 173–75, 176–77

"noche en blanco, La" (Sleepless night) (Roffé), 212n14

nostalgia, 40, 64, 67–68, 78, 115

"Notes on Camp" (Sontag), 185–86, 187

Ocampo, Silvina, 163

Ocampo, Victoria, 24, 123–24, 209n1, 213n12

*On the Way* (*En camino*) (Kupferminc), 87–88

*1–30,000* (Kuitca), 114, 117–18, 120

Orgambide, Pedro, 98

Ostrom, Katherine, 111

otherness: audible, 125; Jewish, xiv, 1, 22, 25, 31, 32, 34, 37–39, 54–56, 73, 76, 99–101, 103, 120, 125, 130, 132, 133, 141, 214n17; overlapping categories of, xiv, 22, 23, 29, 103, 171–72, 175–76, 180, 186–89, 191, 195, 203n6; and state violence, 142–43, 147–48, 165, 167, 169; and visibility, 111, 120–21

*Otro entre otros* (An other among others) (Pelosi), 196

Ottawa Conference of Interamerican Women writers, xi

Partnoy, Alicia 168–69, 204nn11–12, 207n5; *The Little School*, xv, 145, 148–49

patriarchy, 11, 12–14, 26, 37, 45, 59, 72, 134, 182, 189

Pelosi, Maximiliano, *Otro entre otros*, 196

"Pensamientos" (Thoughts) (Gelman), 26–29, 204n12

Peri Rossi, Cristina, 205n17

*perlas rojas, Las* (The red beads) (Dujovne Ortiz), 79, 143

Perlongher, Néstor, 182, 183–84

Peronism/Perón, 2, 49, 76, 149

photography: in Barthes, 104; and the disappeared, 112–13; and family

memory, 42, 60, 68, 69–72, 84. *See also* Brodsky, Freund
Piglia, Ricardo, 20, 163; *The Absent City*, 20
Piña, Cristina, 108
Piterbarg, Ana: *Everybody Has a Plan*, 133–34
Pizarnik, Alejandra, 108–10, 173, 191–95, 214nn18–23; *The Bloody Countess*, 192, 214n19
Plager, Silvia: *Como papas para varenikes*, 83; *Mi cocina judía*, 83–84
*Planets, The* (*Los planetas*) (Chejfec), critical response to, 159–60
*pogrom en Buenos Aires, Un* (A pogrom in Buenos Aires) (Szwarcbart), 98
*polacas, Las* (The Polish girls) (Suárez), xv
Polo García, Victorino, 209n16
Pomeraniec, Hinde, 187
Posse, Abel, *La Reina del Plata*, 164–65
Pratt, Mary Louise, 22, 33, 203n3, 205n16
Prell, Riv Ellen, xiii–xiv
*Prisoner without a Name, Cell without a Number* (*Preso sin nombre, celda sin número*) (Timerman), 148, 149
*Prize, The* (*El premio*) (Markovitch), 132–33, 135, 167
*profundo Sur, El* (The deep south) (Rivera), 96–98
Pron, Patricio, 47–48
prostitution, xiv–xv, 18, 39, 47, 180–82, 189–90, 205n19; in literary texts, 14, 40–45, 68, 70–71, 79, 184, 185, 190, 214n16; male, 187, 213n10. *See also* Liberman; Zwi Migdal
provisional essentialism, 53
pseudonyms, 4, 10, 40, 100–102, 110–11, 184–85, 187

psychoanalysis and Jewishness, 2, 63, 119, 142, 169, 200
punctum, 104, 208n10; deliberate, 104–106, 107, 194

queerness: in Birmajer, 173–75, 177; in Brizuela, 175–77; in Burman, 178–79, 180, 191; in Cozarinsky, 64, 173; in Echeverría, 172–73; and Efron, 187–89; in Feinmann, 177–78; in Girondo, 182–84; in Hofman, 212n20; and Jewishness, 185–87, 189, 191, 196; in Kuitca, 173, 177; in Martel, 5–7, 172; in Pizarnik, 173, 192–94; in Raznovich, 194–95; resignification of, xiv, 12, 171–72, 173–77, 180, 184, 185–87, 196, 208–209n2; in Solomonoff, 196; in Tiempo, 184–85. *See also* homophobia, lesbianism; transgender; transgressive sexuality

race, 14, 187–89, 194; and Jewishness, 48, 204n14; and the modern nation, 2–3, 16–17, 22–23, 29, 55, 110, 172, 201n3, 203n6, 204n12
*Ragged Football* (*Pelota de trapo*) (Torres Ríos), 37–38
Rajca, Andrew, 159–60, 164
Rama, Angel, 28
Raznovich, Diana, xv; *Mater erótica*, 194; "Rear Entry," 194–95
"Real Estate" ("Bienes raíces") (Cozarinsky) 70, 138–40
"Rear Entry" ("De atrás para adelante") (Raznovich), 194–95
Reati, Fernando, 163
Rein, Raanan, 34, 36, 49, 137
*Reina del Plata, La* (The queen of the River Plate) (Posse), 164–65

*Report on the Situation of Jewish Detained and Disappeared During the Genocide Perpetrated in Argentina 1976–1983* (DAIA), 144–45, 149–50, 161–62
Rivera, Andrés, 95, 100; *Kadish*, 145–46; *El profundo Sur*, 96–98
Robinson, Cheri, 212n14
Roffé, Reina: "El cielo dividido," 191; "La noche en blanco," 212n14; *Monte de Venus*, 190–91
Rosas, Juan Manuel, 173, 213n4
Rosenberg, Sara, *Un hilo rojo*, xv, 144
Roth, Cecilia, 102, 103
Rozenmacher, Germán, 56; "*Blues* en la noche," 57–58; "Tristezas de la pieza de hotel," 56–57, 58
ruso, as synonym for "Jew," 19, 20, 38, 111, 134, 191

Sábato, Ernesto, 19–20, 110, 125, 163
Saer, Juan José, 110, 125, 206n6
Salessi, Jorge, 181–82, 213n11
*Sangre kosher* (Kosher blood) (Krimer), 43, 44
Sarlo Beatriz, 22, 26, 182–84, 204n10
Sarmiento, Domingo Faustino, *Facundo*, 22–23
Saslavsky, Luis, 98; *Ashes to the Wind*, 98–99, 206n6
Satz, Mario, 110, 112, 209n16
scholarly good will and objectivity, 50, 206n4
*School for Patriots* (*Ciencias morales*) (Kohan), 134
sea voyage as trope, 4, 14, 15–17, 18, 23, 47, 57, 62, 74, 75, 88–90, 99, 118, 128, 209n19
Sebreli, Juan José, 38
Seidman, Naomi, 186, 187
Semana Trágica. *See* Tragic Week

Senkman, Leonardo, 29–30, 31–32, 49–50, 85–86, 110, 112, 201–202n4, 207n7, 209n16
sexism. *See* misogyny
sexuality, 45, 181–84; as category of analysis, xiii, xiv, xv, 2, 3, 48, 189, 201n2; and criminality, 39–40; in Gerchunoff, 11, 12–13, 173–74; in Martel, 10; in Tavosnanska, 14. *See also* transgressive sexuality. *See also under* anxiety, gender; immigration; Jewishness; modernity; prostitution
"Shabat" (Shabbat) (Krimer), 44
Sharp, David, 205n18
Shua, Ana María, xv, 68, 78; *The Book of Memories*, 74
Sifuentes-Jáuregui, Ben, 184
*Single, Numberless Death, A* (*Una sola muerte numerosa*) (Strejilevich), xv, 148, 149
*Sisters* (*Hermanas*) (Solomonoff), 131, 167, 168
Sitman, Rosalie, 209n1
*Skin of Memory, The* (*La piel de la memoria*) (Kupferminc), 153
*Slaughter Yard, The* (*El matadero*) (Echeverría), 172–73
soccer: and national unity, 34–38, 102, 205n18; and masculinity, 37, 86
Solar, Xul, 26
Solomonoff, Julia, 125, 134, 135; *The Last Summer of la Boyita*, 131–33, 195–96; *Sisters*, 131, 167, 168
Sommer, Doris, 201nn2–3
Sontag, Susan, 213nn12–13; "Notes on Camp," 185–86, 187
Sosnowski, Saúl, xv, 52, 110, 112, 203n7; *Borges and the Kabbalah*, 209n17
*Special Report on Jewish Detained and Disappeared (1976–1983)* (DAIA), 144, 145

Spivak, Gayatri, 53
*Spoils of War* (*Botín de guerra*) (Blaustein), 167–68
state violence. *See* dictatorship; Holocaust
Steimberg, Alicia, xv; *Musicians and Watchmakers*, 68, 73–74, 78, 210n8
*Stock Market, The* (*La bolsa*) (Martel), 4–11, 12, 171–72, 202n7
*Stray Girlfriend, A* (*Una novia errante*) (Katz), 51–52
Strejilevich, Nora, 169, 207n5; *A Single, Numberless Death*, xv, 148, 149
Suárez, Patricia, *Las polacas*, xv
*Sur*, 24, 124, 209n1
*Susana* (Blaustein), 191, 196
Szichman, Mario, 60, 68, 195, 210n5; *At 8:25 Evita Became Immortal*, 45, 60, 71, 208n4; *Los judíos del Mar Dulce*, 68–69, 206–207nn2–3
Sznaider, Natan, 28, 29, 52–53, 91, 204–205nn13–14, 213n3
Szwarcbart, Herman, 95; *Un pogrom en Buenos Aires*, 98

Tablada, La (cemetery), 114–15, 197–99
*Tablada Suite* (Kuitca), 114–15, 118
Tal, Tzvi, 18–19
tango, 34, 100–102, 103, 118, 125
Tavosnanska, Gregorio, 100; *Ydel, el judío pampa*, 14–15, 18, 32, 89
*Tenth Man, The* (*El rey del Once*) (Burman), 59, 60, 92, 93, 94, 95
*tercera mañana, La* (The third morning) (Cozarinsky), 105–106
*That Place* (*Ese lugar*) (Kuperminc), 152
Tiempo, César (pseud. Israel Zeitlin), 111, 184–85, 187; *Versos de una . . .* , xv, 40–41, 184–85, 190

Timerman, Jacobo, 169; *Prisoner without a Name, Cell without a Number*, 148, 149
*To Be a Witness* (*Ser testigo*) (Kuperminc), 112–13
*Todos lo sabíamos* (We all knew) (Kreimer), 127–29, 130
Toker, Eliahu, 40
Tragic Week, 73, 76, 95–98, 208nn3–4
transgender, 174–75, 194–95, 213n5
transgressive sexuality, xiii, 12, 71, 109, 171–96; in Birmajer, 173–75, 176; in Brizuela, 175–76; in Burman, 178–80, 191; in Cozarinsky, 173, 186–87; in Echeverría, 172–73; and Efron, 188–89; in Feinmann, 177–78; in Glickman, 189; in Gorodischer, 189; in heterosexual women, 12, 45, 68, 70–71, 79, 180, 182, 183, 189–90; and immigration, 181–82; in Kuitca, 115–16, 177; in Kusminsky, 178–80; in Martel, 171–72; and modernity, 180–87; and Perlongher, 183–84; in Pizarnik, 173, 192–94; in Raznovich, 194–95; in Roffé, 190. *See also* lesbianism; prostitution; queerness; sexuality
trees: as rhetorical device, 35–36, 73, 79, 80, 86–87, 169, 197, 199; visual images of, 87–89, 153
*tren de la victoria, El* (Victory train) (Zuker), 69, 73, 77–78
*Tres mosqueteros* (Three musketeers) (Birmajer), xv, 1
"Tristezas de la pieza de hotel" (Hotel room sorrows) (Rozenmacher), 56–57, 58
Tsing, Anna, 22

*Una misma noche* (The very same night) (Brizuela), 175–77

*Una tal Raquel* (Some woman named Raquel) (Glickman), xv, 42, 68, 70–71, 78, 79, 109, 189
*Una vez Argentina* (*Once Argentina*) (Neuman), 37, 73, 75–77, 106, 130, 213n8
"Unworthy Friend, The" ("El indigno") (Borges), 110
*Urban Voodoo* (*Vudú urbano*) (Cozarinsky), 186, 213n13
Urbanyi, Pablo, 207n5

Valenzuela, Luisa: *El Mañana*, xiii
*Versos de una . . .* (Poems of a . . .) (Tiempo), xv, 40–41, 184–85, 190
*vida espuma, La* (Seafoam life) (Kupferminc and Fingueret), 153
*Vientos del agua* (Winds of water) (Campanella), 18, 47, 89
Viñas, David, 95, 98, 100; *En la semana trágica*, 95–96
violence: against women, 43–44, 125, 202n11; anti-Jewish, 17, 95, 105, 107, 135, 142–43, 153, 160, 164–65; in Kishniev pogrom, 105, 208–209n11; and masculinity 17; state-perpetrated, 37, 43–44, 72, 135, 142–43, 162–63, 169, 176, 211n6. *See also* Holocaust; Tragic Week
visibility: Jewish, 51, 57, 91–92, 98, 99, 110, 114–15, 120–21, 148, 198–99; and incidental Jewishness, 123–27, 136–37, 141, 160; and invisibility, xiv, 34, 91, 94, 102, 106, 150, 170, 205n17, 211n1. *See also* Jewish legibility
Viso, Olga, 117

*Waiting for the Messiah* (*Esperando al Mesías*) (Burman), 33–34, 58, 59, 92–94, 137, 178–80, 191, 208n2
Wald, Pinie, 73, 98; *Koschmar*, 98
Waldegaray, Marta, 98
Weser (steamship), 4, 15–18, 89
whiteness and Argentineity, xii, 7, 16, 21–25, 27, 29, 50, 124, 186, 201n2, 203n2
women's storytelling: in Cozarinsky, 61; in Dujovne Ortiz, 79–80, 83, 84, 86–87; in Fingueret, 73, 153–54, 158; in Gorodischer, 70, 79; in Krimer, 43–44; in Neuman, 77; as revision, 42, 44–45, 67–68, 70–71, 189–90

*Ydel, el judío pampa* (Ydel, the pampas Jew) (Tavosnanska), 14–15, 32, 89, 100
Yerushalmi, Yosef Hayim, 67, 158
Yiddish, xii, 30, 40, 44, 55, 74, 91, 98, 109, 127, 129, 156, 157, 159, 168, 187, 192, 210n5, 212n16

Zárate, Filomeno, 202n10
Zeitlin, Israel. *See* Tiempo, César
Zivin, Erin Graff, xiii, 201n3
Zuker, Cristina, 79; *El tren de la victoria*, 69, 73, 77–78
Zwi Migdal, 41–45, 189, 202n12

www.ingramcontent.com/pod-product-compliance
Lightning Source LLC
Chambersburg PA
CBHW030536230426
43665CB00010B/914